TALES FROM THE DANCE FLOOR

TALES FROM THE DANCE FLOOR

SACHA LORD

WITH LUKE BAINBRIDGE

MANCHESTER / THE WAREHOUSE PROJECT
PARKLIFE / SANKEYS / THE HAÇIENDA

Harper
North

HarperNorth
Windmill Green
24 Mount Street
Manchester M2 3NX

A division of

HarperCollins*Publishers*
1 London Bridge Street
London SE1 9GF

www.harpercollins.co.uk

HarperCollins*Publishers*
Macken House, 39/40 Mayor Street Upper
Dublin 1, D01 C9W8, Ireland

First published by HarperNorth in 2024

3 5 7 9 10 8 6 4 2

A catalogue record for this book is
available from the British Library

HB ISBN: 978-0-00-865631-7

Printed and bound in Great Britain
by CPI Group (UK) Ltd, Croydon

Dedicated to my mum, Sandra – I still haven't got a proper job, but this seems to be working out OK …

And in memory of Pete Bainbridge, Luke's dad, who passed away while we were finishing this book.

Contents

CONTENTS

2010s
THERE IS A LIGHT THAT NEVER GOES OUT

NOW

CONTENTS

Tracks That Made the Decade

A Tale of Two Cities

'Right, fuckin' listen up ... here's what's happening ... we're going to give you this bag with 20,000 pounds in cash, and you're gonna put on a big night at the Academy for New Year's Eve. Fifteen-hundred tickets, we'll do the door and we'll split the cash fifty-fifty, and you better not fuck it up!'

The guy talking was one of Salford's biggest gangsters. Not someone to be messed with. I was twenty-three, scrawny, and so far out of my depth that I was drowning. I'd not long been promoting student nights and was living in a tiny bedsit, always having my phone cut off because I didn't have twenty pounds to pay the bill. They had bundled me into the back of a car and driven me round town to make me an offer I couldn't refuse, and I didn't understand, either. *Why me? I couldn't do this.*

'But who will we get to DJ?'

'You. You can DJ all night, then we don't have to pay anyone, and make more money.'

Me? 'I can't DJ!'

'The fuck you on about? You're Sasha, aren't you?! You played The Haçienda last month and it sold out!'

I saw a glimmer of light. A possible escape route out of an impossible situation.

'No, I'm not *that* Sasha. I'm not Sasha the DJ, I'm just Sacha, a shitty student promoter. You've got the wrong guy, sorry ...'

'Fuck's sake ...'

The car pulled over, and I was thrown out on to the pavement ...

Like most Mancunians my age, my life is a tale of two cities. Then and now. It has been the best of times, and the worst of times, often in the same week, sometimes the same night. It was a time of euphoric highs and crushing lows. The light and the shade. You don't get a town like this for nothing. Manchester really has been the making of me, and it has so much to answer for the person who I am today.

I've been shot at in a drive-by shooting, bundled into a car by gangsters and had death threats, which was not very acid house. I've been sued and broke, I've had to deal with an army of rats who were high on cocaine, had £130,000 stolen from me during an armed robbery, and have been targeted by a Romanian organised crime gang. Not Balearic, as we say in Manchester.

But I've also been lucky enough to have had some of the most incredible, life-affirming experiences, and to be in the eye of the storm of a musical and cultural revolution. I've gone on to meet many of my musical heroes and have thrown some of the biggest parties that the UK has even seen.

Over the past thirty years, my generation witnessed a musical revolution, as electronic music went from being a niche, underground music genre to arguably the biggest one in the world.

Along the way, I went from a chain-smoking student living hand to mouth, always in danger of having my phone cut off, a visit from the bailiffs or threatened by a gang, to running the biggest nightclub in the world, and the largest metropolitan festival in the country.

We've had some terrible incidents, including tragic deaths at The Warehouse Project and Parklife, which is something you never really get over. No one should go for a night out and not come home again.

I am telling many of the stories in these pages for the very first time.

The Manchester I grew up in is very different to the city it is today. I think some people believe that the reinvention of Manchester started in 1996, after the Manchester bomb planted by the IRA, but the cultural revolution that started with acid house was already well underway before that event.

Manchester has always been a pop-culture city and the revolution of the city is absolutely rooted in that. It's a fundamental part of what makes this the most invigorating and essential place to live: Manchester is the engine room of British music. Even back in the nineteenth century, German immigrants in the city complained that the locals preferred to sing popular contemporary songs rather than listen to the purities of classical music. Manchester is always looking forward. London may have most of the business, but it's Manchester that, more than any other city in the UK, defines the musical direction of this country. I don't think we would have been able to throw the parties and raves in disused breweries, air-raid shelters, and train stations in any other city. The Warehouse Project in particular is inherently Mancunian. It could only happen here.

This is also a city where you can reinvent yourself. You can be who you want to be in Manchester. This is the city where

Morrissey met Marr, Jack met Vera, and Bobby met George and Denis. It's where Engels met Marx, and Rolls met Royce. It's a place where you can make things happen. It's a fascinating, inventive, groundbreaking city that is always moving and makes you feel part of that movement, not a bystander. It's a true city of the people, an egalitarian city, not one based on old money. There's a very little 'old money' in Manchester. This was the world's first industrial modern city, and the world's first post-industrial city. In the words of Tony Walsh's poem 'This is the Place': 'This is the place to do business then dance, where go-getters and go-setters know they have a chance'. That's always been the case, ever since the industrial revolution. Back in 1912, Sir Edward Abbot Parry wrote: 'Manchester is the place where people do things ... "*Don't talk about what you are going to do, do it.*" That is the Manchester habit. And in the past through the manifestation of this quality the word Manchester became a synonym for energy and freedom and the right to do and to think without shackles.' The writer Anthony Burgess, admittedly biased having been born in the city's Harpurhey district, recalled in his autobiography *Little Wilson and Big God* how, for a Mancunian, a visit to London before the Second World War 'was an exercise in condescension. London was a day behind Manchester in the arts, in commercial cunning, in economic philosophy'. I'd still agree with that now.

I went from selling leather jackets on a market stall to promoting my very first student club nights. There's that old saying, 'You've got to see it, to be it'. Noel Gallagher says when he first heard 'Sally Cinnamon' by The Stone Roses, it was a real lightbulb moment. He just knew straight away: 'I can do that. I can write songs like that.' When I first started going to nightclubs I thought, *I can do this. I can't DJ or be*

the singer in the band on stage, but I know I can put the actual
night on. I can be a promoter.

I was just a normal kid growing up. I wasn't a tearaway. I'd
never been in trouble or met anyone who was a member of a
gang. The only gangsters I'd seen were in *Goodfellas*, so my
first year putting on club nights in Manchester was a wake-up
call. We'll get to that later, but there were some hairy moments.
This city was lawless for a long time in the 1990s.

A lot of people are driven on by their childhoods, or their
relationship with their parents, and I guess that I am too. I had
a difficult relationship with my dad, who a lot of the time
made me feel I'd never amount to much, and I think subcon-
sciously that has pushed me on, to prove him wrong. I also
watched him make a bit of a mess of his life and I was determined the same thing wouldn't happen to me.

I still get imposter syndrome, even though I'm not
ashamed to say I've done all right for myself. From living in
a grotty Salford bedsit, I now live in leafy South Manchester, and I get to hang out with iconic music heroes backstage.
But there's still a nagging part of me that says, *You shouldn't*
be here. You shouldn't be running the biggest nightclub in
the world, and one of the biggest festivals in the UK, and
advising the Mayor of Greater Manchester … You should
still be on the market stall flogging knock-off leather
jackets!

This is not a memoir, it's more my view of the rebirth of a city
and a musical revolution over the past thirty years, and how I
was lucky enough to be a part of that. Luck has played a huge
part in shaping my story, although I've worked bloody hard as
well. I think you need both of those to achieve anything. Some
people work their bloody bollocks off all their life, but they

don't get dealt much luck. Some people get dealt amazing luck but perhaps only realise with hindsight and don't put the effort in to make the most of it. I think I had two major slices of luck – the first one was to be born in Manchester, an incredible city to be who you want to be, where you can write your own story. The second was to be born when I was, to be around when the acid house explosion changed the face of nightlife for ever. Blessed was it in that dawn to be alive, but to be very young was heaven. Nostalgia can be a disease, and at The Warehouse Project and Parklife we're always looking forward. We're always building for the future, but we're also absolutely aware we're building on foundations that were laid down in that period. I've been lucky enough to work with some amazing people, who have helped me along the way, not least my business partners in The Warehouse Project and Parklife, Sam Kandel and Rich McGinnis, but also many others who, though less visible, are absolutely key to the success of The Warehouse Project and Parklife.

I've worked with Sam Kandel since 2000, when we first reopened Sankeys. Sam was the one who first came up with the name and concept of The Warehouse Project.

Now felt like the right time to tell these stories for the first time. It's been thirty years since I put on my first night at The Haçienda, and twenty years since I persuaded Manchester City Council to let us hold the first Warehouse party in the country after the Criminal Justice Bill, which sowed the seed for The Warehouse Project. I think we've done a good job over the years of talking about what happens on stage at our events, but I've never really talked about what happens backstage before.

More than anything, this book is a love letter to Manchester, and to the dancefloor.

THEN

1990s
MANCHESTER, SO MUCH
TO ANSWER FOR

The Boy with the Thorn in His Side

If there's one area of Manchester that has been transformed over the past thirty years that I've been running club nights, it's the corridor that runs along the Northern fringes of the city centre, from Cheetham Hill to Ancoats. Most of the significant moments in my clubbing career have happened here, from Sankeys to the birth of The Warehouse Project. Thirty years ago, these were pretty much no-go areas at night. Whole areas of the city where people were really wary of venturing to after dark. When we took over Sankeys in Ancoats in 2000, it was still an urban wasteland all around us. There weren't any street lights and kids in balaclavas on BMXs were always riding around, looking for clubbers to mug. Ancoats now has a Michelin-starred restaurant and loft apartments that go for over a million quid. When we started out at Sankeys, you couldn't buy a pint of milk round there, let alone a Michelin-starred meal.

Cheetham Hill is one of the most historic areas of Manchester. It's where we first launched The Warehouse Project, in 2006, in the old Boddington's Brewery, next to Strangeways prison. But my links to Cheetham Hill go way further back than that. It's an area that has had several waves of immigration, from the Irish fleeing the Great Famine, to the Jewish population in the late nineteenth and twentieth century to migrants from Pakistan and the Caribbean in the 1950s and 1960s, and more recently from Africa and Asia. It's long been home to a lot of Manchester's rag trade, of which my family's history runs parallel with.

My dad's family had been in textiles for generations, my grandad's family originally came from Llandudno, then they moved to Southport. In the late 1930s, grandad somehow managed to secure a massive order from a Swedish company for black fabric. The order was so big that grandad and the business didn't have the money to buy the material up front, so he re-mortgaged his house and borrowed as much as he could from the bank and as many friends and family as possible. He leveraged himself up to the absolute eyeballs to pay for the fabric, and just about managed to do it, but then the order was cancelled at the last minute, which meant he was absolutely fucked. He had a warehouse full of black fabric that he couldn't shift and was about to lose the shirt off his back, go bankrupt, and face having to tell all his friends and family that he'd lost their money. Then the Second World War kicked off, and all of a sudden the British government needed to buy up as much black fabric as they could, to make blackout curtains, which rescued grandad's business. He bought the mill which is now home to a great little nightclub called Hidden that opened in 2015, and he didn't look back from then on.

The guy who opened Hidden, Anton Stevens, used to work for us at The Warehouse Project and is a friend. I actually helped him get planning for the club, as he was struggling a bit, so I rang a copper, another friend of mine, and arranged for him to go down there and help with it. I think a lot of people see The Warehouse Project as this big behemoth with a wall round it that doesn't care about other smaller venues, but that's not true at all. I will always help people at new venues like Anton at Hidden, or Shaun Ryder's son Oli Ryder, who also used to work for us at The Warehouse Project, and now has his own club night, Animal Crossing, and a venue called The Soap Factory, behind Victoria Station. The way I see it, they're not in competition with The Warehouse Project. On the contrary, they actually help us in a way, because they're almost like feeder clubs for us, for new up-and-coming DJs, and also helping develop new audiences.

When I went to the opening of Hidden, back in 2015, I knew it was in the building that used to be my grandad's old mill, but I wasn't quite prepared for the weird feelings of déjà vu I got in there. Even though it had been thirty years since it was in our family, there was still bits that I recognised, like the original wooden panelling, and it gave me chills down my spine. I remember someone seeing the look on my face and saying to me, 'Are you all right Sach?' as I was quite freaked out. It's called Downtex Mill now, but when our family owned the building it was called Fab Lord House, Fab for Fabric, and Lord for our family name. My grandad bought it after the Second World War, and I remember playing there a lot as a kid, climbing over the rolls of fabric. It was real hard work for the lads in the warehouse, because back in those days they had to spend all day wrapping orders of fabric in brown paper and then tie them with string. If they were using string like that all day, it would cut between their fingers, so to harden the skin on their hands they used to piss in a bucket when they got in every morning, and then whenever they stopped for a break or lunch, they would soak their hands in the bucket of their own piss to harden the skin up. Even as a child I thought that was absolutely disgusting. Safe to say it's not a work practice that would pass health and safety regulations these days!

In the mid-1960s, my dad, then in his twenties, took over the business and moved to Manchester where he had an apartment in Appleby Lodge – an old crescent of flats, which is funnily enough right opposite Platt Fields, where I would start Parklife festival forty years later.

At that time, my dad was knocking about with people like the bookmaker Selwyn Demmy and Malcolm Mooney, who were both best mates with George Best. All that gang used to hang out around the area down Bridge Street, off Deansgate, which was then called The Village – George Best had a boutique there and Malcolm Mooney's salon was there. The building that is now Crazy Pedro's used to be George Best's boutique. Selwyn was a right character, who lived in Appleby Lodge, like my dad, and had legendary after-parties at his flat. A big drinker, smoker, and womaniser, my dad was also a gambler, which is how he met that crowd. He was also pretty right wing in his thinking, and a Mason. I look back at who he was and how he lived his life with a bit of disgust really. I'm so far removed from who he was, and his interests, and everything he represented is completely opposed to how I live my life.

Selwyn Demmy also owned a club called Blinkers, where all their crowd used to hang out. My mum and dad actually met in Blinkers. But then I guess they were only ever going to meet in a boozer, because my dad spent most of his life in the bloody boozer.

My mum is from Worsley, which is technically in Salford, although if she was still alive my grandma would kill me if she read that. The worst day of my grandma's life was 1 April

1974 when Greater Manchester was created and all the local borders changed overnight, which meant that Worsley was now in Salford. She had been perfectly happy living on Green Acre Lane, behind the Bridgewater pub, in what had been Worsley, Lancashire. But then the borders changed, and her address became Worsley, Salford, and my grandma never got over that for some reason. She never accepted that she now lived in Salford and not Lancashire.

Our family wasn't musical at all when I was growing up. I can remember the first record I ever bought, in 1979. My dad gave me 50p and I bought 'Video Killed the Radio Star' by the Buggles, who included Trevor Horn, who went on to be the force behind ZTT and Frankie Goes to Hollywood. Like most young kids, I was into chart music like Duran Duran and Culture Club. I remember seeing Culture Club's infamous performance of 'Do You Really Want To Hurt Me?' on *Top of the Pops* in 1982, which was a huge cultural moment. I knew I couldn't mention to my dad that I liked Culture Club and Boy George because it was exactly the sort of thing he would have hated. Being a bit of a reactionary bigot, he would have poured scorn on Boy George, and on me. My dad was exactly the sort of *Daily Mail*-reading little Englander that the Tories try to appeal to with their fake culture wars these days. He would have probably voted for Brexit and absolutely hated the idea of anything 'woke'. His views were almost Nigel Farage-esque.

Boy George later fully embraced acid house when it exploded and he used to go to the early days of Danny Rampling's Shooom when it was still held in a basement fitness centre, and lots of the other really early acid house clubs. He then reinvented himself as a house DJ, after the first of many hiatuses from Culture Club. I've booked him a few times over the years, but I never had a chance to talk to him till recently, when I went to see Morrissey at Hammersmith Apollo. I was invited to some drinks in the green room before the gig and Boy George was there, too, so we got chatting and I told him I remembered that *Top of the Pops* performance as a kid, although I imagine he gets people telling him that every day of his life, as it was such an iconic moment. He was actually really nice, we chatted about him playing at Sankeys and I asked if he remembered playing my event at Granada Studios. He said he did, but I think he was just being kind. Before Morrissey walked on stage, they played 'Johnny Reggae' by The Piglets, and George stood up and started singing along. He also knew all the words throughout Morrissey's set and sang along.

I had a small record collection, mostly *Now That's What I Call Music* compilations, and it was one of those that got me in trouble with my mum one day. Like most schools, there used to be a few dog-eared porn magazines passed around between the kids, and I used to hide my small selection in one of my *Now …* record sleeves, because I thought, *Mum will never look in there*. But my parents then brought my little brother his own record player for his birthday, and he didn't have any records of his own yet, so when I was out one day, he went into my room to borrow some of my records and found the magazines, which – brothers being brothers – he immediately showed my mum. When I got home, she was sat in the kitchen with them all laid out on the table in front of her, and wanted to know where I got them. She was furious and sent me to my room to wait for my dad to get back from work and speak to me. When he got home, Dad walked into my room trying to look stern, but I also noticed a slight smirk when he was telling me off. I actually think that was one of the rare moments in my childhood that he was quite pleased with me.

We were always being told not to touch my dad's stuff, and he had this old brown box suitcase that he stressed we were never to touch or look inside. Obviously, as a kid, if you're told never to look inside something, the first thing you do when your mum and dad go out is peek in it. So, one day when my brother and I were searching in the box, we found the weirdest things. There was this a little apron, and some weird medals, all of which were to do with the Masons, and then we also found these weird little packets. We had no idea what they were, as we were just young and naïve, so we kept one of them out, and asked my mum what they were. They were condoms, so she was obviously not best pleased. It was just another example to us of the mistrust between Mum and Dad.

I remember realising from about the age of eleven, that things weren't going too great with my parents. From as far back as I can remember, my mum and dad were always arguing. My dad would always be moving out for two weeks, and there would be a lot of shouting and screaming. It was really horrible for me and my brother. I remember as a kid going to bed crying quite a bit because I was so upset by it all. We had to move several times and were always moving into smaller houses. My dad had the family business handed to him, he never had to earn it, and he was a bit useless at managing it – squandering the money on drink, gambling, and women.

One of the last houses we moved into before my mum and dad split up sums up his lack of entrepreneurialism and nous to me. The house had a big garden and my dad applied for planning permission to build another house on the land, which was granted. Then, when Mum and Dad got divorced and had to sell the house, my dad forgot about the planning permission, which meant the people who'd just bought the house could pay off their mortgage by selling off half the garden. Dad had just given all that away by not thinking it through.

Mum didn't really work much when I was growing up. She did a bit of sewing and craft stuff, but it was more of a hobby than a business. But as my dad's business failed, my mum stepped up and turned that hobby into a fledgling interiors business, and she became the main breadwinner. Dad was losing money hand over fist and Mum was the one paying the bills. When my dad finally left us, he didn't leave my mum anything, not a penny. He didn't even give her any maintenance till the divorce was finalised. I was seventeen, living at home and doing my A levels, so it was quite a difficult time for me, but not a situation that I wasn't used to thanks to my parents screaming matches. Having failed it four times in Sale, I managed to pass my driving test on the fifth attempt, when someone told me it was easier if you did it in Wilmslow, as the roads were quieter and wider, so I did it there and passed. I had a red C-reg Peugeot, and I used to drive to school, and give my mates a lift there. Then one day a bailiff just turned up with a tow truck, and took my car away, as it wasn't in my name it was in my dad's; I had to tell my mates my car had been taken away, and I couldn't give them a lift anymore, and we were all back to taking the bus to school every day.

Belligerent Ghouls Run Manchester Schools

I'm fully aware that Morrissey was referring to far less salubrious Mancunian education establishments than my first school, a preparatory in south Manchester, when he sang those words about 'belligerent ghouls' running Manchester schools in 'The Headmaster Ritual', the opening track from *Meat is Murder*. I'm also sure a few tiny violins will come out if I say my esteemed school could be quite tough, but the teachers there could actually be just as sadistic as any other school. We didn't have the cane, but we did regularly get smacked with a ruler to the legs. We had to wear shorts every day, even if it was minus five in winter, and would get slapped on the back of the legs if we did anything wrong. The first time it happened to me I was only seven years old, and it was from Mrs Jones, because I refused to drink my daily milk. At 11.15 a.m. we all had to go to the canteen and drink a small bottle of milk, but I hated milk then and still do now. It was the dinner ladies' first job every day to bring the crates of milk in, but if it was a warm day the milk had been sat in the sun for hours by then, making it curdle. I'd had enough one day, my stomach couldn't take it anymore and I refused to drink it. Mrs Jones told me to face the wall and said, 'If you move when the ruler hits you, then you will get it twice.' I was desperate for the toilet so when she did hit me, I did a little piss, and that just made her hit me again with the ruler. Who does that to a seven-year-old? It's just spiteful. The other thing she would do is march you to the toilets if you said a rude word and physically wash your mouth out with soap. I think kids nowadays think it's a myth that they did that, but she actually did it, with soap from the dispenser. Despite all that, I did OK at Prep School. I wasn't a standout pupil, but I was always in the top half of the class. There was one decent teacher there called Mrs Fallon, who spurred me on, and I did really well in her year.

The problem came after I left the prep school, when my parents desperately wanted me to get into Manchester Grammar School, which, looking back, was totally the wrong place for me. I don't blame my parents for that because they thought they were doing the right thing; they even paid for a private tutor to make sure I could get in. The tutor was called Mr Stockton, and he knew all the tricks to play the system to get into Manchester Grammar, that's what you paid him for. One of the things you had to do in the entrance exam is write an essay on something to show your standard of English, and Mr Stockton made me memorise a list of what he called 'a hundred colourful phrases', which I could then slip into any essay and get good marks. I can still remember the phrases today, stuff like 'the moon looked like an incandescent pearl' and 'the tree was twisted and gnarled like an old woman's hand'. It must have worked, because I wrote an essay about a walk in the woods, and slipped in as many of his colourful phrases as I could. I passed the entrance exam and got in. The only problem was I went from being one of the brightest in the class at my junior school to consistently being at the bottom of the class at Manchester Grammar, which gave my confidence a pretty big knock.

I was pretty strait-laced for most of my time at Manchester Grammar. I was the smartly turned-out kid in the blazer with a neat tie, and I even had one of those 1980s briefcases, the box-shaped ones with the gold combination locks on the top. It doesn't get more 1980s than that, really, but it's a weird school bag for a kid to have. Kids going to other schools would have Head or Nike bags, and I'd be getting on the 141 bus with my briefcase looking like a right nerd.

The only subject I really enjoyed at school was art. I used to spend a lot of the lunchtimes in the art room, and I really found solace in it. I just loved doing still lifes of pot plants and things, I found it very zen.

Even though I wasn't a top pupil, I was still a bit disappointed not to be made a prefect in all the time I was at Manchester Grammar. So, when the school got back in touch with me a few years ago, after The Warehouse Project and Parklife had become successful, to ask if I would go and give a talk to pupils, I said yes, but on one condition. That the headmaster stood up at the same time as me and made me a prefect in front of everyone. So, thirty years later, I finally got my prefect badge. My picture is up in the corridor alongside other alumni, like Sir Ben Kingsley.

I don't make a habit out of bearing grudges, but I will make an exception for some people. There was a kid in my year at Manchester Grammar School called Simon, who was a right little bastard, and he used to bully me. I got my revenge on him a few years later, when I was running my student night at Paradise Factory. He came down to the club one night trying to get in when I was on the door, but I recognised him straight away and made him queue up with all the other punters for ages and when he eventually got to the front of the queue I said, 'No, fuck off, you arsehole, you are *never* coming in here.'

The one good thing that came out of Manchester Grammar is that it was an early education in the traditional Mancunian art of blagging it. I knew the only way I could get through was by copying other people's homework and winging it. Blagging is a pretty essential skill for a club promoter, especially when you're starting out, and I guess I first learned that important skill at school.

Although there was a lot about Manchester Grammar School that I didn't enjoy at all, there was one teacher who was a real inspiration to me and who really did change my life. Mr McGinnis, my Art teacher. I don't just say that with the benefit of hindsight, sometimes you only realise later the people who have shaped your life, but I did actually really appreciate at the time how he changed my way of thinking, and opened doors in my mind that I didn't even know were there. I'm hugely grateful to him, because I'm fully aware that not every kid is lucky enough to have a teacher like him, and at that time I really needed his influence. He gave me something I wasn't getting at home.

Mr McGinnis knew what was going on at home with my mum and dad's divorce and, after meeting him at a parents' evening, he also hated my dad as much as I did. My parents had gone round all the teachers and when they sat in front of Mr McGinnis he told them, 'Sacha has actually had a really good year, and is showing some real promise in art.' But my dad just went, 'Yes, but art is pointless, isn't it? It doesn't mean anything. You're never going to get a job or earn any money through art. I don't even know why we're bothering to talk to you.'

So obviously Mr McGinnis hated my dad after that, quite rightly, and had some sympathy for me.

One day, Mr McGinnis made a comment to me about something James Anderton – Chief of Greater Manchester Police at that time – had just done, and how disgraceful it was. Anderton was a real oddball character, and very homophobic, coming out with statements about people with HIV 'swirling in a human cesspit of their own making'. He even had police boats with spotlights searching for gay men on the canals around what would later become the city's iconic Gay Village. He was friends with Cyril Smith and Margaret Thatcher, and often claimed he was doing 'God's work'. He even said that God talked to him directly. Hard to believe that a Chief of Police could come out with such nonsense, but he did, and was backed by Thatcher. He was a laughing-stock to most people and was nicknamed God's Cop. Happy Mondays even lampooned him in a song called 'God's Cop' on their 1990 album *Pills 'n' Thrills and Bellyaches*. I went home that night and made the mistake of mentioning to my dad that Mr McGinnis had said James Anderton was a disgrace, but of course my dad, being a right-wing bigot, thought James Anderton was completely in the right. 'You can tell that Mr McGinnis *he's* the one who is a disgrace!' he said, 'he's a good man, James Anderton.' Of course, my dad would be one of the few people who liked James Anderton. He probably met him through the Masons or something. Looking back, I was beginning to see that there were very different ways of looking at the world, and my dad and Mr McGinnis were definitely showing me two very different views.

One day in 1989, Mr McGinnis gave me a tape by a band called The Man from Delmonte. Although they were a Manchester band, I'd never heard of them but, then again, I'd never really listened to much outside the charts at that time. I loved it and it really opened my mind musically. There was one particular track, 'M.I.C.H.A.E.L.', that was my favourite. I loved the tape so much that when I heard they were playing a gig, I bought tickets to go and see them at the Free Trade Hall. It was my first ever gig and The Man from Delmonte were the support act to some band I'd never even heard of. I just watched them and left and didn't even bother to watch the headliners, but in doing the research for this book, I found an image of a ticket stub for the gig online, and realised that it was actually The Fall who were headlining! So, I could have seen them at my first gig as well, if I hadn't left.[1] That gig was quite a turning point for me: after that I started listening to more alternative music, and got into The Stone Roses, Happy Mondays, and New Order. I stopped being the Manchester Grammar kid carrying a briefcase around and started to hang around places like Affleck's Palace to discover things for myself.

I'm still in touch with Mr McGinnis now, and he said to me once, 'It's OK to call me Steven now, Sacha.' But he'll always be Mr McGinnis to me.

Around the same time in the late 1980s, I had a girlfriend called Celia. We met at a summer camp called Camp Beaumont, at Tabley House in Knutsford, and then started seeing each other afterwards. Celia's family lived at the back of Mere Golf Course, and Rick Astley was her neighbour. He was at the absolute peak of his fame then – 'Never Gonna Give You Up' had been number one in twenty-five countries around the world – and I was desperate to meet him. I would play football with Celia's brother in their garden, and twice deliberately kicked his

---

[1] Many years later, when we first launched The Warehouse Project, I actually had to throw Mark E. Smith out one night as he was being a bit lairy.

football over the fence into Rick Astley's garden, so I could knock on the door to get it back and hopefully meet him, but both times he was out, and someone else answered. Gutted.

Celia was another person who really turned me on to alternative music, especially The Smiths. Celia was absolutely *obsessed* with The Smiths, and a huge Morrissey fan. At the time Morrissey lived with his mum in Hale Barns, a stone's throw from where I live now, and Celia would go round to Morrissey's mum's house on his birthday, knock on the door and give him a birthday card and a small gift of sorts. Morrissey was always really pleasant to her. His sister, Jacky, still lives in that same house now with her sons, Sam and Johnny. I presume she is the Jacky from Morrissey's 2017 album *Low in High School* on the track, 'Jacky's Only Happy When She's Up on the Stage'. And that was the same house that Smiths' band member, Mike Joyce, tried to have repossessed during the court case over band royalties. I've been a huge fan of The Smiths and Morrissey ever since, and Johnny Marr is one of my friends now, but I'm not a huge fan of Mike Joyce, after an incident on social media.

Around 2009, Mike Joyce started following me on Twitter. I didn't have many followers at the time, as Twitter was quite new, and I was like, *Fucking hell! One of The Smiths is following me!* I immediately followed him back, obviously, and the next day he sent me a DM saying, 'Any chance my daughter can come to The Warehouse Project this weekend?' I replied, 'Yes, of course! Send me her name and her mates' names and I'll make sure we really look after them.' His daughter and her friends came down to the club that weekend and, as promised, I made sure they were given VIP treatment. They had a great time. But first thing the following Monday morning, Mike Joyce unfollowed me. I couldn't believe it! I was fuming.

Bigmouth Strikes Again

I was offered a place to do Art Foundation at Manchester Metropolitan University and all I needed to get was two Es in my A levels, but I only managed to get one E (insert your own gag here) so they wouldn't have me. In a way, I'm lucky because that would have set me off down a different path and who knows how my life would have turned out. But I didn't feel lucky at the time.

My mum and dad finally split up, and when they were getting divorced my dad made me sign a document that his solicitor had prepared, to basically get him a more favourable divorce deal. I signed it under duress, even though I kind of knew then it was wrong, and it's one of the biggest regrets of my life, because it upset my mum so much that she and I didn't speak for nearly two years after that. I moved in with my dad and his Scouse girlfriend Jackie, in Dad's post-divorce bungalow.

That was a lost year for me, really. It felt like everyone was going off to university, some were going backpacking around Southeast Asia or Australia, and I was stuck living with my dad and working for him as a door-to-door salesman. Not quite the dream. As if that wasn't bad enough, if I wasn't home by 9 p.m., my dad would lock the door and I would have to sleep in my car on the drive. That happened on a regular basis.

As I've said, my dad had a terrible business sense. His latest idea was selling home-brew kits called Beer Bags. There was a bit of a home-brewing trend at the time, and they were basically weird hessian bags that you could brew your own beer in. But the bags didn't work, and the 'beer' that came out was disgusting, undrinkable stuff. I was the one who was given the short straw of going out and trying to flog them to factories and businesses around Manchester. I would explain how they worked, then leave them with a few, and come back a few days or a week later to collect, and the company would get a cut. It was a shit business idea, especially as they didn't work, so I never got any repeat custom. Later my dad decided to try and convert them into wine bags, and changed the stickers on the front of them, but if anything that was worse.

Dad had me on commission only, so I was going out all day, door-to-door, trying to sell his shit product, earning peanuts in return. My dad's curfew meant that, even if it was midwinter, if I got home a minute after nine, I'd have to sleep on the drive in my car, freezing, till he unlocked the door the next morning at eight and let me in for a shower. I'd then be sent straight back out on the road, selling those shitty home-brew kits.

It was a horrible eighteen months or so. This was 1990. Outside the world was changing and Manchester was the centre of the world, especially in youth culture. It was what the world was waiting for. Madchester and the acid house explosion was happening on my doorstep, but I was trapped in this shitty situation, traipsing round factories being treated like dirt by my dad. Rave on. Fuck me. I knew it was bad at the time, but looking back I can't quite believe I put up with it for so long.

Around the same time, he and Scouse Jackie had a party and invited about forty people around the house. I was told my job was to serve drinks to all his friends, which I did. But part of the way through the evening, after he had a few drinks inside him, and for no reason at all, Dad stopped the music and shouted at the top of his voice, 'WHY DID GOD GIVE ME SUCH A CUNT OF A SON?!'

After shouting this across the room, there was an embarrassed silence and I thought, *What the fuck?* As did most of his mates. A few chuckles and sniggers could be heard, but most people just looked down at their shoes, embarrassed, because it was such a horrible and weird thing to do and say to your own child.

Not long after that, he and Scouse Jackie decided to go on holiday for ten days. 'You're going to have to find your own accommodation while we're away, I'm not having you staying in my house on your own,' Dad told me.

Again, what the fuck? Who would do that to their own son? But I just said, 'Right, fine ...'

'I've changed the alarm code as well,' he said, 'to make sure you can't get in the house while we're away. So don't even bother trying ...'

Nice. Thanks Dad. Before they went away, I wrote down a list of twenty or so combinations that I thought someone a bit simple like my dad might use for an alarm code, dates of birth and other really obvious dates that could be easily remembered. The day they left, I hid around the corner and waited for them to go, then went back to the house and tried the numbers I'd written down. The third one on my list, my dad's birthdate, was right and deactivated the alarm, so I stayed in the house while they were away, and it was actually the only time I enjoyed being in that bungalow. I made sure I cleaned up properly before they came back. The whole house was spotless, and it looked like nothing had been moved. The perfect crime. Or so I thought. Unfortunately, I'd made one significant fuck-up: a forgotten pie in the microwave. I hadn't spotted it when I was doing my last check around the place and he discovered it, uneaten and cold, when he came home.

Dad stormed round to my mum's house, where I was staying, to collect some post or something, and in the street outside he confronted me about the pie. He gave me a load of shit then punched me square in the face before driving off. I never saw or spoke to my dad after that ever again.

Aside from when he punched me, which my mum still talks about to this day, my dad's abusive behaviour was more psychological than it was physical, which can often be worse and leaves unearthed scars. The way he behaved has undoubtedly had a lasting effect on our family, too.

It was 1992, when I was twenty and he was forty-five, that I last saw my dad. He died seven years later at the age of fifty-two – the same age that I am now. At his funeral, my younger brother gave a speech, but I didn't want to say anything about him. Something told me I should be there though, so I just went and stood at the back.

I suspect if my dad had been around to see me make a success of myself with The Warehouse Project and Parklife he would have been proud, even if it were begrudgingly so. But, then again, I don't know because when he was still alive, and I started off promoting club nights, he thought it was an absolutely ridiculous idea. He thought what I was doing was utterly pointless and I was just totally wasting my life.

After that last incident with my dad, I moved back in with my mum for a few months and got a job at Flannels in

Altrincham, then I got my own place, a bedsit in Salford, near my grandparents. My mum thought it might be a good idea for me to be near them so that I was guaranteed a decent meal inside me. I could just walk across Worsley Green to my grandma's and get my tea, which I ended up doing most nights, because she was a great cook. It was mostly comfort food, but always really tasty – things like Spam hash, and meat and potato pie, but my favourite was her egg and chips, which she always did on Saturday. She made the best chips I've ever tasted, although her secret was to cook them in lard, so they weren't very healthy. My grandpa hated them as they were so unhealthy, and he was the opposite.[2]

My grandparents were great to me, and I wish they had been around for a few more years, to see what I managed to achieve.

---

[2] He was only small, but he went to the gym most nights to work out and once won the Mr Lancashire title in a bodybuilding contest!

The Haçienda Must Be Built

The first ever nightclub I ever stepped foot inside, when I was sixteen, was called De Villes and it was on Lloyd Street in Manchester city centre. There were actually two bars/clubs next to each other: De Villes, and one called Lazy Lils, and there was an interconnecting corridor between them, which had the worst sound bleed I've ever heard in all my life, but I just thought that was normal in those days. Lazy Lils was more of a late-night bar, and right in the middle of the floor was a bucking broncho, which just seems surreal now. Can you imagine someone putting a bucking broncho in a club nowadays? You wouldn't get it past health and safety for a start. Let's get everyone hammered and then stick them on the bucking broncho! Recipe for disaster.

The night I went was a Saturday, an indie night, and it was pretty rough. There was chicken wire around the DJ booth to stop things being thrown at the DJs. My mate Pete Armistead, for a joke, went up to the DJ and said, 'My mate says can you put some Bros on?' and pointed at me, and the DJ replied, 'Tell your mate if he doesn't fuck off now, I'll announce that to the club.' I later learnt that the DJ was Alan Maskell, who has owned 42nd Street nightclub for the past twenty years. Years later, when I realised it was him and told him the story, we laughed about it. De Villes was pretty incredible, and a bit of a baptism of fire for me. There was a fight every half hour and things used to properly kick off, but that didn't seem unusual at that time.

I also started to go to a few of the chrome-and-carpet type of nightclubs, mostly Discotheque Royales and Piccadilly 21, where you had to wear a tie to get in. Piccadilly 21 was a weird place; it even had a restaurant in there. I used to sometimes grab a plate of chips on my own halfway through the night, and sit alone, in my tie.

At school, people started to talk about where they were going out, and the cool kids were on about this place called The Haçienda. I was getting stressed at school, because most of the other students were quite focused, and had a plan to get in to a top university like Oxford, Cambridge or St Andrews, and what they would read there, while I still didn't have a clue what I wanted to do with my life. I had a sense that life was slipping away a bit, or that I was getting left behind. I think it was clear to me from the day I started Manchester Grammar that everyone else was more intelligent than me, and by the time I got to sixth form it was clear I wasn't going to university, but I didn't have a back-up plan, and had no idea what should do.

It was the late summer of 1989 when I started to hear about The Haçienda, it quickly became this mythical place that all my mates were talking about, and we decided to check it out one night. Despite everything we heard about the club and the music, the one memo we didn't get was about what to wear. At other clubs I'd been to, like Discotheque Royale and Piccadilly 21, dressing up was necessary for a guaranteed entry. It was still the dark ages, sartorially, where you wouldn't get in if you were wearing jeans or trainers. I thought, *If I'm going to The Haçienda tonight, then I'm going to get properly suited and booted so that I can get in.* I borrowed my dad's suit, my dad's shirt and my dad's tie. What an idiot. We turned up and started queuing, so preoccupied worrying about whether we were going to get in or not, that we didn't even notice at first that everyone else in the queue was dressed completely differently to us. You didn't need to dress smartly to ensure you got in The Haçienda, in fact if you did, you would stand out like a sore thumb. Most people were wearing loose baggy clothing, T-shirts and baggy jeans, sometimes even shorts. We eventually got to the front of the queue and the main bouncer took one look at me and just said, 'Fuck off!' I was absolutely gutted.

After we'd realised the error of our ways, we regrouped (and redressed) before heading back the next week.

That first night we walked into The Haçienda, we actually stopped dead-still, our mouths open, and almost started laughing at the scene in front of us. We had never seen anything like it. Everyone was dancing with their hands in the air, which I'd never seen anyone do before in my life. At the other clubs, the only time you'd dance was when you would kind of shuffle next to a girl you were trying to cop off with. This was something completely different. I'd never seen anyone dance with so much feeling and abandon. Everyone was totally lost in the moment. The weirdest thing was that within half an hour we were on the dancefloor doing the same thing: dancing with our hands in the air. We had no idea that everyone else in the club was on ecstasy – I don't think we'd even heard of ecstasy at that point – the energy and the mood was so infectious, that we just got caught up in it.

I was wearing an Armand Basi turtle neck wool jumper, so I was sweating my tits off, but I felt cool, and one guy even stopped me in the toilets and said, 'Hey Armand Basi, cool.' I'd seen the jumper in L'Homme, Richard Crème's shop opposite Russell & Bromley by St Ann's Square, which I first heard about when Prince was playing a gig in Manchester and the *Manchester Evening News* reported that the shop opened at midnight especially for Prince. My dad knew I wanted the Armand Basi jumper and incredibly he bought it me for my birthday, which was so unlike him. I later learned that it was a fake, and he'd bought it in some dodgy pub in Liverpool.

Most of the other DJs at the clubs we'd been to were mainly playing chart hits, and they were still announcing records and saying, 'Happy Birthday to Sharon!' The Haçienda was something else. Firstly, you didn't recognise any of the music, and it was just one long soundtrack all the night, because the DJs were mixing the records. It sounds ridiculous now, particularly from one of the founders of The Warehouse Project, but I'd never heard a DJ mix records before, and I don't think I was alone in that. Richard Hector-Jones, who went on to work for Bugged Out and as a music journalist, was working in the Eastern Bloc record shop at the time, and he remembers a woman coming into the shop and asking,

'Have you got that record they played at The Haçienda last night?'

'Which one?'

'Well, they only played one record and it lasted all night.'

Because there was no gap in the music, she actually thought it was just a single record that lasted all night! I wasn't quite that confused, but I'd certainly never heard anything like it before in my life. I'd also never seen the crowd facing the DJ, in worship almost. In the other clubs I'd been to, nobody ever paid much attention to the DJ, unless they were moaning to him to play something they liked – the idea that the DJs there were people to be respected or worshipped would have been ludicrous. But at The Haçienda it was different. The DJ seemed to be in control of the dancefloor and the crowd responded with him and followed him.

Unbeknown to me at the time, the DJ that night was Mike Pickering, who was one of the first DJs to start playing house music in late 1985 and early 1986, at his Nude night, with early proto-house records like J. M. Silk's 'Music Is The Key' and Dhar Braxton's 'Jump Back (Set Me Free)'. Mike tells the story that one night at The Haçienda a kid from Moss Side came up to the DJ booth and said, 'Check this out, Mike' and gave him a copy of Adonis' 'No Way Back', which he listened to in the headphones and then immediately stuck on. Mike was going to New York in the mid-1980s to visit Simon Topping, who used to be in a band called Quando Quango, and together they decided to make a Latin house record. They called themselves T-Coy and that record, 'Carino', is arguably the first British house record. It still sounds incredible today. Mike, of course, went on to start Deconstruction records and then form M-People (the M in M-People stands for Manches-ter). I knew absolutely *nothing* about any of this at the time, I didn't even know it was Mike DJing that night. Much later, Mike would be a huge help to us when we first started The Warehouse Project; he helped spread the word and helped bring some of the artists and agents on board. That meant a lot to us at the time, as it felt like a stamp of approval for The Warehouse Project.

Like most clubs back then, The Haçienda shut at two in the morning which always, always left you wanting more – desper-ate to come back and do it again. These days, we run nights till

4 a.m., sometimes 6 a.m., and though at times you can look out and it feels like it's beginning to drag on a bit, that never happened back then because the 2 a.m. deadline left you on a high. Don't get me wrong, we often have nights that finish at five and fly by, but sometimes you get the feeling it might have been better if it had ended an hour or two earlier. A few years later, The Haçienda did get their licence extended till three, but I remember Paul Cons, who used to run the queer night, Flesh, would still finish at two, his reasoning being that everybody would leave on a high together, which was a bit of a gamble, but I think it did pay off for Flesh. It always left people wanting more.

Everyone who falls in love with nightclubs, electronic music, the dancing and the energy has their own epiphany, their own moment when it all just clicks. And though I'm sure younger generations are bored of those of us banging on about The Haçienda, the energy in that place, when it was going off, was just something else, something indescribable. It changed your life. I only hope that The Warehouse Project has created a similar experience for others just like the one that me and my mates had on those formative nights out in The Haçienda.

There were often people there who were wearing amazing designer clothes, but there were also people in there wearing Joe Bloggs or Stolen From Ivor or second-hand clothes. People even wore shorts or bikini tops because it was so hot. Nobody cared what you were wearing. It didn't matter. Nobody was competing with, or comparing themselves to, anyone else. It felt like everyone was on the same vibe, all these different tribes merging to become one, and I'd never experienced anything like that feeling before in my entire life. Something changed in me that night. It was definitely a turning point in my life. A switch was flicked.

I knew I needed to be part of this.

I wasn't even sure what *this* was yet, let alone how I could become part of it. But I knew I wanted to be in it.

I Would Go Out Tonight

The first inkling of the idea to do my own club night came to me in the unlikely venue of Yesterday's, a club in Alderley Edge. I had a mate called Arnie, who was a really nice lad. His family owned Texet in Cheetham Hill, which was a big electronic firm that sold calculators and stuff, so they were quite well off. For Arnie's 21st they hired Yesterday's on a Monday night. I think Arnie only invited about seventy or eighty people but word spread somehow and around 300 kids turned up, a lot of whom he didn't even really know. I remember it, like it was yesterday, no pun intended, when the idea hit me. I was stood there looking at all these people out there on a Monday night when the club wasn't usually open and thought, *I can do this. I could get this many people out on a midweek night. If I could persuade a club in a better location to give me a chance and let me put on a night then maybe there's something in this. I could charge everyone three pounds to get in and I could make it work.* I was still working in Flannels at the time, earning £20 a day, and I was also topping that up by running a stall at the weekends on Stanley Dock Market in Liverpool. I found a factory that had a load of Next leather jackets that were seconds, and I would buy the seconds off them really cheap. The leather jackets retailed at £140 and the seconds I bought only had a button missing or something, so I would get that replaced and then sell them on my market stall for £100. Even if I only sold two all weekend, that would earn me more money than working in the shop all week. But I didn't want to be getting up at 5 a.m. on a Sunday and drive over to Liverpool to sell leather jackets on a market stall in the freezing cold for the rest of my life. I desperately needed something else to do with my life, so I was excited by the idea of putting a club night on. Maybe this could be the start of something. Maybe this could be my way out.

I didn't have a pot to piss in, though. Not a bean to my name. The only way I could make the plan work was to find someone else to put the money up front. I talked to Arnie, who was in right away, and we started planning about where to hold the club nights. Not knowing anyone who went out in Cheshire, I didn't really have much pull on that scene – and everyone I knew went out in Manchester, so we needed to find somewhere in town. Being a bit bolshy, and probably setting our sights way too high, we thought about The Haçienda.

We managed to set up a meeting with Ang Matthews, who was The Haçienda's assistant manager at the time. We were over the moon just to have secured a meeting with her. We couldn't believe it. We thought we were proper little business-men. We were going to a meeting at *The Haçienda*, the most famous club in Manchester, to discuss hiring it. This was beyond our wildest dreams! We turned up at the meeting and it was all surprisingly straightforward. Ang suggested a Monday at the start of July, and we agreed a one-night hire fee for The Haçienda of £1,000 plus VAT.

Arnie and I thought we had done the deal of the century. We really did. We honestly came out of that meeting at The Haçienda walking on air. I thought I was the new Peter Stringfellow. But we'd actually been completely ripped off. They must have been high-fiving themselves in The Haçienda office the second that we walked out of there, saying 'What a pair of clowns!'

What they knew, and we didn't, was that it would be virtually impossible to get enough people through the door on a Monday night in July to cover that hire fee. Arnie and I thought we were home and dry. I think we thought, 'If you book The Haçienda, they will come', right? We soon realised just how wrong we were. In fact, we were fucked. The first absolute schoolboy error we made was, though we were planning a student night, and Manchester has one of the biggest student populations in Europe, we'd booked The Haçienda for the first Monday of the summer holidays, when all the students had fucked off home and weren't around. Idiots. We didn't pick the date, that was the date The Haçienda offered us, and now we realised why.

When we went back a few days later to collect the invoice we dealt with a guy called Jon Drape. That was the first time I'd ever met Jon, and I remember he had his hair in curtains, and was always sweeping it back behind his ears. Half of the lads in Manchester had curtains at that point, and I even had curtains myself at one stage. Jon was usually the one who answered the phone in their office in those days, and I remember he had quite a posh phone voice: '*Hell-o, Haçienda.*'

Little did I know that I would end up working so closely with Jon Drape years later, on The Warehouse Project, Kendal Calling, Parklife and many other projects, but we'll get to that later. I've still got the invoice from The Haçienda for that night, and it's framed on the wall of my office at home, signed by Jon Drape. An invoice for £1,000 plus VAT, which we paid.

Also in the office was Paul Mason, Bobby Langley was kicking about, and Rob Gretton. I never saw Tony Wilson in The Haçienda office, I didn't meet him till much later. I think a lot of people associate Tony Wilson, more than Rob Gretton or anyone else, with The Haçienda. Tony was a public figure. Even in The Warehouse Project office, where we have about twenty-five staff now, if I ask them all, 'Have you heard of Rob Gretton?' I doubt most of them would know who he was, but if I said 'Have you heard of Tony Wilson?' they'd say, 'Of course ... Mr Manchester!'

But people in the know, in Manchester and the industry, know that Rob was the real driving force behind The Haçienda. Rob sadly passed away in 1999; Tony in 2007. Far too young, both of them. But they both left huge legacies in Manchester and in music. Their influence can't be overstated. We wouldn't have the Manchester we have today without Rob Gretton and Tony Wilson. They made us all believe that things were possible. That you didn't have to go far to achieve great things, you could do it on your own doorstep. In fact, it might be better if you did it here in Manchester, running things on your own terms, which you might not be able to in, say, London or New York. I'm pretty sure The Warehouse Project would not have been such a success if it was based in London. There's something inimitably Mancunian about The Warehouse Project.

Anyway, Arnie and I were in a bit of a hole, as we'd already paid up front for the club (well, Arnie had), so we *had* to fill it. We had to find a way of getting close to 700 people into The Haçienda on a quiet Monday night, when the students were away; so we came up with a bit of a scam, a bit of a blag. This was pre-internet days, pre-email, and hardly anyone had a mobile phone, so the biggest way to promote club nights was still flyers. Promoters would hand these out on the street, outside bars, outside other club nights, and also put piles of them in the coolest record shops, clothes shops, and hairdressers around town. Most of those shops would have a table near the door, or a windowsill, or somewhere you could leave flyers. Some of the places would be a bit discerning about what flyers they took – a really cool shop like Geese wouldn't take flyers for a cheesy student night. So, I came up with the idea of going round town, to all these cool places, and saying, 'Hi, we're from The Haçienda and management really want to say thank you for supporting us by allowing us to put flyers in here. We're having this huge party at The Haçienda, and everyone is going to be there – Take That, Manchester United players, *Coronation Street* stars, everyone. We can give you a couple of free guest lists and you can also give us as many names as you like for a £5 discount entry list.' A total lie. The management didn't know anything about it, it was just a blag to try and get as many people through the door. I didn't know any celebrities back then, although I did know Justin Orange, the identical twin brother of Jason Orange from Take That, so I made sure he came down. I thought if anyone moaned and said, 'I thought you said there was going to be loads of celebrities?' I'd say, 'Look, there's Jason Orange from Take That, what more do you want?'

A lot of people were pretty grateful and said, 'OK, cool, thanks', and gave us a list of names. I think we eventually ended up with 787 people through the door and we made about £700, so it was a success in the end.

The funny thing was we didn't go out and go crazy and celebrate. After the club closed at 2 a.m., we went back to Arnie's family's house in Cheadle, where his mum had stayed up and made us some samosas. That's how I celebrated my first ever successful club night: eating a samosa in my mate's mum's kitchen.

Dodgin' the Rain and the Bullets

As far back as I can remember I never wanted to be a gangster. I was a bit of a nerdy kid from the mean streets of Altrincham who went to Manchester Grammar School, my idea of gangsters was the same as the next person. Gangsters were just people in films like *Goodfellas*. They may have seemed cool, slightly romantic figures if your only experience of them was watching Henry Hill or the Krays on the big screen. I had heard of the Quality Street Gang, as they were on the periphery of my dad's social circle. They were a wide loose collective of characters, a lot of them from Ancoats, and you certainly wouldn't mess with them, as their reputation proceeded them. They were proper old school heads, with nicknames like Jimmy the Weed and Jimmy Swords, and they were known and feared throughout town. People would do a sharp intake of breath if they walked into a bar or club and nudge each other. Jimmy the Weed ran The Brown Bull in Salford, where George Best and a lot of journalists and Granada staff, like Michael Parkinson, would drink, and it was famous for after-hours drinking. George Best once went round taking fish and chip orders at a lock-in, then popped out and got them for everyone. Best would even sleep in there sometimes. One of the other haunts was Phyllis's, a late-night-hotel-stroke-shebeen in Whalley Range run by Phyllis Lynott who described it as 'showbiz digs'. Phyllis was the mother of Thin Lizzy lead singer Phil Lynott and his song 'The Boys Are Back In Town' is about the Quality Street Gang and the other characters that would frequent his mum's later night 'showbiz digs'.

Although my dad wasn't close friends with the Quality Street Gang, they could often be found in the same drinking and gambling spots. My mum used to make me get the bus into town after school on Fridays so that I could go to a basement club called Drummonds on Peter Street to collect my dad and make sure he came home for the weekend. He was always surrounded by women and dodgy characters like the QSG.

When you have to face the reality of dealing with gangsters, though, there is nothing romantic about it, trust me.

The modern-day gang problem in Manchester really kicked off not long after acid house exploded at the end of the 1980s, and it was horrible for the best part of a decade – casting a long shadow over the city for most of the 1990s. The gangs were out of control and running the doors at most of the nightclubs. Everybody knew what was going on. The police knew, the authorities knew, the public knew. And anyone who worked in nightclubs sure as hell knew as they had to deal with it on a daily basis. Acid house had changed things so quickly that the police and authorities were just playing catch-up, and promoters like us were left to deal with it on our own. Everyone who worked in and around nightclubs in the 1990s will have stories about the gangs.

There was one bar in Manchester that was owned by someone who was connected to one of the gangs and it was common knowledge that they used to keep guns in the freezer. It seems ridiculous now but that's what Manchester was like at the time. I'm sure there's a criminal element and gang problem of some degree in most big cities around the world, especially in nocturnal businesses that involve large amounts of cash, but it's usually a bit more underground, a bit more hidden away. In Manchester, at that time, it was blatant. It was always there, bubbling away just under the surface. You didn't have to look hard to find it. Some press even started calling the city Gunchester, although no one on the streets actually called it that. Gio Goi, the Manchester clothing label even did a T-shirt with the slogan, 'Manchester – dodgin' the rain and the bullets', like it was something to be proud of.

It's no exaggeration to say the city was like the Wild West back then. It was lawless and out of control. Different gangs and gangsters were running large parts of the city, and often fighting each other over territories, and at times it seemed like they were untouchable.

When I look back now, I can't believe a lot of what happened. I don't know anybody who ran a club night in the 1990s in Manchester who wasn't threatened or intimated, many of them had guns pulled on them or had to pay protection money; quite often people were severely beaten up or kidnapped. Saying that now is really shocking, but what's more shocking, and frightening, is how normalised it was. Instances of pretty shocking, heavy violence were commonplace. You were always hearing that there had been a shoot out on the door of such and such a club, or some other story like that. The gangs themselves didn't make much attempt to keep it secret, either. A lot of the time it was brazen, and happened in full public view, which was almost a show of force from the gangs, to intimidate people. Because they knew they could get away with it at that time. It was almost like, 'What are you gonna do? Who are you going to tell? We can do what we want and nobody in this city can stop us.'

The worst gang violence at The Haçienda was before my time. Because of the gang violence, Greater Manchester Police had first tried to shut down the club in 1990, but Factory fought back by employing the legendary George Carman QC to fight its case and won a six-month reprieve. Not before Carman had to tell the rest of Factory to stop Tony Wilson from constantly shooting his mouth off, famously exclaiming: 'Gentlemen, shut that loudmouth up!'

Shortly after the reprieve, though, The Haçienda decided to close the doors voluntarily, after their new Head of Security was threatened by someone with an automatic gun. 'Someone who was turned away by a bouncer went back and got a machine gun,' recounted New Order's Bernard Sumner. 'He chased the bouncer through the club, cornered him by one of the fire escapes and pulled the trigger, but the gun jammed … the head doorman was chased out of the club by a kid holding an Uzi. The doorman ran out of the back door, jumped in a car, sped home to London and never came back. Poor bastard. That ended everything. The other doormen packed up and left too. Clearly we were fucked.'

DJ, Mike Pickering, even stopped his own sister and friends from coming to the club because he was worried for their safety. It had got to the stage where people were getting mugged at knifepoint in the toilets. It was lawless. One night, Pickering's management team from Deconstruction Records came down to see him DJ and after half an hour they ended up banging on the door of the DJ booth, saying, 'Fucking hell! Let us in here, we're not staying out there, it's horrible.'

On 30 January 1991, Tony Wilson called a press conference on The Haçienda dancefloor and announced the decision to close the club voluntarily:

The Haçienda is closing its doors as of today. It is with the greatest reluctance that for the moment we are turning the lights out on what is, for us, a most important place. We are forced into taking this drastic action in order to protect our employees, our members and our clients. We are quite simply sick and tired of dealing with instances of personal violence … when we opened The Haçienda we never thought we'd have to deal with the sort of people we've had too. We hope, we must believe, we can reopen The Haçienda in a better climate. But till we are able to run the club in a safe manner, and in a way the owners believe will guarantee the role of The Haçienda at the heart of the city's community, it is with great sadness that we will shut our club.

Luke Bainbridge spoke to a lot of the people who were at the heart of that when he was writing his book about the history of acid house. People like Pickering, Graeme Park, Jon Da Silva, Paul Mason and Fiona Allen, who went on to be a comedian and one of the creators and stars of the Channel 4 comedy sketch show *Smack the Pony*, but back in the day worked at The Haçienda and sometimes did the door.

'Unfortunately, the mood in the club changed a lot quicker than most of the punters realised. Because I was working on the door myself and doormen got to know every little dodgy kid coming in there and what they were up to. Violence would escalate quite quickly, and almost every week I'd end up driving someone down to casualty because the ambulance and the police – how can I say this – took their time to turn up whenever we rang them. Either that, or they just happened to be rushed off their feet every time. One kid, a lovely, cheeky chappie, ventured onto someone else's patch and ended up getting stabbed in the leg, just missing a major artery. I was so used to it by that stage I remember taking off my belt to try and make a tourniquet, and as I was doing it I thought, "I only bought this belt today". That's how commonplace the violence had become, that you could have a thought like that while trying to stem the bleeding from a stab wound. The week before, I had seen the inside of someone's skull after they'd been glassed in the club.

Though most people at The Haçienda were still having a euphoric, great time, one night there was a bang and I looked up to see that there was a guy walking across the road towards the club with a gun. The doormen had scattered so I desperately started pressing the button that closed the shutter over the main door, and it was the slowest moment of my life as it came down. I was pleading with the shutter to hurry up and close: "Please, come on!". That's the reality of what went on at the time, and they're only just a few examples. People were either looking away not to see it, or they tried to forget it. But I'm not forgetting it, because it was horrible.'

The last straw for Mike Pickering was when he had a knife pulled on him the night of The Haçienda's birthday. He and David Morales were DJing that night. Pickering was upstairs, Morales was downstairs. He could tell Mike was a bit down at the start of the night and said to him, 'You've not got fed up with DJing have you?' And Mike just said to him, 'Between you and me there's a lot of trouble in here. A lot of gang trouble.'

The main DJ booth at The Haçienda was like a stable door, it was in two halves. The top half of the door was open and some kid from Salford leaned over and grabbed Pickering's beer. Pickering said, 'That's my beer …' and the kid pulled a knife on him. Pickering just said, 'You know what, have the fucking beer,' and shut the door.

Meanwhile, downstairs, someone threw a bottle that smashed just behind Morales, and scattered broken glass over him and the decks. Pickering and Morales both walked out of the booths and bumped into each other at the front door. Pickering said, 'I told you, didn't I?' and Morales replied, 'Man, let's get the fuck out of here.'

They walked out of The Haçienda and Pickering, who had been one of the driving forces behind the club since it started, sadly never set foot in there again.

In 1994, long before the Lowry, the Imperial War Museum North, and the BBC and Media City transformed Salford Quays, I saw one of the gangs in action for the first time. I had just started promoting – it was right after the first night I'd done at The Haçienda – and there used to be a boat moored in Salford Quays called *The Flying Dutchman*, which had been converted into a bar by the owner, Jan. He lived on it, too, and had even converted the cockpit into a little bedroom. Jan must have been under pressure from gangs to pay some protection money, because I remember reading a quote from him in the *Manchester Evening News* saying he was going to stand up to any form of intimidation from gangs.

The boat had a bar down below and there were also some tables and chairs out on deck. I quite liked it and used to go there now and again for a drink. One evening, we were sat outside on the deck, when all of a sudden this souped-up Ford Escort screeched to a halt next to it, and a bunch of guys ran on board and just started smashing the bar up, smashing everything. Then they grabbed fire extinguishers and came up on deck and just started spraying everyone. It was horrible. People panicked and were desperately scrambling to get away from them, women were screaming, and a couple even jumped off the side of the boat into the dock.

I think Jan tried to keep *The Flying Dutchman* open for a little while after that, but the writing was on the wall really, and he eventually decided it wasn't worth it. He sold the boat to the street art and theatre company Walk the Plank, and Jon Drape from The Haçienda actually ended up living on there for a very short time at one stage.

Understandably some people just had enough of the club scene, and they got out. Andy and Mike Mckay were two brothers running clubs in Manchester, around the Gay Village, who inevitably had to deal with gangs, and one night in 1994 some gang members took Andy outside and doused him in petrol and threatened to set him alight. That was the final straw for Andy and Mike. They took the money they had made that night, booked one-way flights to Ibiza, and never came back, or looked back. They established a club called Manumission (with the 'Man' in Manumission referring to Manchester) and it became one of the biggest clubs in the world for the rest of the 1990s, infamous for its sex stage shows, where Mike and his wife Claire would have sex on stage each night, in front of thousands of punters. You wouldn't get away with that in Manchester on a wet Wednesday night. Manchester's loss was Ibiza's gain.

After our first Scandalous night at The Haçienda, I had got the promoting bug and was beginning to think I had found something I might be good at. We did two further nights at The Haçienda that year – a fresher's ball in September then a student Christmas party in December. That was when I began to realise the harsh reality of promoting club nights in Manchester in the 1990s was that you had no choice but to work with the gangs and people who ran the doors at the clubs. It was a nocturnal minefield and you needed to know who you were dealing with and how best to work with them and keep them on your side, because if you didn't have them onside you were fucked.

At that time, Damian Noonan ran the door at The Haçienda, and he had a fearsome reputation. Everyone knew who he was, including the punters, especially any punters who had unintentionally got on the wrong side of him. My fresher's ball event in September had sold out, and when I turned up on the night Damian asked me how many tickets I'd done. I told him it was completely sold out. 'OK, how many tickets have you got for me?'

'I don't have any. I had about fifty left over, but they're all at home.'

'Where do you live?'

'Chorlton.'

He called one of his guys over and said to him, 'You're in your car tonight, aren't you? Run Shrimpy back to his house in Chorlton, he needs to pick up some fucking tickets for me ...'

Damian's nickname for me was 'Shrimpy' for some reason. I never had the balls to ask him why. I was living on Cromwell Road in Chorlton at the time, but I was bright enough to know I didn't want Damian and his crew knowing where I lived, so I got the bouncer to pull up on a road parallel to Cromwell Road, jumped out and ran down a random person's drive as if it was my house, then jumped over their back fence and into my garden, so they never knew where I lived.

Our next night at The Haçienda was the student Christmas party at the end of 1996. It sold out again, but this time I'd made sure to keep some tickets to give Damian to sell. I also roped in my old friend J-Boy to dress up as Father Christmas and rented him the outfit from a fancy-dress shop. As soon as Damian saw J-Boy dressed as Father Christmas he said, 'I'm having that suit at the end of the night. I'll use it for my kids on Christmas morning.' We thought he was joking, but at the end of the night he demanded J-Boy give him the suit.

'But it's only rented,' I tried to protest, 'I've got to return it on Monday.'

'I don't give a fuck.'

'What am I going to tell the fancy-dress shop?'

'Tell them Damian Noonan's got it.'

I wasn't going to argue with Damian. J-Boy had to take the Father Christmas suit off there and then and give it him. The thing was, he only had boxer shorts on underneath, so I had to drive him home in his underwear in December, freezing his bollocks off.

Not long after I started promoting, there was the incident I mentioned in the introduction where I was bundled into the back of a car by a couple of Manchester's biggest gangsters and made an offer that I couldn't understand, let alone refuse. They tried to give me a bag with £20,000 cash in and wanted me to put on a big night at the Academy for New Year's Eve. I knew I couldn't do that; I'd only just started promoting.

Damian had a fearsome reputation, and I was as scared of him as everyone else, but I also got on well with him on some level as well. I was having a bit of trouble with a rival student promoter called Paul Bennett at the time. He was a cheesy student promoter who was quite a bit older than me, a mature student in his early thirties, who lived in student halls. He had a massive team of students working for him and he was getting them to rip all my posters down and bin all my flyers, and it was really affecting my nights and losing me a lot of money. He was trying to just wipe me out completely. I tried various things to combat it, and I was at the end of my tether. I decided to phone Damian up and tell him I had a problem with this rival student promoter.

'Come round to my house tomorrow Shrimpy, I'll sort it.'

When I got to Damian's house, he had a huge baby pink leather suite and the biggest TV I've ever seen.

'Right, what's the problem Shrimpy?'

I explained the situation with this Paul.

'What do you know about this guy?'

'Not much. I know he lives in Dalton Ellis student halls, and he drives a dark blue BMW M3.'

'OK, give me his number ...'

I gave Paul's number to Damian, and he rang him up.

'Is that Paul? ... It's Damian Noonan here. I'm sat with Sacha; he's been telling me that there's a problem between you two. Well, if you've got a problem with Sacha, then that's a problem for me. If you don't leave him alone, I'm going to come and find you, smash you and your dark blue M3 through the doors of Dalton Ellis student halls, got it?'

I never heard from Paul again. Never spoke to him or saw him ever again. He obviously got the message, because he just disappeared.

There were running battles between various gangs and factions about running the doors of different nightclubs at the time, but I just tried to keep my distance from all of those battles. The key thing was not to let them know too much about you that they could use against you. I certainly didn't want anyone knowing where I lived, because then you always had the worry that they could turn up on your doorstep.

One of the problems in the 1990s was that clubbing was a purely cash business. *Everything* was run on cash. Punters paid cash for tickets, cash on the door, and cash over the bar. What gangs and criminals wanted more than anything was cash, and in particular, cash that can't be traced. Nightclubs back then were nocturnal businesses dealing with large amounts of untraceable cash, so they were obvious targets for gangs. Especially if they could control or take a cut of the lucrative drugs trade that was being done in a lot of those clubs.

Thankfully the past is a different country, gangs did things differently there. Nowadays things have completely changed since the dark days of the 1990s. The police and authorities have a much better handle on things than they had then, when they were simply playing catch up. These days we work hand in hand with the police, authorities, and council. But to be honest, one of the biggest things that has changed is there is hardly any cash changing hands anymore. Almost all payments are done by card or contactless now, so there simply isn't large amounts of untraceable cash around to be targeted. When I can think back to the amount of cash that went through some of our nights and events in the late 1990s and early 2000s, it's unbelievable.

Shaun Ryder from Happy Mondays thinks *The Wire* is very true to life in the way that gangs move on to legitimate businesses, or seemingly legit businesses, and quite a few of those gangsters from the 1990s and 2000s have done that. A lot of them are now dead, including most of the main figures whose names were enough to strike fear into anyone, but of those who are left, quite a lot of them have gone legit. They're not going round threatening people physically anymore; they're making money in other ways.

Come Home

After my first successful nights at The Haçienda, I started looking around for another venue I could use on a regular basis. I thought I could do a weekly student night, but I wouldn't be able to fill The Haçienda each week. I needed an alternative and managed to get a meeting at Home.

Nobody talks about Home much anymore, or certainly not as much as they bang on about The Haçienda, but Home was a really important club in the early to mid-1990s. Home was launched by Tom Bloxham, who came to Manchester as a student, and first started out selling bootleg posters in Affleck's Palace. Tom went on to found Urban Splash, a ground-breaking property company who were one of the first to start turning Manchester's derelict old mills into loft apartments in the 1990s, and then across the country. Tom also went on to be the Chairman of Manchester International Festival and trustee of the Tate and Manchester United Foundation. He was already a really impressive character when I met him at Home, and you could tell he was going to play a big role in shaping the future of the city. He also stood out because he was quite a sharp dresser. While most of us were wearing baggy clothes and dressing down, Bloxham and Wilson were the only ones round town who were wearing Yohji Yamamoto suits.

Although house music was now pretty established, and the basis of most of the biggest club nights across Manchester and the country, student nights were slower to catch on.

By the time I started promoting student nights in 1994, students were more clued up, and getting bored of the still pretty formulaic nights that hadn't changed for years. You would get half an hour of 1970s music, and then half an hour of 1980s music and then a few more modern tracks like 'Jump Around' by House of Pain or maybe something by The Prodigy or Cypress Hill. I could probably list you fifteen of the songs that would always get played. To me it was pretty obvious that there was a big gap for someone (me) to do a student night that was more dance-music orientated. Even if it was the more accessible end of house music, and not something really under-ground. So, I started a night at Home with my friend Jonathan Newman, who I called J-Boy, and it started to do well almost immediately.

I was made to feel really welcome at Home. I was still living in the bedsit in Salford and Home became a bit of a home from home. The building at Ducie House had some really creative people working out of it. So What Arts, Simply Red's management team led by Elliot Rashman were in there, plus the *Jockey Slut* offices, led by John 'Johnno' Burgess and Paul Benney, who had just started doing a night called Bugged Out at Sankeys, and who I still work with at The Warehouse Project to this day. 808 State also had their office in there and they were really friendly and supportive, too. All of a sudden I felt that I was part of the Manchester music scene, albeit a very small cog in the machine at the time, but almost everyone made you feel welcome. The manager of Home was called Joe

Strong, who had been one of the original managers of Ministry of Sound. There was also a really lovely guy called Simon Calderbank who ran a night called Foundation, that was really successful there. There was a really good crowd at Home. The only person who looked down on me was Mick Hucknall, when he came in the office. He just seemed a bit arrogant and pretentious.

It was also at Home that I saw cocaine for the first time. The drug of choice for many people was changing, and that definitely brought about a change in the mood in clubs as well. From the collective euphoria of the early halcyon days of ecstasy and acid house, things had gone slightly darker. In the early 1990s cocaine wasn't very widespread, but by the mid- to late 1990s it seemed like it was everywhere. The collective mood of a club full of people on ecstasy is very different to the collective mood of a club full of people on cocaine. Particularly the cheap street gak that seemed to be everywhere at times.

At that time, I was just a one-man band, really, and would even go out and flyer all my nights and do everything myself. I didn't even have a computer, let alone a website or email. All I had was my basic Ericsson mobile. I would run everything from that one phone, and some weeks I couldn't even do that because it had been cut off because I hadn't paid the bill, because I was skint. I was still living a hand-to-mouth existence really.

When the student nights got established, Tom Bloxham asked me if I could get a bit more involved with the weekend nights. It was then than I became more exposed to the gang trouble they were having. There were two incidents in particular that stand out. The first one was when twenty guys from Salford walked up to the club all wearing balaclavas. They just went through the whole club, smashing the place up, and obviously scaring the life out of the punters; they just walked out, and nobody could do a thing. It was all because they wanted to run the door and if they weren't going to be given the door, then they were going to cause as much trouble as possible.

The other incident was when I got caught in the crossfire of a drive-by shooting and was very lucky to survive. I was running the guest list on a Saturday night, and I was stood outside by the bouncers, with the guest list on a clip board. We heard it before we saw it and looked up to see a car flying round the corner and a gunman leaning out and opening fire. The bouncers immediately realised what was happening and ran inside and shut the steel doors, but I must have been a bit frozen to the spot, like a rabbit caught in the headlights, and I was left on my own stood outside, still holding the fucking clipboard in my hand. Thankfully all the bullets somehow missed me, but you can still see the bullet marks clearly on the corner of Ducie House to this day. Every time I walk or drive past and see them it sends a shiver down my spine and takes me right back to that evening.

After the drive-by shooting on the Saturday evening, Tom Bloxham called and chaired a meeting on the Monday morning. Tom was pretty hands-on with the club at that stage, and while he was talking and discussing how we should handle it, I could see Joe Strong, the manager, writing something down on a piece of paper. I just thought he was taking notes, but when he'd finished writing he pushed the piece of paper across the table to Tom. In hindsight, I realise that it was a resignation letter. Joe said, 'Sorry, Tom, I've got a family to think of. I can't do this anymore, I'm off' and got up and left. That was the last time we ever saw him, and I've no idea what happened to him. He'd just had enough and walked away. He wasn't the only one.

I was still a kid at this stage. I was only twenty-three. A year ago, I'd been working in a clothes shop for twenty quid a day, and living at my mum's, and now I was having to deal with gangsters on an almost daily basis.

I remember Tom Bloxham telling one of the gangsters in Home one night, 'Listen, don't come in the club and threaten me. You know where my office is. I'm there every day from nine to six, so if you got a problem come and see me in there and we'll sort it out.'

The doors at Home were being run by Mickey Francis and his firm, who were known as Loc 19. They were old Manchester City hooligans, and one of them only had half an ear, because he'd lost the other half in a fight. At the time they were taxing me fifty pence for every person that came through the door on my nights. I charged £2.50 (£3 for non-students) and they took fifty pence off me for each person. It probably doesn't sound like much, but if I had 600 in attendance, I had to give Loc 19 £300 (about £700 in today's money), so they were probably taking half my profit.

Problem is, I would have good weeks and bad weeks, especially when the students were on holiday, but they didn't give a fuck if I'd had a bad week. They still wanted paying a decent amount on bad weeks, even if I didn't have the numbers. Some weeks I wouldn't make any money at all, I was literally putting the night on and doing all the work, just to hand over whatever I made straight to the gangs. One of my DJs at the time was a guy called Leaky Fresh, who was from Moss Side. He was a really lovely cool guy – tall and good-looking, with braids. Leaky had a really laid-back manner, and a way of charming women. He was a great DJ, too, and he'd actually been in the World DMC Championships in 1989, which is like the World Championships of DJing. At one stage, when I was having a few bad weeks, he could see what was going on, so decided to help me out, as it was no good for him if the nights became unworkable because he wouldn't get paid, either. Leaky called a meeting with one of the head doormen from Loc 19, a bloke called Warren, in his little record shop in town. There was a record store in the Corn Exchange downstairs near the entrance of Konspiracy called Underground Records run by two guys, but it had a small backroom where Leaky ran his own little shop from. Leaky managed to convince Warren to give me a few weeks grace from paying Loc 19, otherwise the night would be finished, and I would go bust. I was really grateful to Leaky for calling that meeting and trying to help me out, but I knew it was only a temporary reprieve. They would soon be demanding money again. Although I never considered leaving Manchester, as some people did, I knew I was going to have to leave Home.

Paradise Factory

After I'd decided to leave Home, I found myself in Paradise.

Located on Charles Street, behind the old BBC building on Oxford Road (fifteen years before the BBC moved to Media City in Salford), Paradise Factory was located in the old Factory Records headquarters. At the heart of Factory's halcyon days in 1989, Factory famously bought the building and spent a fortune converting it into their new offices, including an infamous boardroom table, suspended from the ceiling. After Factory went bust in 1992, Peter Dalton and Carol Ainscow bought the building and set about converting it into a nightclub, which they called Paradise Factory, in a nod to the building's history. Carol and Peter's partnership had first made their name with the opening of Manto bar in the Gay Village in 1990. Before the arrival of Manto, the Gay Village was a rough collection of pubs based around the canals and red-light district, and had a pretty seedy reputation, not helped by the bigoted God Cop James Anderton, who had regularly targeted the village and came out with homophobic comments. Manto started the revolution of Gay Village, it was the architectural 'coming out' of the village. Unlike the old-school queer pubs like the New

Union, that kept their business hidden within, Manto was on full display, with floor to ceiling windows.

Peter and Carol were really important, pioneering figures in the development of Manchester in the early 1990s, and they could also be pretty formidable, particularly Carol, who sadly died in 2013, aged just fifty-five, after battling a brain tumour. Peter was a great supporter of mine in those early days, Carol perhaps less so. I was petrified of her.

I was still pretty naïve at the time, I was only twenty-three and had been putting on club nights for less than a year when I moved to Paradise Factory, and on my first night there I went up to the head doorman, Roy, to find out how much he was going to tax me.

'How much do you want off me?' I asked him.

'What you mean?' replied Roy, 'Aren't you paying the club a hire fee, like?'

'Well, yeah,' I said, 'but don't you want something off me as well?'

I had just presumed that was the norm after my dealings with the bouncers at Home. 'They used to take fifty pence a person off me at Home, and it was killing me some weeks, so can we do forty pence a person?'

Roy just looked at me.

'What … the doormen used to tax you on the door?

'Well, yeah.'

Roy just laughed. 'Nah, I won't do that. Just give us a drink at the end of the night if you've done well.'

I liked Roy and got on with him, and even used to give him £50 at the end of each night, which doesn't seem that generous now, but he was happy with that at the time.

Paradise Factory was great. I ended up working there for seven years, which is an eternity in clubbing years, and I loved it. I ran two nights there – Release and Shooting Stars. Release was the first one I started, and that ran from 1994 to 2001, so I had several generations of students through the doors. Its success, I think, was down to two things: first, we didn't patronise the students when it came to music policy – we didn't follow the formulaic approach of other nights going on in town that had a mixture of 1970s and 1980s classics, we played decent house music, even if it was the more accessible type of house music, rather than underground – and second, I was all over the promotion. There were roughly 60,000 students in Manchester at that time, and I did everything to make sure that every one of them knew about Release at Paradise Factory.

On the music side, most of the credit at my Paradise nights can go to one guy. I began to book a DJ who I honestly hand-on-heart believe is one of the most underrated DJs of his generation, certainly in Manchester and the UK, Dave Booth.

Dave had been a DJ in Manchester since way before I had started going out to clubs, in fact since I was at primary school. Dave started out DJing in the 1970s at a club called Pips, which was a hugely influential Manchester venue located near the old Corn Exchange, right by where the National Museum of Football is now. Joy Division did their first ever gig at Pips, and Dave was the DJ at that gig, so it doesn't get any more seminal than that. A generation later, he was also a tour DJ for The Stone Roses and played for them at a lot of their landmark gigs, including Spike Island. He also played at many other clubs including Playpen, Isadora's, The Haçienda, and Garlands in Liverpool. Dave tragically passed away in 2020, although it was nice to see all the tributes that were paid to him from everyone including Peter Hook, Ian Brown and 808 State, and to know that he was really appreciated by people who mattered. Even though he never truly got the wider recognition he deserved, I've never seen anyone who could control a room and a dancefloor quite like Dave Booth could, and he certainly got the respect of everyone who was involved in Manchester's clubbing scene at the time.

The manager of Paradise Factory back then was a guy called Andy O'Dwyer, and although I wasn't being taxed by the bouncers, he *did* start taxing me.

At first, I didn't say anything about being taxed, as I thought I was pushing my luck working there anyway, so I just grudgingly accepted it, but after a while I got more and more pissed off with handing over £700 to Andy every week, so I complained about the situation to Peter. At this stage, I was making probably £500 or £600 a week, still just about getting by, but then I had costs to cover as well. (Andy was making more money than me most weeks!). Peter and Carol wanted proof that he was taxing me, so they asked me to phone him up and try and negotiate with him and record the conversation. I did that and when I played them back the recording, and they had proof of what had been going on, Andy was sacked.

I was still doing all my own promotion for most of the nights, standing outside clubs and bars, night after night, handing out flyers and talking to people and spreading the word. One night when I was out doing that, I met a girl called Elisa Marchionne.

Though she had grown up in Cheshire, Elisa was half Italian: her dad came from a small village called Carpineto, up in the hills of Pescara. Elisa was doing a course in window design in Italy, where her family was from, but was back home for the holidays. We went out on a date and quickly became an item, and then she started working with me on the nights, and we became a team, and I was no longer a one-man band. It was Elisa who really managed to get the student market nailed when it came to our promotion. She was the real driving force behind that, and she ended up with teams of students working for her, getting the message into all the student halls and unions. We even managed to borrow the keys to some of the halls, from one of the cleaners, in exchange for a bottle of whisky each week. We managed to leave flyers and posters actually inside the halls, where none of our rival promoters could get to, and they could never work out how we managed that.

Elisa and I ended up getting married in 2000, and although we later split up, we're still on good terms, and she is still part of The Warehouse Project and Parklife team.

One week, I decided to give away a car at Release, as a bit of a gimmick. I promoted it beforehand, and on the night everyone who came in was given a raffle ticket, and we announced the winner towards the end of the night. It was only an Orange Ford Escort, that I had bought through AutoTrader for £400 or something. Paradise Factory had these big service doors on the side of the building, so I just opened up those doors and drove the car onto the middle of the dancefloor and had it there all night till the raffle. It was all a bit tongue in cheek, just a silly gimmick. But what I hadn't thought through was that in those days everybody still smoked in clubs, and obviously the car was full of petrol. It was a huge fire risk – a health and safety nightmare. Peter Dalton didn't find out what I'd done till the morning after, and then he went fucking mental at me. He hit the fucking roof, and to be honest, he was right. It was pretty bloody stupid of me. But then, nobody else had said anything on the night either.

A similar thing happened at The Haçienda once, when they thought it would be a good idea to have a full-size ice cream van in the club. They drove it in through the service doors on

Whitworth Street West, but then a fire officer happened to turn up and just went, 'What on earth? That's full of petrol and people are smoking in here!', so they had to take it out immediately. Being The Haçienda, they pushed it outside, siphoned all the petrol out so it wasn't a fire risk, and then pushed it back in, to get round the fire officer.

One of the other battles I had with Peter Dalton at Paradise Factory, was when I had the idea of a foam party, but he kept saying, 'No, no, no. You're not doing a foam party. No way.' But I was desperate to do one, and kept pestering him, and in the end I just wore him down and he said, 'For god's sake! OK, you can do one foam party next week, but it's a one-off, Sacha, and don't ask me again after this!' We went ahead and did it, and it was a total sell out, and a huge success. It was a bit grubby, the Paradise Factory, to be fair. Most nightclubs and late-night bars are. Punters just can't tell usually because it's usually dark and loud when they're in there but trust me if you went in your regular nightclub during the daytime you would be shocked at how dirty it was, and how it stank of stale beer. The morning after that foam party, Peter rang me up first thing and said, 'You can do a foam party every week if you want … that's the cleanest the club has ever looked!'

Foam parties are not as easy as they seem. The first time The Haçienda had one, they hired in a foam machine and Paul Mason, the manager, was fixing it to the balcony and trying to get it to work. He managed to switch it on, but had it facing the wrong way, so the highly concentrated foam mixture shot straight into his long, curly hair. Poor Paul had to walk down Deansgate in the rain, back to his flat at St John's Gardens for a shower, with this trail of foam coming off his head behind him!

The other night I ran at Paradise Factory, called Shooting Stars, ran on Thursday nights and took its name from the Vic Reeves and Bob Mortimer TV show that was hugely popular at the time. The idea was that we would have a guest celebrity every week, the kind of celebrity that would appear on Vic and Bob's show, and the flyer would give a clue as to which celebrity was going to appear that week. We had all sorts of characters – from Timmy Mallett to Howard Marks to Katie Price to Margarita Pracatan, the Cuban singer who used to appear on Clive James's TV chat show. Timmy Mallet was great; he went round the club and was interacting with all the students. Katie Price, the notorious Page 3 model turned up pissed, and all she really did was get on the mic and say, 'Do I make your cock go hard?'

Bob Carolgees with Spit the Dog was a bit tricky. After we had agreed a fee, Bob's agent said, 'Do you want Spit to come as well, because there will be an extra fee for him?' Of course I wanted Spit! That's who I thought I had already booked. Who is Bob, without Spit?

I booked Howard Marks, the famous drug dealer, one night. His book *Mr Nice* had just been released and was a huge bestseller. The only problem with that night was that there had just been a huge drugs raid by the police on Paradise the weekend before, and after the raid, Peter Dalton rang me up and said, 'You're going to have to cancel Marks, we can't have him appearing at the club just after we've had a drug raid.' But I knew it was going to be a massive night, as Howard was so huge at the time, so I persuaded Peter to let us go ahead, and thankfully it passed without incident. The students absolutely loved him. Quite a few punters had brought ready-rolled spliffs for him to autograph, which he was happy to do, and he told a few stories about his exploits smuggling coke from South America, and they lapped it up.

After I'd been at Paradise Factory for a while, the door was taken over by a guy called Ratty from Wigan. Ratty seemed quite quiet when I first met him. He was in his late twenties, over six foot and built like a tank. He had short blond hair, and he was no stranger to a sunbed. All his crew were from Wigan and Preston, and had broad Lancashire accents. Although he seemed quite quiet, you definitely wouldn't want to get on the wrong side of him. After taking over from Roy, Ratty ran the door for quite a few years at Paradise Factory, till after I stopped doing nights there. He had to deal with people trying to intimidate him and take the door off him, but that was almost expected back then. One night I was walking down Charles Street to the club and the whole street was thick with smoke, and I couldn't work out where it was coming from till I got closer to the club, when I realised that a gang had firebombed Ratty's Mercedes convertible, and it was smouldering outside the club.

There was another particular incident when an Egyptian guy was trying to muscle in and take some of Ratty's doors from him. One night Ratty and his right-hand man decided to make matters clear to him and took him to the bridge over the canal on Charles Street, by Paradise Factory, and held him over it by his ankles, threatening him. Unfortunately, Ratty's right-hand man sneezed while he was holding him and dropped the poor guy in the river. He seemed to get the message.

Granada: From the North

After a couple of years at Paradise Factory, I was getting more ambitious, and increasingly feeling the need to do something bigger. I needed to. I had to. I really wanted to prove to myself, and to everyone else in Manchester, that I was capable of pulling off something bigger than student nights. But there was also a need to start making real money, because I was still living hand-to-mouth, week-to-week, getting my phone cut off now and again because I hadn't paid the bill and receiving the odd unwelcome visit from a bailiff about some other bill I hadn't paid. It was no way to live, and it was also reminding me of my life when I was a teenager when my dad was in financial trouble, and everything started getting repossessed. I had to find a way to make a gear change, to step things up a little.

I started looking around for a possible venue and came up with the idea of doing a night at the Granada TV Studios Tour. Back in the 1990s, Granada was still based in the city centre, at the bottom of Quay Street, near where the new Factory International building is now. It was the brainchild of Granada's David Plowright who had envisaged it as a 'Hollywood-on-the-Irwell' (the River Irwell runs alongside the site) and originally opened in 1988. The exterior was a replica New York street scene, which was supposed to look a bit like Times Square, with yellow cabs and huge neon signs. Inside there were various mock sets from past Granada productions including Baker Street from *The Adventures of Sherlock Holmes*, the giant room from *Return of the Antelope*; and then the main attraction for most people was the actual *Coronation Street* set that they used for filming. You could walk down the famous cobbles and even pop in and have a pint in a mock-up of the Rovers Return. In 1997, they added Skytrak, which was the world's first flying, solo roll-ercoaster: a single person was strapped in and suspended, in almost the same position as a hang glider would be, and then 'flew' round the theme park.

I thought it could be a great place to do a huge party, but when I initially approached Granada they weren't fully convinced about the idea and they also told me, 'Look, it's company policy that we only work with blue-chip companies.' At that stage my little operation was still more chips and gravy than blue chip, so I needed to bring someone else in to convince Granada to take a chance on the event.

I had already done a couple of nights at The Haçienda that were sponsored by Tim Cox, who owned a Häagen-Dazs fran-chised shop in St Ann's Arcade in Manchester. He only ran that one shop, he didn't really represent Häagen-Dazs or anything, but I thought if I brought him on board we could use the Häagen-Dazs name to get us in the door at Granada. I also misguidedly thought that Tim was loaded and might be able to help with cashflow. I subsequently learnt he was as skint as me, and his image was all a bit of a front. But Tim and I agreed to be partners on the first event with a fifty-fifty revenue split. Most importantly, badging it as a Häagen-Dazs event did the trick and got us in the door at Granada. They still had their reservations and I had to continually reassure them, but we were in the door and started to set plans in motion.

It was the first time the Granada Studios Tour had ever done an event like this. They had previously hosted a queer event, but that had been quite a bit smaller, nothing on the scale that I was planning. Rightly so, they had their concerns about protecting their brand and reputation, particularly about the risk of any stories in the press about drug use. Granada was a household name, a family name, the home of *Coronation Street*, and they didn't want that name being dragged through the mud or being attached to any controversy; they had their staff and security all over me and the event. We weren't really running a lot of the show, Granada were. We booked all the acts, promoted it, sold the tickets, and put the production in, but when it came down to the nuts and bolts of running the actual venue, the bars, and the security of the venue, Granada kept all that in house.

I was continually reassuring Granada that I had everything under control and all the preparation was going to plan, but to be honest, I was flying by the seat of my pants and making it up as I went along as I'd never run an event like this in my life.

I brought in Colin Sinclair to look after the production side of things for me. Colin owned a club called The Boardwalk on Little Peter Street, which had opened in 1986 and ran till 1999, and was a great club for most of the 1990s – Dave Haslam, having first made his name DJing at The Temperance Club on Thursday nights at The Haçienda, did a long running club night there on Saturdays called Yellow. Colin's dad owned the building that the Boardwalk was in and there were rehearsal rooms in the basement that everyone from Simply Red to Happy Mondays had used. Oasis had a rehearsal room in there for two years before they got signed, writing most of their first two albums in there.

I really liked Colin and got on with him. We used to have our planning meetings in Oliver Peyton's restaurant, Mash and Air, during the day. Colin got a guy called Andy Stratford to do all the heavy lifting and legwork on the production and put the PAs in (Colin wasn't the type to get his hands dirty) and he did a really good job.

As ever, we had some real issues with gangs around the event. Damian Noonan wanted to do the security but the Greater Manchester Police were totally against that. At that stage they were trying to get to grips with the gang issues. One of the problems was that Damian's door team had recently done an event at G-Mex, when the police knew they had basically let all their mates in, and there was blatant drug-dealing going on in the venue. I had to have a meeting with the council and police, and Damian sent along his right-hand man, but the police officer present said to him, 'Under no circumstances are you going to get to run the security at this event, and I'm instructing Granada now, to that effect.' It got really heated and I realised I was way in over my head at this point. I'm the type of guy who always makes sure I'm under the speed limit, and if a police car is behind me when I'm driving I start worrying even though I've done nothing wrong. But here I am, still only in my mid-twenties and caught in the middle of a stand-off between the gangsters and the authorities. Damian's representative just stood up, stared at the police officer and said, 'I'll be reporting back to Daddy.' All Damian's crew used to call him Daddy. He threw his business card on the table and said, 'There's my card, you will be calling me in a few days' and walked out. I was shitting it and said, 'Oh, my god, is that a threat?' And the police officer said, 'Yeah, they do this all the time.'

In the end, the door was run by Mark Logan from Showsec, who we still work with to this date – he is responsible for the security at The Warehouse Project and Parklife. The Granada Studios Tour was also the first time I realised why Dunbury Spring Water seemed to be strangely popular in licensed premises around Manchester. There was a member of Manchester City Council's Health and Safety team, who lived somewhere out near Buxton – famous for their spring water – and had a stream at the bottom of his garden. This guy's wife would spend all day bottling water from the stream, and then sticking the labels on they had printed that read 'Dunbury Spring Water', like a Northern version of that episode of *Only Fools and Horses* where Del Boy starts supplying restaurants with freshly bottled 'Peckham Spring' water. Although Del Boy wasn't a member of the council's Health and Safety team!

Two days before the event, this health and safety officer turned up at Granada Studios Tour, in his official capacity, to sign off my licence for the event. His opening gambit was something like, 'Good to meet you, now, what water are you selling?' It seemed a strange first question to ask.

'I've no idea,' I replied, 'we don't run the bars, Granada do ...'

'Oh, OK. But you will need water for all your production staff and artists, won't you?' He asked me, pointedly.

'Er, yeah, I guess so.'

'A couple of pallets should do it? ... It just so happens that I'm in my van today, and I've got a couple of pallets of Dunbury Spring Water with me. So, I can drop them off while I'm here, and give you an invoice?'

'Er, OK.'

'Great ... well, everything seems in order here, so I'm happy to sign off the licence.'

That's how it worked! If you went out in Manchester back in the 1990s and remember buying a bottle of Dunbury Spring Water from The Haçienda or one of my events, and thought, 'Dunbury Spring Water? I've never heard of that before?' now you know where it came from. If you ask any promoters or club managers from that time, they will laugh about that, and were quite possibly 'persuaded' by the Buxton resident that it might help get their licence signed off if they were to stock Dunbury Spring Water at their event. I can assure you, that would not happen these days.

I had brought in Ang Matthews from The Haçienda, and her boyfriend Billy Idle, to programme the event and book all the DJs. It was a step up from the talent I was used to booking. We'd gone from booking John Harlow, Ashton-under-Lyne's finest, to Jeremy Healy, Farley Jackmaster Funk, Boy George. I think we paid the headliners about £5,000 each, where I was used to paying DJs around £250.

A lot of DJs on the bill were people Ang and Billy knew already, like Jeremy Healy. One of the other headliners was Nigel Benn – the professional boxer – who for a short period back then had a second career as a DJ. He played in the Baker Street studios, where they filmed *The Adventures of Sherlock Holmes*, and even I will admit he wasn't great. I remember standing there and overhearing two lads in front of me talking and one of them asked the other, 'This is terrible, is he actually DJing with his gloves on?'

Jeremy Healy had also taken a booking in Swansea the same night, and we ended up doing a live link up from Granada to the venue in Swansea, and during his set, every now and then, he would hold up a sign that said, 'Hello Swansea'. I can't imagine it was the greatest experience for the poor crowd in Swansea, just watching that on a feed from Manchester!

Ticket sales for the event had been incredible, though. Capacity was 4,500 but I accidentally sold 5,200 tickets and took £150,000 on ticket sales. Overselling it really was accidental. I was selling tickets through various outlets around town, and even though I'd rang up and told them it was sold out, some of them carried on selling till I picked up the leftover tickets, as they wanted their cut. The problem was, the entrance at Granada had full-length turnstiles that automatically counted people in, so I had to find a way of getting the extra 700 people in without them being counted. In the end, when we had got 4,000 people through, I got Andy Strat to fuse the electronic turnstiles, so they stopped working and then all the punters had to come shuffling in through the manual gates. Granada were never the wiser and never knew exactly how many people we had in there.

The Skytrak rollercoaster was predictably a bit of a disaster on the evening. All these drunk punters were getting on it, and then flying around above the crowd like Superman, and inevitably half of them would be sick on the crowd below, so we had to close that down after less than an hour.

The crowd itself was quite a commercial crowd, quite mainstream. Much more Discotheque Royal than Warehouse Project. We actually had to throw out a couple of students that evening after we caught them having sex in Jack and Vera's backyard. They knew exactly where they were, and they must have been big *Corrie* punters. They'd deliberately gone to Jack and Vera's and were having sex next to Jack's pigeon shed. We saw it on CCTV and couldn't believe our eyes. *Next to Jack's pigeon shed?* You wouldn't have thought that was the sexiest place, would you? I can't remember exactly what they said when we kicked them out, but they weren't embarrassed at all, I think they were actually quite proud of what they'd achieved

75

and thought it was definitely worth getting chucked out for. I doubt it's a tale they'll tell their grandchildren, though. Or maybe they will if they're massive *Coronation Street* fans too. No pigeons were harmed in the event.

This really was a turning point for me. It was the first time I had made any proper money, and I managed to pay off all my bills, and was still left with £10,000 in the bank. I was fluid. That might not seem like a fortune to some people, but I felt like a millionaire right there. It gave me belief that I had something to build on.

Never Invite Bouncers to a Wedding

On reflection, it probably wasn't the wisest idea to invite a bunch of nightclub bouncers to my wedding at a genteel golf club in Cheshire. I mean, a bunch of big bouncers from Wigan that liked to party hard at a posh wedding in Cheshire – what could possibly go wrong?

It was August 2000, and I'd been working with Ratty and his boys for quite a while at Paradise Factory, and we'd just given them the door for Sankeys, so we were pretty friendly at the time.

Elisa's parents, Fiore and Lynn, were pretty well connected in Cheshire, and they invited a lot of the Hale and Bowden posh 'set'. They had a business selling high-end Italian furniture to the local ladies who lunch, and that was their circle. The wedding was quite a high-end affair at Mere Golf Club, which is really hoity-toity, and just near where Rick Astley and my first girlfriend lived. It was a mixture of posh Cheshire set, and then forty-eight Italians from Elisa's dad Fiore's home village of Carpineto. Most of Elisa's relatives didn't speak English, and were farmers from rural Italy, not the rough streets of Naples; so to come to a big city like Manchester was a bit of an eye-opener for them.

There was a weird mix of demographics there already but then, in the middle of that mix, there was the Paradise Factory table, with Ratty and his crew and Peter Dalton, and a few others. I noticed pretty early on that their table was getting rowdier and rowdier, which I should have expected really. They were clearly there to have a good time, let's put it that way.

It so happened that our wedding was the night before Captain's Day, which is like golf's FA Cup Final, and the biggest day of the venue's year – a huge annual showpiece event. So obviously everyone at the golf club will have been building up to Captain's Day for months, with extremely detailed preparations to make sure everything was perfect.

Just after the speeches, as it was getting dark and the party was about to get started, management came looking for me, and they were absolutely livid. Unfortunately, Ratty and his boys had stumbled across where the golf buggies were stored, god knows how, and had somehow hot-wired them. They were out on the golf course, speeding up and down the fairways and doing handbrake turns and donuts on the greens. 'We tried to stop them,' fumed the manager, 'but they just told us to fuck off.'

So, the night before the golf club's big showpiece event, Ratty and his mates had ripped up the turf on some of the greens. To say the manager was apoplectic is an understatement.

Unfortunately, things only got worse from there on. Fiore and Lynn had put up all of his Italian family in the Bowden Hotel and organised a coach to take them back there from the club. But Ratty found out that Elisa and I were staying at Mere Court, a small quaint country-house hotel on the outskirts of Knutsford. So Ratty and his crew gatecrashed the Italians' coach and told the coach driver in no uncertain terms that he was driving them to our hotel first. Apparently, they were singing songs and being really boisterous on the coach, and Fiore told me later that all the Italians were a bit intimidated.

After the coach driver dropped them off, Ratty and his crew were determined to carry on partying. It was now about one in the morning, and it was only a small quaint hotel, but Ratty and his crew were really going for it, and having a proper party, getting up to no good, being boisterous, and playing music too loudly. The first knock on the door came from some poor teenager who worked behind the bar, who had been sent up to tell the group to turn it down, but when Ratty answered the door and this kid saw this guy the size of a brick shithouse, he just looked and said, 'Er, it doesn't matter.' They must have sent up about three or four different staff to get the music turned down, and in the end they just gave up. I don't think the hotel dared to bar Ratty and friends the next morning, but I think we knew they would never be welcome back there.

Fiore's poor family from that little town were probably scarred for life, just like the greens on the golf course from the hijacked buggies!

Flyposter Wars

When I initially met Dave Vincent in the late 1990s, I thought he was an arrogant little Cockney, with a big mouth and little manners. Which is exactly who he was back then, as I'm sure he would be the first to admit. But apart from being arrogant and annoying, he was also a bloody good promoter. (I'm sure he'd be the first to admit that too!)

Dave was a proper Cockney. He came from a rough estate in Stepney and had quite a tough upbringing. He and his mates had their fair share of brushes with the police as teenagers. I don't think Dave had seen much life outside of London, till he went to visit a mate of his called Avi, who was at university in Manchester, and it opened his eyes a bit. Dave went on to move to Manchester and became a mature student at UMIST. While he was a student he quickly fell into promoting club nights as well, and by the time I met him he was selling out big nights and had become one of my rival student promoters in Manchester. One of the things that helped Dave in the early days of the late 1990s, was that he knew quite a lot of the London DJs, especially in the growing garage scene, and he was one of the first to offer them gigs outside London. He started to do pretty well, and by the time I got to know him a bit better, around 1997, he had a night on called Colours at The Haçienda, which was regularly selling out and had a good reputation on the clubbing scene. He also promoted Ministry of Sounds nights there.

Dave, it's safe to say, was a character. He was larger than life, and you would always be hearing crazy stories about what he was up to. He was obsessed by Danny Tenaglia, and he was involved in one of the first mad stories I heard about Danny. Dave had booked Danny to play the Academy in Manchester, and he had to collect him from Sheffield first, because Danny had just been performing there. Dave, being obsessed, offered to drive over to Sheffield and pick him up himself. Snake Pass, as it is known locally, is a road that runs over the Pennines and Peak District from Sheffield to Manchester, and it's really exposed to the elements, so high in the peaks, and often gets closed off due to bad weather. That night it was snowing and visibility on the roads was awful, as Dave and his mate Jools were driving back over the top with Tenaglia, in Dave's little Clio. It was pitch black, and as they came round a blind bend, they hit a cow that was in the middle of the road. It was a large cow, and it ended up stuck across the bonnet of the Clio, and Dave and Jools had to jump out and drag the cow off the car before they could carry on. Tenaglia must have thought, *What the fuck have I got myself into?!* God knows what the poor cow thought too. I believe it was still alive when they dragged it off the bonnet, hopefully it survived to tell the tale.

Towards the end of the 1990s, Dave and I were in direct competition, and we would play dirty tricks on each other; anything we could do to try and get one up on each other. He had an office in Beehive Mill and now and again I would phone up his office and disguise my voice, I'd say something like, 'There's a group of us who were planning to come down to Colours this week, but is it true it's been cancelled?'

'No, why would you think it's been cancelled?'

'I've just seen your posters up in Chester and it's got a big 'cancelled' sticker across it.'

'What?!?'

Dave or one of his team would then fly out of his office in Beehive Mill and drive down to Chester, Stockport or Bury (I'd always choose a location which was a bit of a drive, to make it more of an inconvenience for them) to check on his posters, and they would lose a day's work and promoting. It was a pretty low trick, looking back, but he absolutely gave as good as he got back by pulling similar stunts on me, too. Most promoters would. Promoting was a dog-eat-dog world back then, so everyone was playing a little bit dirty. You had to. I knew for a fact that Dave or his team were tearing down my posters, and as soon as he was putting up posters, we would go around town pasting our posters over his. If I knew he was out in Bury that day, putting posters up, I'd go round after him and rip them down before the paste had even dried, or post mine over his.

It's hard for young kids and promoters nowadays to understand just how important flying and flypostering was back in the day, but before social media it was the main way of promoting your night. Email didn't even exist when I started promoting. Well, it maybe existed, but I didn't even have an email address and most of the punters I wanted to reach definitely didn't have one. I didn't have a website. I didn't even have a computer! I just ran everything through my mobile phone. That was my office. My mobile phone and my Filofax were the only office I used back then. I still use both. I must be one of the few people running nightclubs who is still using a Filofax in 2024, but it's just habit. I've got the same Filofax I had twenty years ago; I just buy a new diary insert each year.

These days almost all of our promotion for The Warehouse Project is done online and we have a full-time social media team in the office. The only time we would really do flypostering now is maybe at the start of the season, to announce the line-up. But back in the 1990s and early 2000s, there was no social media. Flyers and flypostering *was* our social media, and they were hugely important to nightclubs. There was almost a direct correlation between how many posters you managed to get up around town and how many paying punters you got through the door. Obviously which artists you booked also had a huge effect, but flypostering was almost as important. Didn't matter who you had booked, if you didn't paper the town then you wouldn't sell out. In the early days, me and Elisa would sometimes spend all day flyering, go home for tea, then back out till 2 a.m. in the freezing cold and rain putting up posters in the dark, dodging the police. After a while, I started flypostering during the day in a high-vis jacket, and the police would just drive past and assume I had permission as it was so brazen.

Most of the flypostering in and around Manchester was controlled by Kev and Vinny back then, who were real old-school characters. They weren't gangsters but they knew *everyone*. I really liked Kev and Vinny, but I didn't use them all the time, as I never wanted my poster to just be one in a row of twenty other posters, jostling for attention. I always wanted to find a way to stand out and use different sites. I did use them sometimes as there was kind of an unwritten rule that everyone would use Kev and Vinny at some stage, they were kings of the flypostering world in Manchester in the 1990s.

I always got on well with them and they even invited me shooting and horse racing with them. They were both really into shooting, and I don't mean clay pigeon shooting; they would go on proper old-school country shoots in Cheshire and come back with a brace of pheasants or grouse. Kev and Vinny lived amazing double lives. Monday to Friday they would be grafting the streets around Manchester, dealing with club promotors and sorting any problems out on the streets, dealing with some pretty rum characters ... then they would spend their weekend hanging out with Lords and toffs on their incredible rolling estates in Cheshire, shooting grouse. I never went shooting as it didn't appeal to me, and I have no idea how they got into that scene. Kev and Vinny are now retired, but their nephew Keith set up his own flyer and promotion company called Exposure in the 1990s and he's still running it now; everyone knows him as Keith Exposure or Minced Beef. Lovely lad and a big United fan.

Kev and Vinny had some rules they would stick to about not flyposting on glass windows and bus stops, but back then I didn't really give a fuck. I wouldn't dream of doing anything like this now, but I was still young and determined to make my nights work, no matter what, so I would flyposter everywhere. After he had left The Haçienda, Paul Mason moved in with his girlfriend, Jo, on the ground floor of Sally's Yard, one of Urban Splash's first developments, just off Oxford Road. He got up one morning, drew the curtains open, and it was still dark. He thought, *What the fuck?* and went outside to investigate, only to find out that someone had completely flypostered over the windows of their flat. He was absolutely fuming. To add insult to injury, he then got up on a ladder with some soapy water to try and remove the offending flyposter, and as he was up the ladder, a police car pulled up behind him and started to caution him for flypostering. 'It's my bloody flat!' said Paul, 'I'm trying to get the bleeding thing off, not stick it up!'[3]

Dave Vincent also didn't stick to fly-posting etiquette, and the tit for tat between us was getting a bit ridiculous, so one day he called me and said, 'Listen, why don't we have a chat and see if we can work together, because we can't go on like this, we're both spending half our time battling each other instead of trying to fill nightclubs!'

We arranged to meet at the bar Generation X, for a bit of a summit meeting, where we both agreed we were wasting a lot of time and money on competing with each other, and that we should try and find a way to work together instead. We had quite a lengthy talk about how we could move forward, then Dave suddenly looked at his watch and said, 'Shit, I'm gonna have to go, it's Patsy my girlfriend's birthday tomorrow and I've got stuff to organise.' I was like, 'Wow, that's a weird coincidence it's actually Elisa's birthday tomorrow as well.' Dave looked at me and said, 'When's your birthday?' I said '26th January' and Dave went white and said, 'Fackin' hell. That's my birthday too!'

Which was a bit of a weird coincidence, and we bonded a bit over that, and decided we were going to work together. Our birthdays were about the only thing we had in common, as Dave and I were very different characters. He was a wide boy Cockney, I was Manc. He'd wear the same clothes for days, while I tried to be a bit more groomed and even ironed my jeans each morning. I tried to be diplomatic, but he was a

---

[3] I never knew this story till Luke told me while we were writing this book, but I think that may well have been me who pasted a flyer over his window. Sorry, Paul.

bull in a china shop. I'm quite fussy about what I eat, and try to be healthy, he would just grab a greasy donner kebab at 4 a.m. I was always prompt; he was always late. Dave just wanted to throw the best party ever, I was more about making sure we could run a tight ship and a proper business. But despite all our differences, we did have a bit of respect for one other and thought we could each bring something different to the mix. Dave was running Colours and Ministry of Sound in Manchester and had great contacts with DJs, and pretty good relationships with a lot of the big names, but he was living in London. I had a lot more contacts than Dave on the ground in Manchester. We decided to pool our resources. For the first few months we were just scouting around, trying to find the right opportunity. We had a few good ideas and some pretty daft ones too, but still hadn't found the right thing.

Then one morning, Dave rang me up really excited, like a little kid saying, 'Look, I've not slept a wink, I've had this mental idea …'

'Go on …'

'Instead of doing nights together, why don't we open a night*club* together?'

'Because it would cost a fortune …'

'I don't mean build one. Hear me out. I've already spoken to Andy Spiro this morning … and we can go and have a look at Sankeys if you want …'

'Sankeys? … *Are you fucking mental?*'

2000s
STRANGEWAYS HERE WE COME

'This Area is More Fucked Up Than Detroit!'

Sankeys originally opened its doors in the summer of 1994. It was set up by Rupert Campbell and Andy Spiro, inside Beehive Mill in Ancoats, and the name of the club came from the fact that the Mill had historically been used to manufacture soap. Rupert and Andy had been in a band together and were running Beehive Mill for the building owner, Joseph Steinright, turning it into a space for designers, small record labels, and other creatives. Beehive Mill was an outpost in an urban wasteland at the time, there was nothing else round there. They managed to convince Joseph to let them open a club inside the mill, a month before I first held my own club night, across town at The Haçienda in 1994. They had a tricky first few months, and nearly went bust within the first six months of opening their doors, but the turning point was when they gave the Friday night to Bugged Out, a club night run by the editors of *Jockey Slut*, John 'Johnno' Burgess and Paul Benney. Johnno and Paul didn't even have a name for the night at first. Johnno says Sankeys suggested the names 'Soap Opera' and 'Okey Dokey' to them, but they eventually chose the term 'Bugged Out', which they borrowed from a techno artist's description of his own music in *Jockey Slut*. Bugged Out was an overnight success, with the in-house residents James Holroyd and Rob Bright being joined by big guest names like Justin Robertson, Underground Resistance and Derrick May. Daft Punk even played some of their earliest shows there, before they took to wearing their helmets.

Ancoats in the early 1990s was unrecognisable to the place it is now. There can't be many places in the Western world that have changed as much over the last thirty years. In the mid-1990s it was still a desolate wasteland. That probably sounds overly dramatic to younger readers, but it really isn't. Desolate wasteland is being polite. Anyone who went to Sankeys back in the day will tell you what it was like and will have a war story or two about making the perilous half-mile journey from there, back to the city centre. There were no street lights and almost every building was derelict.

Historically, Ancoats had been Britain's first industrial suburb, when it was the centre of an industrial revolution. Manchester was the first modern city in the world, and Ancoats was its industrial heart, especially after the opening of Rochdale Canal in 1804, which saw huge mills springing up and dominating the area, and tightly packed housing for the workers. By 1815, Ancoats was the most populous area of Manchester, but also one of the poorest. L. S. Lowry would often visit Ancoats in his day job as a rent collector, and painted some of his famous street scenes there, as mentioned in the lyrics to 'Matchstick Men and Matchstick Cats and Dogs', the No.1 from 1978 by Michael and Brian: *He painted Salford's smoky tops/ On cardboard boxes from the shops/ And parts of Ancoats where I used to play'*.

It was written by the band's Michael Colman, who lived with his mother and siblings in Britain's last workhouse, in Ancoats, when he was growing up. One of Lowry's paintings of the area, *Ancoats Hospital Outpatient's Hall*, depicts the hall where Michael went to be treated after being mugged when he was only eight, and sadly lost his eye as a result. The Smiths also made a reference to the area, when Morrissey's pitched-up backing vocals on their 1986 single 'Bigmouth Strikes Again' were accredited to the *nom de plume* Ann Coates.

After Britain's cotton industry slumped in the 1930s, Ancoats never truly recovered, and by the 1960s slum clearances removed a lot of the housing, which left behind a barren wasteland. By the early 1990s, Ancoats was still empty. Once you crossed Great Ancoats Street, Manchester's very own 8 Mile (or half mile), there might as well have been a note on the map that said 'Here be monsters'. People who hadn't been to Sankeys before would be walking down the darkened streets saying, 'Where the fuck are we going?' Detroit is famously desolate, once the industrial heartland of America, but after the race riots in 1967 fuelled the 'white flight', the city's population halved, leaving swathes of the inner city derelict and abandoned. When the legendary Detroit-based DJ, Derrick May, was booked to play Bugged Out at Sankeys, he arrived, got out of the car, looked around him, shocked, and said. 'This area is more fucked up than Detroit!'

Fast forward to the present day, and Ancoats has loft apartments that go for over a million and a Michelin-starred restaurant, Mana. The set menu at Mana is £195 a head, and wine pairing is another £140 a head. £195 gets you 'A series of servings reflecting the season at the time of your visit. Produce at its peak is enhanced by methods of preservation from seasons past. Fermentation and fire are the widest pillars of our kitchen.' While we were writing this chapter of the book, Jay Rayner, the esteemed restaurant critic, was raving about the epicurean qualities of Ancoats in the *Observer*, describing it as 'a fast-developing district of boozy and edible promise, where the industrial past has been repurposed for the service industry present. You'll never want for a negroni or a chilli-spiked Gordal olive in Ancoats.' You couldn't buy a can of coke round there in the early Sankeys days, let alone a negroni, and if you got spiked it certainly wasn't with a chilli Gordal olive. Jay Rayner was reviewing the Edinburgh Castle, which back in the 1990s was a really rough pub, run by Jimmy Swords, one of the Quality Street Gang, but is now yet another great pull to the area.

In the years they were running Sankeys, Andy and Rupert were dogged by issues with gangs, like most clubs in Manchester at that time. Unfortunately for them, their time at Sankeys was probably the nadir of gangland trouble in Manchester. The gangs had permeated everything and, in the end, Sankeys, Home and The Haçienda all closed within a year of each other. Creativity in the city was being stifled by the presence of gangs and the Greater Manchester Police still didn't have a grip on the culture of the gangs, and there were also a few bad eggs in GMP at the time. Spiro tells a story about how they tried to work with the police to combat the gangs, but soon realised there were some old-school coppers who were more than willing to turn a blind eye to the crime. After he got increasingly frustrated by two CID officers, who came down to the club but refused to do something about a gang member who was in that night, he complained to their commanding officer, who he knew was concerned about the gang situation. The next day, Spiro was in his office, when the door was kicked open and the two CID officers stormed in, grabbed Spiro, and pinned him up against the wall, threatening him for going above their heads, and making threats about what they would do if it happened again.

It wasn't just nightclubs that were getting squeezed by the gangs either. Oliver Peyton, who is now one of the judges on the BBC's *Great British Menu*, decided to come to Manchester after his huge success in London with the Atlantic Bar and Grill. In 1996, he opened Mash and Air, a futuristic four-floor bar, restaurant and micro-brewery, on the edge of the Gay Village, which was way ahead of its time. Because it was the place to be seen after it opened, it soon attracted the attention of the gangs. Oliver and his sister Siobhan, who ran Mash and Air on a day-to-day basis, were pretty shocked with what they were faced with. Siobhan knew that Spiro and Sankeys had their issues with gangs and would sometimes ask Spiro for advice. One night she rang him up and said she had well-known gang members on one table in the restaurant, and a group of CID officers on another table. The gangsters actually sent over a bottle of champagne to the CID, who gratefully received it and waved their thanks. When the gangsters finished their meal, they simply got up and walked out without paying, in full view of the CID and there was nothing Sarah and her staff could do to stop them. When Sarah told Spiro this, he said, 'Are the CID still there? Put the champagne on their bill, they drank it.' She did that, but the CID refused to pay for it either, saying, 'No chance. We didn't order that champagne, the other table did, they just sent it over to us.'

There were so many incidents like that, making running a restaurant impossible, let alone a nightclub. In the end, in 2000, Oliver Peyton threw in the towel and went back to London.

The gang's grip on the area got too much for Rupert and Andy too, and it was a huge shame for Manchester and the UK clubbing scene in general when Sankeys closed. It might have only been open for four years, but it had left a strong legacy. I could absolutely see why it was so attractive to Dave, and why he was so excited about the idea of reopening it. But by the time he came to me with the idea, the club had laid dormant for two years.

To be honest, I wasn't sure that reopening Sankeys with Dave was a remotely feasible idea at first, or that we could get a licence to open the club either, but Elisa persuaded me that we should at least try. For the first few weeks I just went along with the idea to humour Dave. I thought it was such a mental idea that it would soon become apparent that it wouldn't work, and the whole plan would just go away. Instead, it became more and more real as time went on.

Dave had made some good connections with people who worked in the City and found three investors who were willing to put money into the club. They were city boys who had done well for themselves but also liked to party. Between them, they put £38,000 in, which was the entire budget of what we had to reopen Sankeys.

Originally, there were going to be three partners in the club – myself, Dave and John Hill, who used to run a club night called Golden. John was a really lovely guy from Stoke, and Golden was one of the top club nights in the country at the time. But John was fully aware of the gang problems that had plagued Sankeys during its first incarnation and, in the end, he got cold feet about coming in with us. He just didn't want all the stress (of which there is a lot) and risk hanging over his head and told us, 'I can't do this. It's too risky in my opinion. I'd still love to do Golden on Saturday nights, but I don't want to be involved in the running of the club.'

We had to go to Manchester Magistrates' Court to get the licence for Sankeys to reopen, and we really didn't have a clue till the day of the decision if we would get it and be able to reopen. In the end we did, but it was touch and go, and plenty of people couldn't believe we'd succeeded, including one of the magistrates who, after the licence had been approved, turned to his colleague, exasperated, and said, 'I cannot believe we're allowing Sankeys to open again!'

Daryl Butterworth, who at that time was Head of Licensing for Greater Manchester Police, was also in the Magistrates' Court that morning to hear the outcome. Afterwards, he came over to me and said, 'Listen Sacha, you will only *ever* see the blue lights *once*.'

What he meant was, at the first sign of trouble, the police would be called to Sankeys to shut us down.

We've Found the Keys

Once word got out that Dave and I were reopening Sankeys, everyone in Manchester thought we were, not to put too fine a point on it, absolutely mental. All the trouble that the first Sankeys had gone through was well known throughout the city and the club was seen as a poisoned chalice. Everyone really missed Sankeys, but nobody thought it was feasible to reopen it, or wanted to take the risk of doing it themselves. The clubbing world were more excited about the news of the club reopening, but still thought we were a bit crazy to take it on.

Although we had some financial backing from our investors, £38,000 is not a lot of money to open a nightclub, even back then. We really were working on a shoestring. We hired everything and bought nothing. From the sound system and the lights to the glasses for the bar … Everything was borrowed. Firstly, for cost reasons, we just didn't have the money to buy everything, and secondly because we didn't know how long the club was going to last, it made sense to hire things rather than invest in them. At least for the first few months, while we saw how things panned out.

Dave suggested we bring in a young promoter called Sam Kandel, who he had worked with previously on his club nights, as Promotions Manager for Sankeys. Like me, Sam had put on his first ever night at The Haçienda, but he was only fifteen at the time! He obviously hadn't let The Haçienda know exactly how young he was, or they turned a blind eye to it. Weirdly, Sam still has his first contract from them as well, like me, and it's also signed by Jon Drape, who we would both continue to work closely with in the future. Sam then worked with Dave for a couple of years while he was doing his A levels, helping out with promotion, before he went off to Birmingham University when he was eighteen. While most people chose their university on the strength of the course, or the reputation of the establishment, Sam chose Birmingham simply because he'd managed to secure the Friday-night slot at Bonds nightclub (also home to Miss Moneypenny's), so he could continue his promoting career while studying. Coincidentally, the week Sam graduated and left Birmingham, he ran into Dave outside Affleck's Palace in the Northern Quarter, after having not seen him for a couple of years. Dave told him about the plans for Sankeys and persuaded him to come join us as our Promotions Manager. I'd never met Sam before, which is odd because he grew up pretty near me in Altrincham, and although he was a few years younger than me, we immediately hit it off and became quite close pretty quickly. Sam had also been a regular at Sankeys in the early days, showing up there every Friday night for Bugged Out, and knew the club inside out, meaning he knew exactly what made it so special and what it would take to capture the magic once again. Sam was a brilliant addition to Sankeys, but I had no idea at that time that we would end up being business partners for almost two decades.

Although Sankeys had only been closed a couple of years, two years in clubbing years is a lifetime. It had really been missed, by Manchester and the whole clubbing world, becoming a bit of a mythical place, so we came up with the following tagline and built our promotion around that for the reopening: 'We've found the keys'. The 500 key-shaped invitations that were sent out to VIPs were embossed with gold.

The police warned us that if we brought any of the gangs in to work on the door that they would shut us down immediately, no questions. Things were beginning to change a little in Manchester already, and the police had a better handle on the gang situation, but some members of these gangs still wanted to run the doors at clubs, because if you run the door of the club, then you also run what goes on inside.

Everyone who knows me, and anyone who has been a regular at The Warehouse Project over the years, knows that I like to stand on the door at my own events as much as possible. That way I can see what the crowd is like as they come in, which gives you a sense of what kind of night it's going to be but is also good to keep an eye on numbers. Back in the day, I also used to do it to make sure that the bouncers and security weren't dicking about. But I was warned by police and my own security that it would be too dangerous to do that, at least for the first few months after Sankeys reopened, as I might be a target for the gangs who didn't get the door.

We worked bloody hard in the month leading up to the reopening, and by the final week we still had people working on site in the club. In the end, Dave and I took turns sleeping there, so that one of us could always be at the club, twenty-four hours a day. Just to make sure Sankeys was ready in time.

The night before the big launch, I was asleep in bed when I got a call from Greater Manchester Fire Rescue, telling me there had been a bad fire at the club and asking me to come down to assess the damage. I couldn't believe it. I jumped in my car and picked up Dave, from the flat he was renting around the corner from Sankeys, on the way. When we got there, we couldn't believe what we found. The electricity substation right behind the club had deliberately been blown up. One of the gangs, angry about not being given control of the door, was determined that if they couldn't run the door, then they weren't going to let Sankeys open at all. They had come down in the middle of the night, thrown a mattress over the steel fence surrounding the substation before pouring petrol over it and setting it ablaze. The whole substation was ruined. Unbelievable. Dave and I were so exhausted by this stage that when the guy from the fire service was explaining what had happened to us, we both just burst out laughing, and couldn't stop. The whole thing was surreal.

Obviously it was pretty scary that the gang had gone to such extremes, but it wasn't going to stop us. What the gang obviously didn't know is that Sankeys actually had its own generator. A hangover from when it had been a mill. So, although the substation had gone down, and the rest of Ancoats was pitched into darkness, Sankeys itself was absolutely fine, and we opened the next night as planned.

Because the rest of the area was still in complete blackout, Sankeys stood out even more as a beacon in the urban wilderness. We felt like we were in our own little bubble, having this full-on rave in the middle of an otherwise derelict dystopian landscape. Somehow, it made the opening night even more special.

Then reality set in. The atmosphere around the club and the office was really tense for the first few weeks. We were wary that at any time we might be targeted by gangs. For the first three months, one of my security team, a guy called Dave

Power, would pick me up from home at the start of the night and then drop me off at home again at the end of it. It was his idea of mitigating risk. It's not much fun having to look over your shoulder on the way home every night. Trust me.

We had to employ a General Manager to be the licence holder for Sankeys, as neither Dave nor I were allowed to hold the licence at the time, as neither of us had passed the exams. The first few people I asked were scared off by the trouble Sankeys had previously had and didn't fancy taking on that stress. But one guy who was up for it, and was another great addition to the team, was James Cassidy. I'd known James for a few years since I ran nights at Paradise Factory, when he was one of the bar managers there. He saw the opportunity to step up at Sankeys and grabbed it, and he became our GM licensee. James was great. He was about my age, a big Irish guy with a long ponytail and he didn't take any shit from anyone, including Dave, who could drive him crazy at the bar with all his hangers-on wanting free drinks. Dave used to call James 'Anthat' because James used to finish every sentence with '… and that.' At the end of every night, when the music stopped, James would stand in front of the DJ booth and shout to the whole club, 'Ladies … Gentleman … unless you're coming home with me … fuck off!'

One of the other legendary characters at Sankeys was Crazy Paul, who we inherited from the first incarnation of the club. Paul was in his sixties, but he looked like he was in his eighties, he had a huge head of white hair and a big white beard, and glasses, so he looked like some sort of mad professor. The kids at Sankeys loved him, especially the first time they saw him, they couldn't get over the fact that this guy who looked old enough to be their grandad was working there, and obviously as into the music as they were. Paul loved working the lights, he saw them as his little babies, he treated them like family. He also loved speed and would sometimes spend all day Sunday in the club, still up, going round singing to himself and taking the lights down individually and polishing them. He eventually fell out with Dave and I after we decided the lights needed an upgrade, and we replaced them without running it past Paul first. He went absolutely ballistic at us, you would have thought we had sold his own children, but to Paul that's what they were, and he never forgave us for that.

At the same time as we were reopening the club, I was also still running my student nights. I had no idea how Sankeys was going to pan out, so needed to make sure I had a back-up plan, just in case. So, Elisa more or less took over the day-to-day running of the student nights, while I focused on Sankeys. A week or two after the club reopened, I was at Discotheque Royale one night when I recognised their head of security and started chatting to him. He was asking me how it was going at Sankeys. He had a pretty fearsome reputation and was notorious for giving people a dead hard smack. Instead of punching people, he had this signature slap instead and I knew he was connected to one of the main gangs, so it was pretty obvious that he was trying to glean some information from me. I told him it was going fine, and we hadn't had any trouble, but that was probably because the police had set up surveillance on the club and had plain-clothed officers in the building opposite the club every night it was open, watching and documenting everything that happened at the club. It was complete bollocks. Although the police were genuinely keeping an eye on the club from a distance, they certainly didn't have any covert officers watching the door all night, but I thought if I put that out there as a rumour and word got back to the gangs, that might put them off if they were thinking about putting any more pressure on us.

Are You Tribal?

Dave Vincent had been a regular at the original Tribal Gathering in the early 1990s, and it was an event that held mythical status for him. He told me about a time at Tribal Gathering where he had taken something that made him convinced that he was a giant. It was only when the drugs wore off that he realised he'd just pulled his tracky bottoms up too much. A very Dave anecdote.

In 1999, just before Dave and I started working together, he had bought the rights to the Tribal Gathering name, and really wanted to bring Tribal Gathering back. As the first step in achieving this, he came up with the concept of doing Tribal Sessions on Friday nights at Sankeys. It sounded great on paper, but after we reopened the club and launched Tribal Sessions, it was a real slog for the first few months. Tribal ran every Friday and the DJs Dave was booking were great, including people like Andy from Portishead, but we just couldn't get the interest, we couldn't get enough punters through the door – around 200, 300 at the most – and the place looked empty. As well as losing money, it just wasn't happening.

The tagline for that night was, 'Are you Tribal?' Unfortunately, the answer to that from most of Manchester, at first, was a big fat No. They definitely did not consider themselves Tribal.

At the turn of the Millennium, the Northern Quarter was just starting to change in a big way, and obviously it was right on our doorstep, a five-minute walk away (although that five minutes did involve you taking your life into your own hands). It should have been a decent potential market for us, but the Northern Quarter was pretty cliquey and, ironically, quite tribal. Just not in our sense. We felt like we were out on a limb a bit, and we thought maybe that was part of the problem and why the Friday night wasn't taking off as planned. Dave and I just weren't in with the cool crowd, and we decided we should make more of an effort to get 'in' with the Northern Quarter crew.

A bar called Cord had just opened, and a lot of the music scene had quickly coalesced around that, people like Luke Una (who lived above it), all the Fat City and Grand Central crew, plus all the Manchester music mafia that worked for record labels and promoters like Twisted Nerve, Ear to the Ground, Paper Recordings, plus people like Chris York from SJM concerts, Richard Hector-Jones, Rob Bright and James Holroyd from Bugged Out!, everyone who worked in key shops like Oi Polloi, Eastern Bloc, and Piccadilly Records, plus members of bands like Doves, Crazy Penis, Alpinestars, and Alfie. Cord was owned by Paul Astill (who years later would design The Warehouse Project office), Pete Orgrill, and Simon Cooper, and they had quite cleverly deliberately targeted that nascent Northern Quarter crowd when they opened, and they'd done a really good job of it. Not least by having a wall of tankards behind the bar, engraved with the names of all the people in the music scene they wanted to be regulars, and it worked.

Dave and I were definitely not part of that crowd. There was never going to be a tankard engraved with 'Sacha' or 'Dave' behind the Cord bar. It didn't bother us personally, but we did think it might help our Friday nights and the business if we made a bit more of an effort to get 'in' with that crowd. One night, we decided to go down to Cord to try and ingratiate ourselves. We walked in there and I immediately felt super self-conscious. I'm sure it wasn't quite like this in reality, but in my head when we walked in it was a bit like those scenes in Westerns where someone walks into a bar: the music, the balls on a snooker table roll silently before stopping dead, and smoke fills the air. I felt like everything went a bit quiet when we walked in, as if everyone in there was thinking, *What the fuck are they doing here?*

I walked up to the bar and ordered a Coke, and Dave in his loud cockney voice, said, 'Can I have an Advocaat and lemonade, please?' Once Dave said that I knew we weren't going to be accepted as part of the Cord crowd. We never went back after that night.

Back at the club, we called a Tribal Sessions summit meeting to discuss what we were going to do. Dave was determined to make it work somehow. 'We need to have one last go at making Tribal work, and give it everything,' he stressed. He went away and came back having booked Dave Clarke for the main room downstairs, and Bob Sinclar for the upstairs set. Sam went to town on promotion for that night, and I mean he *went to fucking town*. There was not a lamp-post, phone box or an electricity box in Manchester that wasn't plastered with a poster advertising 'Tribal Sessions with Dave Clarke and Bob Sinclar'. I can still remember the artwork for the poster now. It sold out, and it was a brilliant night, and we all had a huge Tribal sigh of relief. That was it then, we were away. Golden kept us going for the first six months, but when Tribal kicked off as well, it really felt like Sankeys was back in all its glory, where it belonged.

What became apparent, which was slightly annoying to me, was because Tribal was booking the 'cool' talent, that a snobbery emerged between the people who went to Tribal and those who went to Golden. On Saturday nights, Golden had DJs like Lisa Lashes and Judge Jules, and pulled in a different, largely female crowd, with girls in fluffy bras, that the Tribal crowd looked down on. It wound me up a bit because I loved Golden. Not necessarily because of the music, but because it was paying the bills. Tribal was losing a fortune to begin with. There was also a bigger bar spend at Golden nights, and there was a good reason for that.

As the night became successful, the Tribal crowd quite quickly became quite, well, I guess, 'tribal'. There was a really close group in the centre of it, and Dave became like their cult leader. His ego began to grow when Tribal Sessions really started to take off. I hadn't seen that side of him before. That clique of regulars started calling themselves The Tribalists and used to wear face paint and Native American tribal dress. You'd never get away with that now. There were about twenty Tribalists and they were a law unto themselves, and Dave let them get away with murder, they could do whatever they wanted. They were there every week, always on the guest list, never paying for entry or drinks.

We didn't have a dressing room, green room, or VIP area, so backstage was basically just the Sankeys office. I used to go into the office on a Monday morning and there would be remnants of powders all over my desk, empty drug wraps and other leftovers from the weekend's partying and it would more often than not be the Tribalists who were responsible, rather than the guest DJs and their entourages. I had constant run-ins with the Tribalists and I'm sure the dislike was mutual. They saw me as the boring fun police, pouring cold water on the party. I just wasn't 'Tribal', in their eyes. I didn't mind people partying, I mean it's a nightclub at the end of the day, but I also wanted to make sure Sankeys was successful as a business as well, not just an excuse to party. The Tribalists could be lawless, and I used to lose my rag with them, saying, 'At least clean the fucking desks when you're done.'

After they had finished at the club, the Tribal clique would head off to these after parties, which often went on till Monday morning. I never went, but I would hear stories about them playing weird games, like Hungry Hippo. I would ask, 'What's 'Hungry Hippo'? It turned out, this was a more druggy and less wholesome version of the children's game. It involved them all sitting about in a circle as one person sat in the middle of the group with their mouth open so that everyone else in the surrounding circle could try and throw pills into their mouth.

One night at Tribal Sessions, after we had closed, I was getting ready to leave at about 4 a.m., I was just waiting on James to give me all the figures, when I noticed what looked like a piece of steak in the middle of the dancefloor, and I thought, 'Who the fuck has brought a steak into the club?' But, as I walked over and looked more closely at it, I could see that it was actually a rat (or the remnants of what used to be a rat). Because Sankeys was in an old mill, we would often get the odd rat or two. We didn't have a vermin problem, but like every old building you would get a rat every now and again. This poor thing must have tried to make a run for it across the dancefloor at some stage in the night, possibly trying to escape the Tribalists, and it had got trampled on instead because it was a rammed night, the kids had just been dancing on this dead rat all night, pulverising the poor little bastard to pieces. The only way I could tell it had been a rat was when I looked closely enough to see the poor little fucker's tail. Thank fuck the Tribalists didn't see it – they would have probably taken it to their after party.

In 2001, Dave organised a big joint birthday party for his thirtieth and my twenty-ninth. Dave wanted it to be a gangsters and molls fancy-dress party, and he hired a barge for the night that set off from Castlefield. The second the barge set off, it became clear it was going to be a really debauched affair, which is not quite what I had in mind. After about half an hour, I'd had enough and asked them to pull over to the side of the canal, and me, Elisa, J-Boy and his wife got off. We scrambled up the bank and suddenly realised we were in the middle of Salford, dressed in 1930s fancy dress, but we managed to flag down a taxi, and decided to go back to Sankeys. When we got back there, we were in the courtyard outside, still in our comedy fancy dress outfits, when a gang of about thirty turned up, walked straight past the bouncers on the door into the courtyard. I was at the end of my tether at that point, and without thinking through the ramifications, I just walked up to them and said, 'Can you not just leave us alone? You're ruining the night for everyone.' One of them threatened to stab me, and on reflection I was pretty lucky that they didn't react, but thankfully they just left.

Put on the Red Light

Golden had a really great run; it had single-handedly kept Sankeys afloat in those early days. But by 2001, the numbers were starting to dwindle, and it felt like the night was running out of steam. The sands were shifting beneath its feet, and the music world was moving on a bit.

We knew we wanted to make a change and move slightly away from the trancey feel of Golden, so we looked for ideas for a new Saturday night, and at the start of 2002 we decided to go to the Miami Winter Music Conference for some inspiration, to see and meet new DJs and make some contacts in the industry.

The Winter Music Conference started in 1986, and by the 1990s the five-day blowout was a huge chemically enhanced *bonhomie* for the dance music industry, with thousands of DJs, producers, label execs, agents, and promoters, like us, converging on South Beach, from all over the world, hustling and partying hard. My perception of Miami was pretty limited to be honest, it was probably mostly based on *Miami Vice*, so the trip was a real eye-opener, swapping the mills and street lights of Ancoats for the pastel-coloured hotels and palm trees of Miami.

It goes without saying that it was a lot more glamorous than going out in Manchester. If you were going to Pacha in Miami you had to make a bit more of an effort than if you were just popping down to Cord bar or Sankeys. I'd never been to a club outside of Manchester before this trip, which people might find ridiculous. I'd never been to a club in Leeds, Liverpool, or Sheffield, let alone London, New York, or Ibiza. The only time I'd been to Ibiza was on holiday with my grandparents when I was a little kid. I've still not been since. To be honest, I never really saw the attraction. It always seemed like too much of a busman's holiday for me. I spent my whole life in clubs, I didn't want to then go on holiday to visit even more clubs.

When I walked into Pacha in Miami, I'd never seen so many ridiculously incredibly good-looking people in my entire life. It was more like being at a fashion show than a club. We were hanging out with people from the industry, like Charlie Chesters, Dave Beer, and other agents that we knew, and were invited to some amazing parties. Dave Vincent and I had always dressed very different. Like with many things in our lives, we had a different sartorial outlook. I was more clean-cut, while Dave had this baggy look going on, which I just didn't get. I'm sure he thought I dressed oddly as well. When we were in Miami, he spent the whole time in baggy shorts, white socks, and sandals. One night when we were going out, I couldn't help but say something.

'C'mon Dave, you need to make a bit of an effort ...'

'Nah, fack off, it's a London thing.'

'It's not a London thing ... it's a shit thing.'

Miami was pretty wild. Dave had brought two of his mates with him, Theo and Beans. I don't think Theo and Beans went to one club all week. Dave would come to meetings with me, and to the clubs to check them out too. But Theo and Beans? They just stayed in that suite all week.

While we were in Miami, we met up with a big agent who represented a lot of iconic music acts. He has calmed down a lot now, but back in the day he had a huge reputation as a bit of a party animal. We met in his hotel room, where he did a massive line, then called up the hotel reception and kicked off with them because he hadn't been able to withdraw money from the cash machine in the lobby. After a while, the staff on reception explained that the main problem was that the machine downstairs he had been trying to withdraw money from was actually a payphone, not a cash machine.

There was a Silver Diner across from our hotel and we ate there for every single meal. Breakfast, lunch, and dinner. Talk about Brits abroad. It's a bit embarrassing looking back now, but we weren't exactly epicureans back then. One night when we were in there with the agent, the waitress came to take our order.

'I'll have a cheeseburger please,' I said.

She looked at the agent and he said, 'Ketamineburger!'

The waitress just looked confused and said, 'Sorry?'

'Ketamineburger!' he roared.

'I'm not sure what you mean by a Ketamineburger, sir.'

'Just bring me a cheeseburger and I'll show you!' he replied.

When the poor waitress came back with his burger, the agent said, 'I'll show you how to make a Ketamineburger ...' and in front of her, he lifted the top bun off the burger, produced a little bag of ketamine from his pocket, sprinkled it on top, and sat the bun on top before taking a big bite, with a smile.

We all looked on in shock.

While we were over there, we went to see Danny Tenaglia do an incredible twenty-four-hour set at Space, which even by Miami standards, had a reputation for its marathon raves, running parties into the following morning and evening. We had to get there at the start of the set, and there was one track on loop for the first two hours, gradually getting louder and louder and louder, and when it eventually kicked in, the whole place went fucking mental. I've never seen a reaction like it. Next thing I know, the agent was at the side of the stage, wearing this lovely black cashmere jumper, and suddenly lifted up his jumper and set fire to all of his chest hairs. What the fuck?

Security rushed in and were patting him down to make sure they were OK. It was his party trick back then, apparently, to set all his chest hair on fire, and it wasn't the first time he'd done it.

This agent is still one of the biggest ones working in the UK today but is completely different to how he was twenty years ago back in Miami, and we still work together, booking loads of their artists for Parklife and The Warehouse Project with him. He has always been really good to us, and is really on it when it comes to the next big thing. In the very early days of Sankeys, he called us up, all excited and said, 'I've got this brilliant new band from New York, they're gonna be huge. Nobody's heard of them yet, but I've got them coming over to do a couple of early gigs and they'd be great for Sankeys, they're called Scissor Sisters, I'll send you a tape.' He sent this tape up to us, but we weren't keen on the music, and hated the name, so we didn't book them. After saying no initially, he even said that we could book them for just £500, which wouldn't have even covered the cost of their train from London. We even turned him down then. Scissor Sisters, of course, then exploded and went absolutely huge. We'd turned them down for £500 and, only a year later, Renaissance paid £1,000,000 to book them!

After we came back from Miami, we had the idea for our new Saturday night: Red Light. We wanted to sex things up a bit, get away from the trancey feel of Golden and – it sounds ridiculous on paper I know – but we wanted to bring a bit of Miami to Manchester. We couldn't bring the weather, but we could bring the soundtrack. Dave started booking DJs like Danny Tenaglia, Felix Da Housecat, Erick Morillo, Jacques le Cont and that second wave of Chicago house DJs like DJ Sneak, plus the best British DJs at that time like Xpress-2, who were absolutely fucking amazing.[4]

We came up with an idea for these provocative-looking, sexy flyers for Red Light. We used pixelated images of couples in various carnal positions, the most explicit of which was a man taking a woman from behind. When it was pixelated on the flyer, you could just about make out what was going on, so it was more suggestive than anything. But what we didn't realise was when we blew it up to huge poster size, from a distance it didn't look quite so pixelated after all, it looked a lot more graphic, bordering on pornographic. The posters went up all around Manchester, and possibly caused a few car crashes, or near misses, from goggle-eyed blokes who couldn't

---

[4] We had no idea at the time, but in 2020 Erick Morillo was arrested for assault and sexual battery. He was found dead at his Miami home on 1 September 2020, three days before his court case was due to start. After his death, nine other women came forward with accounts of being assaulted by him.

avert their gaze. They also ended up with me getting banned from my favourite Thai restaurant.

Kevin and Vinny were flypostering for us at the time, primarily targeting Sale and Altrincham more because they knew Sam and I lived there. It's the oldest trick in the flypostering game: make sure you've got a heavy presence near the club owner's home and office, and they'll presume you're doing a good job. There were more of these soft porn posters around Altrincham than anywhere else.

There is a great Thai restaurant in Altrincham called Phanthong, next to the market, which I really loved. It was owned by an elderly Thai couple who I got to know quite well, and they were really friendly to me. But that all changed one night when I went down there just after those Red Light posters had gone up around Altrincham. Chorchaba, the wife, had seen the posters all over Altrincham, and was really offended by them and absolutely furious with me. 'Sacha! Your posters are disgusting, they are *filth*! They should not be allowed. I am *disgusted* with you! Get out, *get out* of my restaurant!' she fumed.

I tried to reason with her and explain, but she was having none of it. The restaurant is still there now, and I think that I'm still barred.

We booked Danny Tenaglia to do a twelve-hour marathon set, which we were all super excited about. It felt like we had completed the Red Light circle, as seeing his marathon set in Miami had been one of the original inspirations for our very own slice of Miami in Ancoats. Dave was absolutely obsessed with Tenaglia. Obsessed. Dave was always in the DJ booth at Sankeys, he'd be in there all the time at Tribal nights and bring girls in there with him, or some of the Tribalists. The thing is, the DJ booth downstairs at Sankeys wasn't that big, so though some of the DJs didn't mind if they were in a party mood, some of the others, who took everything more seriously, used to get really fucked off about it if Dave and his crew were in there with them. Tenaglia's manager knew all about his antics, having dealt with him in the past, so he demanded a stool outside the door to the DJ booth, and he sat there for the whole twelve hours. Didn't move once. Just to make sure that Dave couldn't get anywhere near Tenaglia.

Eastenders Comes to Sankeys

One of the weirdest episodes at Sankeys was when *Eastenders* came to film an episode on location in 2002. I'm pretty sure it must also go down as one of the weirdest episodes of *Eastenders* in its history.

It was a one-off episode set in Manchester, which was a departure for *Eastenders* for a start. We were contacted by a location manager from the BBC who wanted to hire Sankeys to use as a one of the locations for the episode. We agreed a hire fee of about £7,000 for the week they were filming, but we didn't know anything about the plot before they started filming and had to sign an NDA (Non-Disclosure Agreement) so we couldn't even tell anyone that the BBC were filming there.

When it did go out on-air, the episode focused on the characters of Ricky and Bianca, who had been out of *Eastenders* for a few years by then and were returning for a special feature-length episode only. Bianca was living in Manchester and working for a character called Vince (played by Craig Charles) who ran a nightclub (played by Sankeys), but he was also a drug dealer. When the programme aired, everyone was intrigued to see what the episode would be like and how

Manchester would be portrayed when it first broadcast. Truth be told, it did feel a bit like the city was typecast a bit. Within the first five minutes, Luke Una was texting Luke Bainbridge saying, 'Raining and gangsters FFS!'

There was a really rough pub next door to Sankeys, run by an Irish guy in his sixties, called Shaun. He had a pretty unorthodox approach to running a pub, life, and interior decor. There was always scaffolding *inside* his pub. God knows why. He was forever ripping up floorboards and taking ceilings down, and the place always looked like a working building site. It just didn't look safe, which meant that hardly anyone ever went in there. Shaun also lived right above the pub, and we could see into his bedroom from the Sankeys office. He quite clearly had a penchant for ladies of the night, and we saw a few things from our office that I'd rather not have seen, let's put it that way.

When the *Eastenders* crew arrived on site, they mostly filmed in the evenings, so it looked moody and desolate. Once Shaun saw all the BBC trucks, he must have seen a possible pay day. He started blasting pro-IRA songs out from his pub, really loud, which was obviously interfering with the filming, meaning the BBC had to stop filming so that they could go and ask him to turn it down. He flat-out refused at first, so they had to plead and negotiate with him, and in the end I think they had to give him £1,000 to get him to turn his music off so they could finish filming without any more IRA background music. They had no choice. He probably spent it on more scaffolding and ladies of the night.

We weren't around for filming, so even though Craig Charles's character Vince was using my desk throughout the filming, I never got to meet him, although we did have a couple of incidents with him a few years later. When he played Kendal

Calling in 2011, he was booked to headline the Thursday night, then on the day of the gig he said he couldn't do it because the *Coronation Street* filming schedule had changed, and he was now filming first thing on Friday morning. I was sat in 'Event Control', which is really the command centre of an event while it is running, and I was listening to this conversation about getting Craig Charles a car back to Manchester. He had previously been caught in a tabloid sting, smoking a crack pipe in the back of a taxi while watching porn, so without even thinking I came out with, 'Make sure there's a crack pipe in there for him too!' There was a deathly silence and then I turned round and saw his management were sat there too. *Shit.* I had to apologise and explain to them I was only joking.

The Legend Returns ...

After Tribal Sessions had really taken off and started to smash it, Dave pushed for us to do a Tribal Gathering Weekender. This was his baby. He'd always wanted to throw a party like this ever since he had been to the original Tribal Gathering parties, and he was determined to pull it off. The original Tribal Gathering didn't mean as much to us in the North, but to Dave, it was like the Holy Grail. I think in his eyes, the weekender was like the passing of the baton from the hallowed old guard to Dave, and he was now the new guardian of the Holy Grail.

Bugged Out had thrown a weekender in Prestatyn a couple of years earlier, which was already a legendary addition to the clubbing history books, although perhaps not for all the right reasons. Run by Bugged Out and Chris York from SJM, they had a great line-up, including the Chemical Brothers and other amazing Balearic offerings, like the Doves playing an acoustic set in the on-site pub on the Sunday to people who had been awake for days. I was quite keen on avoiding such tales of extreme hedonism, and actually making a profit from the event. Dave, as usual, just wanted to throw the ultimate party.

We chose to do it at Pontins in Southport, which had been the home of Southport Weekender since the early 1990s. The promo flyer we produced was a bit OTT, to say the least. It declared:

The Legend Returns TRIBAL GATHERING The Weekender 2002

Mountains they traversed, over oceans deep and wide, the Tribal legend returns, to bridge the dance divide.

The flowery Tribal text continued inside ...

Come with us ...

Tribal Gathering, pioneers of the multi-arena dance festival, has not been seen on the event circuit since 1997. Just as the tribal movement was hailed as one of the world's fastest growing phenomena, suddenly, almost overnight, it strangely disappeared from the scene. After the legendary 1997 Kraftwerk show, the organisation that had long been regarded as the 'People's Party' was gone. As it left, cloaked in a veil of mystery, a dark corporate cloud descended on the scene.

Now in 2002 while 'super-clubs' continue to produce massive multi-arena festivals with 100 DJs and a million flyers, there now comes time for a new beginning. After five years in the wilderness, the Tribal legend finally returns with an intimate event for 4,000 people, encompassing all the things that first attracted us to dance music. Tribal Gathering is back with the unique creative experience to push the boundaries once again ...

We managed to get the front cover of Manchester's *City Life* for the event, which Luke Bainbridge was Editor of at the time, and Dave insisted we do a Tribal-themed photo shoot. It was

Dave, me, and Greg Vickers, dressed in full Tribal gear, around a tepee, and managed to drag poor Grandmaster Flash and Justin Robertson into the photo shoot too. The facial expressions in the photo tell the whole story. Dave's face is contorted like he's snarling 'Come onnnnnn!', Greg and I just look a little bit unsure about the whole thing. Justin and Grandmaster Flash look like they would rather be anywhere else.

City Life interviewed a lot of the main DJs including Sasha, Justin, Flash, Erol Alkan, and Ashley Beedle. Grandmaster Flash had just DJed in front of the Queen at the closing ceremony of the Commonwealth Games – 'When the Queen invited me, I was very happy about it. I didn't understand it, but I came ... It was the biggest event ever played by a DJ. A billion and a half people. It should be in *The Guinness Book of Records*.' Sasha was very complimentary about Sankeys, saying: 'It's without doubt the best sound system in any nightclub in the country. I'd go as far as saying that the sound in the booth is the best I've ever heard when it comes to playing and mixing records. To my mind they have the most amazing crowd at the club since they reopened. And I love David Vincent. He always bends over backwards to make me feel welcome when I come to Sankeys.' Erol Alkan's Trash was the coolest club night in London at the time, but he was a bit of a wildcard for us at the time, as he wasn't the usual Tribal booking, it was a bit of a departure from our usual music policy. He's a brilliant DJ, and twenty years later he's still a regular at The Warehouse Project, especially on Bugged Out nights. When he was asked what his chalet would look like at the end of the weekend, he said, 'I'm actually notoriously tidy and tend to leave hotels in better shape than when I find them.' Sadly, that would not be the case with the Tribalists and a lot of the punters, who would take a more Balearic approach to chalet life.

The security we used for the events was a squad of ex-Marines that were recommended to us by Southport Soul Weekender, who had used them several times before and said they had kept everything in check, and they'd never had any trouble. The Marines took everything very seriously, as you'd expect. When I first turned up on site, they were doing exercise routines and were always shouting at each other. They had this one guy in charge, and when he barked an instruction, they'd all shout back 'SIR, YES, SIR!' like the recruits in Stanley Kubrick's *Full Metal Jacket*.

The marines were fully prepared for any eventuality, including watching for people jumping over the fence to get in under the cover of darkness. Everyone was searched on the way in, but because Southport was quite close to Liverpool you would have Scouse gangs sending people over the fence after dark as drugs mules, to avoid the searches on the way in. The Marines were wise to that and had come armed with night-vision goggles and would lie down in the grass, scouring the perimeter for Scouse drug mules clambering over the wall. It all seemed a little over the top to me.

Dave had wanted to be a comedian when he was younger and still loved being the centre of attention. He had come up with this spoof character called Ketaman and embraced it as an alter ego. I didn't quite get it myself, but I guess it was an in-joke among the Tribalists, and I wasn't part of their gang. He had this whole outfit with a cape and an eye mask and everything. In Dave's eyes, Ketaman was the Tribal superhero. He had first introduced him at Tribal at Sankeys, and I'd tried to persuade him it wasn't a good idea. If I was leaving slightly early, I'd pull him aside and say, 'Dave, I'm off now, please don't get Ketaman out.' But within twenty minutes of me leaving and driving home, I'd get a call from James Cassidy to say, 'Ketaman's out ...'

The thing was, Dave now decided he wanted to develop his alter ego and add additional characters for a comedy show at the Weekender. Alarm bells started ringing with me from the off, but once Dave had his heart set on something, there was nothing you could do to stop him. He brought in his friend Jules and a couple of the Tribalists to play other characters, and they were rehearsing in the Sankeys office in the week or two before the event. From what I could tell, Dave conceived it as a way of lampooning what he saw as the 'cocaine set' that he felt had ruined clubland, because in his mind the Tribalists were the keepers of the flame, the warriors keeping the true spirit of acid house alive. Some bollocks like that anyway. He had all these props made, including a huge credit card, and a 10ft-long £10 note. The thing about in-jokes is that they don't translate. To make things worse, Dave decided to put the show on just before Sasha's headline set. It was a recipe for disaster. When the time came, I was stood just to the side of the stage with a few other Mancunian heads, including Luke Una, Richard Hector-Jones, and Marc Rowlands. The room was absolutely rammed with a crowd desperate for Sasha to come on. Instead, Mad Mike and his cohorts came on and started this apocalyptic acid house cabaret. It was an absolute car crash. Imagine if Vic 'n' Bob did an acid house spoof of *The League of Gentlemen* and you're still nowhere near. The crowd started booing and I thought, *Oh god*. Luke was there and says it was one of the most bizarre, astonishing things he's ever seen, and he wasn't the only one. Anyone who was there will tell you how weird and misjudged it was. No one could believe it, and at the same time, no one could look away. The booing just got louder and louder. The kids were peaking and were desperate for Sasha to come on, they didn't want this car crash cabaret of in-jokes. In the end, the booing got so loud, that they had to cut the show short, and troop off with their Tribal tails between their legs. I did feel sorry for Dave, because he'd put so much effort into it, and no one likes to be booed off, but it was a doomed idea from the start.

The Tribalists had always been keen on their after-parties, and the promotional material that we put out for Tribal Gathering even encouraged it.

> *The party will last for two nights and three days, over five rooms and four serious sessions. Not only that, but when the main room shuts down at 7 a.m. each morning, a thousand after parties explode into action in the chalets surrounding the main complex. This Tribal Village will become the home of the Tribalist community.*

I'd not looked back at the flyer for the Tribal Gathering Weekender for the best part of twenty years till we started working on this book, but when I dug it out of storage and read that back I honestly couldn't believe what I was reading. Nowadays, on any event we run, there's detailed planning for the mass exit with security, police, and the relevant authorities on how we're going to manage the customer flow after the event, and make sure it's as peaceful as possible, and everyone gets home safely, with minimal disruption to the wider local community. But at Tribal Gathering Weekender, the promo was actively encouraging everyone to carry on partying after 7 a.m., and to 'explode' into the next day. Un-fucking-believable. No wonder it got out of control ...

As dawn broke, the head of the Marines came and woke me in my chalet, to tell me, in a sorry voice, that they had lost control of the site. I went outside into the dawn light and was faced with an acid house Armageddon. The hardcore Marines had well and truly lost their grip on the situation. You could hear parties from every block, people were lying around on the grass in various states of undress, others were throwing themselves out of top-floor windows, and in the middle of all this, my business partner Dave, was speeding round on a moped, dressed as Ketaman, firing rockets and fireworks at everyone. It was chaos.

The 'chalets' were two-storey accommodation blocks and, as expected, a lot of the kids went mental once they got back to their chalets and continued the partying. Music was blasting from every chalet. A few people trashed them, others threw mattresses out of windows. People started jumping, off their heads, out of the upstairs windows, onto the mattresses below. Of course, the Tribalists were right in the middle of all this, and even Greg Vickers, our resident DJ, got involved. He was one of the ones throwing himself out of the top-floor window, and actually ended up hurting himself quite badly. Who would have guessed that throwing yourself out of an upstairs window while off your head could be dangerous?

While all this was going on Dave, who on paper was supposedly one of the responsible people in charge, was charging about causing even more mayhem, still dressed in his Ketaman outfit, complete with flowing cape. He had somehow found a mini moped, and armed himself with a load of fireworks that he got passed security, and was speeding round the site on this moped, with his Ketaman mask on, and his cape flapping behind him, firing rockets and fireworks at the Marines, his own security team.

The First Warehouse Party

In 2003, we decided to hold the first warehouse party in the UK since the much-criticised Criminal Justice Bill had been passed by John Major's government in 1994. We didn't know it at the time, but this was the event that sowed the seed of an idea that would eventually become The Warehouse Project. The original idea came from an insane one-off club night we went to at The Haçienda in March 2001. Not the real Haçienda, because that had been shut for four years by then, but a deconstructed-reconstructed Haçienda inside a warehouse in Ancoats, just around the corner from Sankeys.

In 2000, film director Michael Winterbottom was in Canada shooting *The Claim*, his adaptation of Thomas Hardy's *The Mayor of Casterbridge*, and got snowed in while doing a recce in a remote logging town. After getting frostbite, he decided he wanted to make his next film closer to home and decided, 'Let's do something about Manchester, Tony Wilson, The Haçienda and Factory Records'. He signed up Steve Coogan to play Tony Wilson and then brought in the brilliant Frank Cottrell-Boyce to write the script for what became *24 Hour Party People*.

Naturally, Winterbottom wanted to shoot some scenes for the film in The Haçienda. But in classic Factory timing, the original Haçienda had been knocked down just months before, reduced to rubble to be turned into flats, like every other building in Manchester back then. The developers of The Haçienda site even had the nerve to put a huge banner on the side of the new flats, which declared, 'Now the party's over, you can come home', which was sacrilege to some of the old congregation for whom it had been their church. One day, a famous Manchester DJ drunkenly pulled the banner down in a rage, took it back to his home and hung it from his sixth-floor flat.

By the time Winterbottom wanted to film some scenes for the film in the club, he'd never see The Haçienda. It didn't exist. So, it had to be rebuilt. Having made the decision to do that, the film crew were on the hunt for a suitable location somewhere in Manchester, and eventually came across a warehouse in Ancoats on Pollard Street, which was owned by Carol Ainscow, the property developer, who I knew and had already worked with because she owned Paradise Factory. Winterbottom decided the best way to film The Haçienda scenes would be to throw an actual club night in the rebuilt venue. Partly because they wanted to try and get it to look authentic and partly because the film crew fancied spending some of the budget on a huge fuck-off party. Luke was in and around the filming quite a lot, and even played a music journalist in the film, and he witnessed first-hand the cast and crew were partying impressively hard. More than once a member of the cast turned up to film a scene having not been to bed the night before. Let's just say there was a lot of method acting going on during the making of *24 Hour Party People*. Luke still has the original invite to the party on

Friday, 2 March 2001, which is Fac 451. The invite declares: *'What do you have to say to that? Yes, we will have to "build The Haçienda" for ourselves.'*

There were lots of rumours going around town before the party, about who would be DJing and what the venue would be like. Obviously it was the hottest ticket in town and there was much consternation about who had managed to get their hands on tickets and who hadn't. Those who had been the real regulars back in The Haçienda's heyday justly felt that they had more right than anyone to be there, but it had been a dozen or so years since the club's heydays, so they all looked a dozen years older (some of them looked a lot more than a dozen years older, thanks to their recreational habits) so that wouldn't have looked right on screen. Because the production team could only fit in so many people on set, they were never going to be able to please everyone. Somehow, they managed to keep the exact details of the night secret, so none of us knew quite what to expect when we turned up.

In fact, it was an incredible night. The production team had spoken to Ben Kelly, the original designer of The Haçienda, and got hold of the original plans for the club, recreating it exactly as it was during its prime in the 1980s. It was so weird. It was incredible. It was only the main room, so there were no stairs down to The Fifth Man and the Gay Traitor, and the door that led to the original toilets was in the right position, but it just led out to some portable toilets. Everyone spent the first half hour walking round pointing at stuff, saying, 'Wow, it looks just the same!' After the novelty wore off, people just got down to partying hard.

What was quite strange was that everybody fell into old habits, so you would see people you recognised dancing in the same places as they used to in the original Haçienda. As if that wasn't weird enough, you also had all the actors playing Tony Wilson, Joy Division, New Order and Happy Mondays walking around and partying. Half the real musicians, people like Bernard Sumner and Peter Hook from New Order, members of A Certain Ratio, Mani from The Stone Roses and the real-life Tony Wilson were also walking around. Not to mention Sean Harris, who played Ian Curtis, and looked just like him, which was a particularly spooky glitch in the Mancunian matrix, given the real Curtis had died two years before the original club was built, and never saw inside the actual Haçienda. Steve Coogan was in character as Tony Wilson and made a speech from the DJ booth for the film. I was stood outside when he arrived, and even though he was dressed as Wilson and not Alan Partridge, people started shouting 'A-Ha!' at him.[5]

Coogan's night was more bizarre than anyone's, and he partied hard too, as he later admitted in an interview with the *Guardian*: 'I got goosebumps when I walked into the re-created Haçienda. One of my first gigs was there in 1986, supporting my brother's band, the Mock Turtles. There was no legendary last night as depicted in the film. I got my climactic speech for that scene out of the way with a clear head, then took half an E. It was – what's the fashionable word – an immersive experience. We weren't particularly well behaved.'

That night was so wild, brilliant, and hallucinatory that for the rest of the weekend everyone who had been there was in a bit of a daze.

I was as blown away as everyone else, and over the weekend started to think about the amazing space, and how it seemed

---

[5] Coogan's memories of growing up watching Wilson on television had been partially his inspiration for Alan Partridge.

such a waste to use it for just one night. Wouldn't it be a great idea to hire the reconstructed club and throw some parties in there? Since I already had a relationship with the building's owner, it seemed like an absolute no-brainer. All the people who had been there for the film's one-night party and loved it, were just a tiny percentage of the tens of thousands of clubbers in Manchester and beyond who would love a unique chance to party in the deconstructed-reconstructed Haçienda. *Who wouldn't?* We began to get really excited about the possibilities and even started thinking about line-ups.

Unfortunately, by the time I managed to get hold of Carol the following week, to ask about hiring the set, she told me it had already been knocked down. I couldn't fucking believe it. They had flattened the whole set the day after filming. We'd never see the reconstructed Haçienda again. It didn't exist. It had been built, but then, for the second time in a year, The Haçienda had been knocked down.

Mutability is our tragedy, but it is also our hope, as Boethius the Roman philosopher (played by Christopher Eccleston) tells Coogan's Wilson in 24 *Hour Party People*. After we had got over the initial shock of the film set being knocked down, we thought, *Well, why don't we do we throw a huge party there anyway?* It took a while to plan, but Carol was up for it in theory, and I verbally agreed a hire fee with her. Stupidly, I never confirmed it in writing, which would come back to haunt me. The council were less enthusiastic than Carol, and in the weeks leading up to the event I felt like they were trying to block us in every way possible.

When we started planning, we were almost looking backwards for inspiration, in order to move forward. Not to The Haçienda, but to the original UK warehouse raves. We wanted to give a nod to the M25 orbital raves (that Orbital took their name from), and the Blackburn warehouse raves from the halcyon days of acid house. I was too young to have been to the Blackburn raves, and so was Sam, but Dave had been to some of the original orbital raves.

We decided from day one there would be no permanent structure in there. All the bars were on the back of trucks. We also had some nods to the original warehouse raves with the production, like sourcing a 'vintage' laser from the 1980s. We did what we could to recreate that vibe and that feel. The whole clubbing scene had got a bit shiny and glam, and we wanted to remind people of its roots.

When we first got on site there was a mammoth clean-up operation to be done. There were two old, battered Portakabins, which had possibly been used by the film crew and then left there. Pollard Street was just on the cusp of the red-light district, and the Portakabins had been adopted by the local sex workers who would take their clients there. Others used them to shoot up in. They were in a right state, so in the end we had to send the diggers in to crush them.

The week of the event, licensing came down and said we needed an extra fire exit in one of the huge walls, so we had to knock a huge hole in one of the walls. Unfortunately, there was an old persons' home a little way away, and the new hole meant that the sound would be travelling directly towards it. So, we had to source a truckload of hay bales from a farmer and build a wall of hay against the exterior wall to soak up the sound.

It was such a proud moment for me personally when we finally got the licence for the event, and I decided I wanted to thank the people at Manchester City Council who had helped it happen. I had given them a namecheck personally in the Tribal warehouse programme, so as soon as they arrived back from the printers, I drove round town and dropped a few off to the relevant people, saying, 'Thanks again, this is a great thing for Manchester, and we've given you a namecheck in the programme'. Unfortunately, I hadn't checked the programme fully, and it was only when I got home that night and was looking through it that I noticed Dave had inserted a full-page advert for a Ketaman DVD. Under the banner 'Special K presents ...' There was big picture of Dave, dressed as Ketaman, pretending to do a line through a traffic cone. I couldn't believe it. My blood ran cold. I'd personally dropped these programmes off to all the powers that be at Manchester City Council, with a full-page advert for Ketaman. I was really worried that they might think we were completely taking the piss out of them, and it could sabotage the event, and even be the end of my career. (Remarkably, no one at the council ever mentioned it, so maybe they didn't even see it.)

With three days to go, Carol rang me and asked me how it was going. I told her everything was fine and that we had sold out in advance. 'Great', Carol said, 'I need you to come and see me in my office.' I went over to see her at the old Daily Express Building on Great Ancoats Street, where her office was, with Daz Jameson, our Production Manager.

'So, you've sold out?' Carol said, 'How many tickets have you sold?' We had sold 12,000 tickets in advance, but I didn't like where this conversation was heading, so I decided to play it down a bit and said '8,000'.

Carol said, 'Right, I want another £10,000 in that case ...'
'What for?!'

'Let's call it 'inconvenience' ...'

I tried arguing and negotiating but Carol was ruthless, and I ended up having to agree to give her another £10,000. I had no choice; she held all the cards because we only had a verbal agreement, and we couldn't afford to lose the venue three days before the event. It was an expensive lesson. Even if you know someone and have worked with them for years, if you have agreed something, make sure you get that agreement in writing. Get it in black and white, otherwise you're leaving yourself open, and they can fuck you over.

There was no online banking then, so I couldn't just transfer her the money. I didn't have £10,000 in the bank to do that anyway. Everything was cash in those days, and that was what Carol wanted, so I had no choice but to somehow find ten grand in cash to give her that very same day. I drove off and went round Eastern Bloc, Piccadilly Records, and all the other places that were selling our tickets, collected the ticket money, and went back to Carol with a bag full of the cash.

The final issue before the event was the council again, when the licence officer came down to inspect the site on the day of opening. He looked around for a bit, asking a few questions before finally asking, 'Where are your sniffer dogs?'

We'd agreed that we would have sniffer dogs on the door, and he wanted to make sure we had them. I'd asked Ratty, our head of security, to organise them, so I rang him to see what was happening.

'Ratty, where are the sniffer dogs? Licensing are here and want to see them.'

'I'm just picking them up now, I'll be there in half an hour.'

He finally turned up nearly two hours later with the most unlikely-looking bunch of sniffer dogs you've ever seen. There were four of them and they all looked like they'd come last in the local village dog show (or were cast-offs from a *Beano* cartoon). One of them was a Pomeranian for god's sake. They didn't look like they could sniff out a juicy bone, let alone drugs. Bizarrely, and thankfully, somehow the licensing officer was happy when he saw them and signed off the licence. I later found out that

Ratty had completely forgotten to organise sniffer dogs, so he'd just got his bouncers to drive round Preston, where they lived, and just grab random dogs from people's gardens!

Dave had booked almost all of the artists, but we also brought in Rich McGinnis from Chibuku Shake Shake in Liverpool to book one of the rooms. That was the first time we'd ever worked with Rich, but he would later become a partner of The Warehouse Project and Parklife. I'm not sure what the artists were expecting before they turned up at the event. We had existing relationships with most of them by this stage, through Sankeys, but none of them had played an event like this before, as there hadn't been a proper warehouse party in the UK since the 1990s. The only artist who saw the venue before the event was DJ Sneak, who happened to have been playing Sankeys a couple of weeks before, and Sam drove him down to take a look. He stood in the middle of the empty warehouse, blown away. 'Shit man, this is so dope! Ya know what … this shit is going to go down in history!' he told Sam.

We had coaches full of punters arriving from all over the country for the event, so it was busy from the minute the doors opened. The one young kid that sticks in my mind is this poor lad who was on a coach from Middlesbrough or somewhere, and within an hour or so of the doors opening, he'd gone to use a Portaloo, and his mates had pushed it over when he was in there. By the time he managed to get out he was covered in shit. One of our staff did try and clean him down a bit and then he had to just sit on the coach till 6 a.m. and wait for it to set back off again. Poor bastard.

I'd asked Tony Wilson to turn up and give a speech from the stage, as I thought it was a nice link back to the filming of *24 Hour Party People*, when Coogan gave a speech as Wilson. He turned up in this long raincoat and security didn't know who he was so, thinking he was a local homeless person, wouldn't let him in at first. They radioed through saying there was someone saying he was Tony Wilson on the front door, and I had to go down and get him in. He didn't stay long, Wilson was never one to hang around and party, but he seemed to enjoy it and appreciated what we had managed to pull off. We really appreciated him showing up, it was always like getting a blessing from Mr Manchester when he turned up at your events.

It was one of the most bizarre, wildest, and most brilliant events that we've ever put on. Anyone who was there that night felt the same: emotional, ecstatic, confused, and celebratory. Looking back, we really were out of our comfort zone in so many ways, and it's a miracle that we got away with it and eventually came out the other side.

Elisa was running the cash office, which was located in a room up some metal stairs – I presume it was the foreman's office back in those days, because from that room you could see the whole dancefloor, so the foreman would have been able to see the whole factory floor. We had a security guard at the bottom of the stairs, and one at the top, and we also had clear visibility of the stairs, so could see if anyone unauthorised was trying to come up. The cash was taken up there for Elisa to count, throughout the night. There were 12,000 people in there, spending cash all night. There were no card machines, so Elisa had to hand count £250,000 that evening. Quarter of a million. I remember her telling me that by halfway through the evening, her fingers were tingling, and she felt like she was losing the feeling in them.

Nowadays, particularly since the pandemic, almost all payments are cashless, which makes such a huge difference to big events. Back then, holding a large amount of cash was a huge security risk, particularly with the gangs still knocking around. It would obviously be all used notes, and therefore totally untraceable, which made it even more attractive to anyone who might want to rob you. The more money you have on site in cash, and the longer you are holding it, the more chance you have of getting robbed. I decided one way of getting cash off site safely was to use some of it to pay all the DJs and suppliers on the night. It was all legit, everything still went through the books, we just asked all the DJs and suppliers to arrive with their invoices and then paid them there and then. It was a simple security measure to reduce the risk of us being robbed at gunpoint, though it wasn't completely without drama at times ...

We were using a PR guy from London for the event, a lovely guy, and he came up to me at one point in the evening and said, 'Here's my invoice, can I get paid?' and I said, 'Sure, no problem', and took him up to the cash office. We had two bouncers on the door, one outside, and one inside. I took the PR guy in, who gave Elisa his invoice, but she was counting out his payment when we suddenly all heard this huge sniff from behind us. We all looked round at the same time and the security guard who should have been guarding the inside of the door was doing a massive line of coke off the table. The PR guy looked at me and said, 'This *really* is fucking acid house, isn't it?'

I just said to the security guard, 'What the *fuck* are you doing?' and he just looked at me with this big shit-eating grin on his face.

When the party finished at six the following morning, I realised I'd made another error. The club night had started at 2 p.m. and run till 6 a.m. and at Sankeys we always booked the security to finish twenty minutes after doors closed, so I'd done the same with the Warehouse party, but the egress took slightly longer than expected, so by the time I was ready to leave, about 6.45 a.m., I was stood outside and all the security had long gone. Nowadays, Pollard Street is a really nice part of Ancoats, with great restaurants, bars, and coffee shops, and a brilliant artisan bakery called Pollen. Back then, there was nothing and taxis refused to pick up passengers from around there, because the drivers had been robbed at knife point so many times. So, I'm stood on a street corner in Ancoats with £100,000 in cash in a rucksack at 6.45 a.m., and all the security staff have fucked off home, which is not a good situation to be in. There was only myself, Elisa, and a guy called Charles Herbert, who used to drive the DJs for us, so I told Charles I had all the cash on me, and he said he would drop me off on his way home.

Because it was a Sunday morning and a bank holiday, the banks didn't open till Tuesday morning. Forty-eight hours away. This meant I had to keep £100,000 in cash on me for two days. Elisa and I lived in Warburton, just on the edge of Partington at the time, and I knew if the wrong people knew were we lived we would be in trouble, as they could put two and two together and figure out we had the takings. Elisa and I spent the next two days with the curtains closed and the lights off; we didn't once let the rucksacks of cash leave our sight. We just sat on the couch with the curtains drawn wearing the rucksacks. I didn't even take if off when I went to the toilet. Elisa cooked dinner wearing hers. We were both bloody terrified of something happening.

On the Sunday evening, I got a call from Darren Jameson.

'Where are you?'

'I'm at home.'

'OK, meet me at Lymm services as soon as you can.'

'Why, what's wrong?'

While Darren and his crew were de-rigging and cleaning up the warehouse, they had found a box containing £5,000 in cash. I'd tried to contain the cash system as much as possible, and we had a system where people had to use tokens at the bar, so none of the bars took cash, but that meant there were boxes of tokens and cash flying back and forth between the upstairs office, and somehow one of the boxes had got mislaid and not made its way there. Fair play to Darren, we might not even have noticed that was missing if he hadn't told us.[6]

First thing Tuesday morning, I was waiting by the door to the bank for when it opened. I've never been so relieved to see a bank door open, never been so relieved to see any door open.

I often think back to that event with fucking fear because we were so so *so* out of our depths. We did not have a clue what we were doing. Why the gangsters didn't come and ruin it for others, I've just no idea. While no one was taken ill, it was a huge success.

Creamfields were very upset with us and wanted to make sure we didn't do it again on an August bank holiday, as Jim King told us he thought we took 5,000 tickets off them. Because of the financial success, too, it made us think differently about the benefits of doing big statement events like that versus the endless slog of managing weekly club nights.

People who were at that first warehouse party still mention it to me. With the benefit of hindsight, I think we all began to believe our own hype a little bit after that. It was a huge thing to pull that off when everyone said it wouldn't happen, we wouldn't sell enough tickets, issues with the council, and Carol taking an extra £10,000. Perhaps we became slightly arrogant and thought we'd done something really fucking special and

---

[6] I gave him a few hundred quid as a thank you.

possessed the Midas touch. Dave most definitely did. He went on a different trajectory after the Tribal Warehouse party.

We are often asked why we didn't do it again, but we couldn't do it again on that site, because that warehouse was torn down, to (you guessed it) build new flats. We looked at other places, but never found somewhere that could match up to that original warehouse because it was so special.

The other knock-on effect was because we had been focusing so much of our efforts on the Warehouse party, Sankeys suffered. Not just because our focus was elsewhere, but also because when you take 12,000 people out of your potential market of customers, like we did that weekend, it doesn't just affect that one weekend, it affects a couple of weekends either side. In a way, our success had taken away from other successes. Like I said earlier, we only needed a couple of bad weekends for Sankeys to really start suffering financially, and we'd taken the wind out of its sails for the best part of a month. It also affected the second Tribal Weekender, because there was no way that could live up to the Warehouse party, and it all felt a bit flat after that.

After the huge success of the Warehouse party, we wanted to do another one, but unfortunately the same warehouse wasn't available. After a lot of searching, we found the old Bauer Millet showroom behind G-Mex, that they were moving out of. Most people in Manchester know the Bauer Millet site. It was a garage showroom that sold high-end cars, but you weirdly never saw anyone in it. I'm a bit of a petrolhead, and I've bought a few silly cars over the years, but even I had never been in there. We did the deal with Laurence Millet in the showroom, and he was a pretty old-school car dealer. He was about sixty, always suited and booted, and wore a lot of gold about himself. Glasses, watch, bracelet, everything he wore was gold, and he had very strong aftershave. I've never met anyone wearing that much aftershave. He was a bit like a Mancunian version of Swiss Toni from *The Fast Show*. I'm sure renting his showroom to us to put on a party was very much like making love to a beautiful woman.

We put on a New Year's Day party for 1 January 2005, and I think we were one of the first to do that, to put on a New Year's *Day* rather than New Year's Eve party. It was also one of the first Haçienda reunion events. The club closed in 1997, so it had been shut for seven years by that stage, and we were the first to bring the resident DJs Mike Pickering and Graeme Park back together on a bill. That was the first time I properly met Mike Pickering, who would go on to be a really good friend of The Warehouse Project when it launched, and Graeme Park, who is lovely, and we still work with to this day. Peter Hook wasn't very happy when he saw the artwork for our event (this was before he started putting on his own Haçienda reunion events) and I had to go and meet him and pay him £5,000 so we could continue with the event.

That was also the first time I met 'The Lieutenant', when Jon Drape brought him in to work on the production side of the event. The Lieutenant is obviously not his real name, but he prefers to move in the shadows rather than court publicity, so he didn't want his real name in this book. The Lieutenant has been around in Manchester since the late 1980s. He's earned his acid house badges. He's definitely not a gangster but he's well connected around Manchester. The Lieutenant has worked with us ever since and is an integral part of The Warehouse Project. I would go as far as saying he is my eyes and ears on the ground.

Meanwhile, Sankeys was continuing to struggle a little. Especially throughout the summer months, when the students had gone home. We didn't realise it then, but looking back at it now, the Warehouse party was the beginning of the end for Sankeys. We just didn't see it through the strobe lights.

Leaving Sankeys

By the spring of 2006, I was getting increasingly demoralised by what was happening at Sankeys. It was very clear that Dave and I had, shall we say, very different priorities.

It had become blatantly obvious, to me at least, and it was affecting the business. He was living in London during the week but coming up to Manchester every weekend and partying heavily for forty-eight hours. Behind my back, and when I wasn't there, it had become a bit of a free for all. Dave was like a kid in a sweet shop. Actually, worse, he was the naughty kid that co-owned the sweet shop. He saw Sankeys as his own private playground, and he invited lots of other naughty kids to party there all weekend, every weekend, often at our expense. It was no way to run a business, in my eyes. From my perspective, it seemed like Dave wasn't really interested in running a business and just wanted to throw the best parties. It didn't seem as if the cost or practicalities mattered to him at all and I was still seen as one thing: the fun police.

It had all gone too far.

As I mentioned, after the success of the Tribal warehouse, I think we were all slightly guilty of getting ahead of ourselves and believed our own hype, but with Dave it was next level. He went off and decided to do a Tribal Gathering charity event on his own in Luton, which was supposed to raise money for Syria. He actually described himself as the 'Bob Geldof of dance music' at one stage, and he thought the event was going to make a huge difference. Unfortunately for Dave, he hadn't really got a proper organisational structure in place, the whole thing collapsed around him, and they had to pull the entire event at the last minute.

After the debacle of the Tribal Gathering charity event that never happened, Dave seemed to double down on his partying, and it was becoming really detrimental to the business. He bought a penthouse in central Manchester, five minutes' walk from Sankeys, and had a lap-dancing pole installed for his after-parties.

There were so many incidents where he went too far. Too many straws that broke the camel's back. When the super club Home (in Leicester Square, London) went bust, we bought their Phazon sound system from them for £78,000. When they'd opened, Home had made a huge fanfare about their specialist, state-of-the-art sound system, custom-built by a guy called Steve Dash, from New York. Steve had built the original Phazon system for Twilo nightclub in NYC, where Sasha and Digweed were residents in the 1990s, so this sound system was a huge deal, and when Home went out of business Dave was determined we would get it for Sankeys.

Stupidly, we hadn't bothered to measure it to make sure that it would fit into Sankeys before we bought it. Fortunately, when it was delivered, it just about fitted into the club, and I mean *just* about. The ceiling in Sankeys was much lower than Home, and when we finally managed to install it there was only a tiny gap between the system itself and the ceiling.

Because it was such a specialist system, we had to pay Steve Dash to come over from New York and install it. Steve was a pretty unique individual. When he arrived in Manchester to install the system, from what I could tell, Steve spent a week sitting in the middle of the dancefloor, listening to white noise, and making very tiny adjustments to the levels. I couldn't work out if he was taking the piss out of us.

Once Steve had spent that week setting up the sound system, he left us and went back to New York. You'd have thought everyone would've been quite protective of the fabled Phazon sound system that we'd just installed, but no. Not long after Steve had gone, I left the club one night at 3 a.m., and as soon as I'd left the building, some people went absolutely mental and threw a huge party on the dancefloor, flinging jelly and talcum powder about the place. Some of the powder got into the speakers and damaged the system, and we had to get *another* specialist in to fix it.

That was typical of the problems that Dave's partying was causing at the time. He was a brilliant promoter, and his knowledge was first rate, but his hedonism was affecting everything. We would have a promoters' meeting every Monday afternoon, and Dave, who had usually been partying all weekend and hadn't been to bed for seventy-two hours, would quite often fall asleep during the meeting, with his head down on the table. He and I had worked together really well for a good few years, but it's hard to maintain respect for someone if they put partying above business and fall asleep during important planning meetings. Especially if that person is supposed to be one of the leaders of the business. It would be like all the players turning up at Manchester United on a Monday morning to find Alex Ferguson or Roy Keane asleep when they should have been leading training or having a debrief on the weekend's game.

During the last eighteen months or so of my time at Sankeys, all the fun had gone out of it for me, and it became a slog really. As a business it was beginning to limp on hand-to-mouth, week-to-week, and I think we all realised that the clock was ticking. All of us apart from Dave, that is, who probably still had the blinkers on a bit.

I decided I wanted to get out of Sankeys. I *had* to. I couldn't handle Dave's behaviour anymore and our relationship had deteriorated so much that I was now at my wit's end. I rang Mike Chilman our main investor and said, 'We need to do something about Dave, he's out of control.'

I felt bad about going behind Dave's back to Mike, but I didn't know what else to do. Shortly after, Dave randomly bumped in to Mike in London, and Mike said, 'What's going on Dave? I've had Sacha on the phone blah blah blah ...' Dave hit the fucking roof at me going to Mike behind his back, and everything just went turbo. The following week, Mike called a meeting with Dave and I at the Lowry hotel in town, to try and sort things and clear the air, but it quickly became apparent that it wasn't going to be sorted and the air wasn't clearing. It seemed the only way out was for Dave to buy me out, or me to buy him out. We both agreed to go away and spend the weekend thinking about our options. I honestly think Dave thought that despite it all we would kiss and make up again the following week, but I'd had enough and on the Monday morning I said, 'Right, I'm off ... make me an offer.'

Dave was pretty shocked, but we agreed a deal with each other directly. He could buy my share of the business. As part of the deal, Dave didn't want me to set up another nightclub in Manchester in direct competition with Sankeys. After that, we went down the legal route. Dave had taken other advice and now thought the deal wasn't a fair price after all. After I had declared I was leaving, Sam Kandel and Kirsty Smith both decided they would leave at the same time because they had both had enough as well. We began to talk about what we might do next, and one of our first ideas was acquiring a few rundown properties and doing them up. We came up with the name 'Ugly Duckling Group' to reflect the idea of taking old buildings that were real dumps and transforming them into something special. We quickly realised that we didn't have the money to do anything of any sort of scale, so we would need to find something to finance the project.

Our initial idea was just to throw a handful of nights, which would give us enough capital to start the business properly. I thought between four and six parties would do it, but very quickly the idea started to snowball. The three months from September to Christmas were always the best part of the year at Sankeys, and the rest of the year was usually a struggle, so we thought, *Why don't we just find a warehouse that we can put parties on for those three months a year?*

It was actually Sam who came up with the name and concept for the project. He was living with Krysko at the time, and the two of them stayed up really late one night, putting the world to rights, and talking about ideas for our new warehouse project, when Sam suggested running it for the final three months of the year, and said, 'Why don't we just call it The Warehouse Project.' When he told us the next day, we loved the name, and began to put plans into action and I put some money in to get us started.

We found an image on Google of a random warehouse that looked really cool and moody. We had no idea where it was,

I'm not sure it was even in Manchester, but Sam and Rich added it to The Warehouse Project proposal they were sending out and taking to artists and their agents.

On my final night at Sankeys, Dave wasn't even there, which was a bit of a blow considering the years we'd spent building this together, but indicated how damaged our relationship was and what little respect he actually had for me. Dave was actually on a plane to South America, heading off to *find himself* deep in the rainforest.

Having frowned on Dave's hard partying at Sankeys with his acolytes, that final weekend I just didn't care. It was my last night at Sankeys, and it got pretty wild. The bar was a bit of a free for all. It was a Red Light night on a Saturday, and everyone knew it was my last night so I DJed at the end of the night. Well, I didn't DJ, I just selected ten of my favourite tracks and Krysko actually played them for me. New Order's 'Blue Monday', Prince's 'Controversy', and The Smiths' 'Panic'. Not very Red Light at all, but the crowd loved it. I've got a picture of me at the end of the night, with long hair, wearing a headband. Not a great look.

One of the people working at the club at the time was a guy called Wayne, who was also leaving. Dave had caused Wayne no end of headaches, and he wasn't Dave's biggest fan. So, we had a little backstage party afterwards, and Wayne asked if he could borrow the office I shared with Dave for a couple of minutes. I said, 'Yeah, if you really want.' I had no idea what he was going to do.

Dave's office 'chair' was a hollow cube, and Wayne just took a shit on the floor, and put Dave's cube over it. I never heard from Dave about that, he probably thought it was me who did it.

Dave and I were still having a legal ding-dong, going back and forth over our agreement after the relationship between us had broken down beyond repair. It was costing both of us an absolute fortune in legal fees. He hired lawyers, I hired lawyers, and the whole experience was just one big, horrible exercise, especially after we had built Sankeys together and were both proud of what we'd achieved.

Because neither of us were keen on dragging out the negotiations any further than they already had been – the only thing we *did* agree on! – we both agreed to walk away and head off to do our own things. Dave would continue with Sankeys, and I would embark on something new. Sometimes, you just have to know when enough is enough and call it quits as it's not always worth the hassle. In the end, we both agreed to walk away.

I'm not sure what we would have done otherwise. We would have probably opened The Warehouse Project but with me behind the scenes, rather than being the public face of it.

The Warehouse Project was the future. We knew it.

This City is Ours: The Birth of The Warehouse Project

Although I was hugely excited about our plans for The Warehouse Project, there was one slight issue that we needed to sort before it could all kick off: we didn't have a warehouse.

We had the *project* bit of The Warehouse Project, we knew what that was and that was all great, but we still didn't have an actual bricks and mortar *warehouse* to put the project in. While Sam and Rich were down in London, giving the big speech to all the agents and the wider industry, getting them all excited by showing them the picture of a random warehouse they had downloaded from the internet, it was my job to scour Manchester and find an actual warehouse that we could use. I looked all over the city, speaking to estate agents and developers, and even driving down random streets in deserted parts of town to find somewhere. There can't have been many empty warehouses in Manchester that I didn't take a look at.

Then one day, I read a story in the *Manchester Evening News* about Boddingtons Brewery closing down, and an idea began to take hold in my mind. The brewery was a Mancunian landmark, on the outskirts of the city centre, at the foot of Cheetham Hill, between Strangeways prison and the Arena. Boddingtons had been brewed on the site for over 250 years so the beer had long been one of the symbols of Manchester, and they played up to that image in the 1990s, calling themselves the 'Cream of Manchester' and running a famous TV advert with Manchester as Venice, starring Anne Chancellor (who shortly after being the face of Boddies went on to star in *Four Weddings and A Funeral*) who grabs a pint from a passing gondolier, sips it and declares, 'By 'eck, it's gorgeous!'

Shutting down the brewery and moving it out of Manchester and into Wales was a huge moment for the city, and more than symbolic for everyone who worked there. It was a proper old-school workforce and generations of families (mostly men, their fathers and grandfathers) had worked there, so it touched a nerve when you saw pictures of them leaving the brewery for the last time, carrying cardboard boxes with their personal effects away with them. The brewery was a huge site, right in the centre of Manchester, and it now lay there empty, and I thought we could turn it into a positive story for the city. It kind of played into the Ugly Duckling idea of giving something a new lease of life, and I thought maybe we can turn this sad moment into something different. It's the end of one thing, but the start of something new.

I didn't think about this connection at the time, but Luke pointed out that Factory Records decided on the name Factory because when they were planning their first club night in the summer of 1978, Manchester was in a post-industrial slump. There were 'Factory closing' signs all over the city at this point, and they wanted to buck that trend and have a 'Factory opening' one instead. I suppose there was a similar spirit in what we were thinking. We wanted to breathe life back into the nightlife of Manchester. OK, it was business, I won't shy away from admitting that. But we did also want to put something back.

I found out that the building was now owned by an old-school Iranian Jewish guy called Mr Hakim, and I went to see him and explained we wanted to put a few dance parties on in the building. I didn't really go into much detail, and I think in his mind they were going to be some sort of tea dances such as people threw in the 1950s. He was pretty traditional, and I decided the best policy was a 'need to know' basis, and not explain who Felix da Housecat and The Chemical Brothers were. We agreed to pay Mr Hakim £60,000 to rent the warehouse for the whole season.

We took over the old brewery site in June 2006 and had three months to clear out all the old machinery and turn it into a venue. It was a lot of work to do in that time span, and it didn't help when a group of travellers then moved onto the site, presumably because they could see the worth in stripping out some of the old scrap metal. Mr Hakim went down to bargain with them to get them to move off site, and I told him 'Whatever you do, don't pay them off ... if they won't leave, we need to get the authorities involved.'

But Mr Hakim wanted to tackle the situation head on and get it resolved, so he ended up paying them to move off site. Lo and behold, three days later, another bunch of travellers had moved on site, obviously being tipped off that there was money to be made, and they wanted paying off too. This time he went with my suggestion, and took the legal route, and we managed to get them moved on, but it meant we lost vital time to get the site ready.

Jon Drape was our Production Manager, as well as the person in charge of turning the Boddingtons site into a

My very first photo shoot
for my school, 1981.

Manchester Grammar School,
1983. Butter wouldn't melt.

J.L.P. Concerts present

THE FALL

**The Man From Delmonte
& The Sandmen
Thursday 13th July 1989**

FREE TRADE HALL, PETER ST. MANCHESTER
DOORS OPEN 7.00pm
Tickets £5.50 advance

PLUS BOOKING

Nº 112

Ticket stub
from my very first
gig. I went to see
The Man From
Delmonte and
left before The
Fall came on.

A collection of some of my
early student night flyers. None
of these will be found in the
Design Museum any time soon.

meet the stars
@
shooting
stars

who will it be?
launch party thursday 25th September @
Noto5*Paradise*

THIS WEEKS CELEBRITY CLUE: international american based star, she likes a cocktail

meet the stars
@
shooting
stars

who will it be?
thursday 9th october @
Noto5*Paradise*

THIS WEEKS CELEBRITY CLUE: If you don't love him, he'll spit at you!

meet the stars
@
shooting
stars

who will it be?
thursday 16th october @
Noto5*Paradise*

THIS WEEKS CELEBRITY CLUE: MI5, MI6, mafia dealings, 43 passports, just out of prison,
he likes a smoke · he's nice

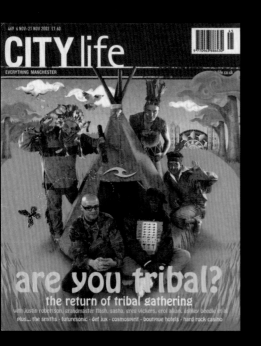

469 6 NOV–21 NOV 2002 £1.60

CITY life
EVERYTHING MANCHESTER
life.co.uk

are you tribal?
the return of tribal gathering
with justin robertson, grandmaster flash, sasha, greg vickers, erol alkan, ashley beedle et al
plus... the smiths · futuresonic · def lux · cosmospirit · boutique hotels · hard rock casino

The infamous *City Life* shoot promoting
the return of Tribal Gathering in 2002.
Justin Robertson and Grandmaster Flash
don't exactly look thrilled to be there.

Me and Mum in The Haçienda
at one of my early student
gigs. Mum is holding a bottle
of Dunberry Spring Water
(see story on page 73)

Krysko, me and Dave Vincent (l-r) in the DJ booth at Sankeys.

	Saturday 25 November			Saturday 25 November
THE RACKING HALL			**THE BOX**	
10:00:	Mike Pickering		10:00:	Residents
11:00:	New Young Pony Club		11:00:	Reverend and the Makers
11:30	Annie Mac		11:30	Residents
01:00	Klaxons		12:00	DNCN
01:30	Erol Alkan		01:30	Black Strobe
03:00	Mylo		02:30	Optimo
04:30	Switch			

Set times for a night during the inaugural Warehouse Project season in 2006.

WHP streaker during 2 Many DJs set.

The dancefloor at WHP, doing its day job. Store Street was a car park during the week, and we had two hours every Friday to turn it into the country's best nightclub.

When the lights went up, and everyone had gone home, we had to turn it back into a car park again.

Mark Ronson taking a well-earned break after his set at WHP in 2007.

Me and Liam Gallagher, backstage at Parklife when he headlined in 2018. Liam joked to his fans about renaming the festival Parkalife.

Me and Snoop Dogg hanging out at Parklife when he headlined in 2014.

Pharell Williams at Parklife in 2018. There was a slight moment of panic in Event Control when this happened, as he hadn't warned us he was going to invite the audience up on stage.

Me (far left) and The Prodigy, taken a WHP, before the sad passing of the immensely lovely Keith Flint (next to me in the pic) in 2019.

Goldie, in the mix at WHP.

Preparing for The Haçienda day as part of United We Stream, which I launched during lockdown in 2020.

A drone shot of the return of Parklife after Covid, in 2021. It's possibly my favourite photo of Parklife.

Me and Boy George backstage at a Morrissey gig, Hammersmith, 2023.

The WHP family, on the last ever night at Store Street, including me Krysko (back, far right), then next to me, Kim O'Brien, my business partner Sam Kandel, and Rich McGinnis, with WHP photographer Sebastian Matthes crouching, far right, next to my ex-wife Elisa.

This is just two random punters at WHP, but I've always loved this picture. Something about it captures the mood of WHP for me.

The main room at WHP, Mayfield Depot, 2023.

Parklife is now the biggest metropolitan festival in the UK.

groundbreaking nightclub, the man who had to make sure we *could* organise a piss-up in a brewery, if you will pardon the pun. He did an incredible job in turning it round in a few short weeks, but we were all working blind a little bit. We didn't really know how the venue would work till it opened. We'd never done anything like this before, nobody had, really. Nobody had turned an industrial site like this into a nightclub. It was technically 'the two-warehouse project' for the first season, as we split the old brewery into two warehouses, one slightly larger than the other. The larger of the two was where the actual Boddies had been brewed for centuries, and was known as 'The Racking Hall', the other was the cold store where the kegs were stored, and we called that 'The Box'. Most of the events used both, but some more intimate events just used The Box.

That whole year was a baptism of fire for the entire team. I would never have admitted it at the time, but nearly twenty years later, I don't mind saying that there were points where it felt like the whole thing was hanging by a thread, and other times where it felt like a game of Whac-A-Mole. One problem would pop up, and by the time we had dealt with that, a different problem had jumped up somewhere else behind our backs. It was relentless.

Tony Wilson and Factory Records used to talk about 'praxis'. It's the idea that you do something because you want to do it, and only after you've done it do you realise why you did it, and what it meant. We had an idea of what The Warehouse Project was in our heads, and on paper, before we started that first season, but it was only by actually doing that first season that we found out what The Warehouse Project truly was, and what it could become; which bits worked, which bits didn't, who the crowd was, and what they would respond to. The kind of artists who would work in a space like that, and those that didn't translate as well.

When we first announced The Warehouse Project, we were pretty bolshy in our teaser campaign, which declared: *For twelve weeks, this city is ours ... Manchester is back.*

We didn't announce the location at first, as we wanted to maintain an air of mystique and keep people guessing. We also wanted to stress that it was only going to be here for twelve weeks, as we wanted to make sure people felt the urge to check it out before it disappeared.

When we finally put out the flyer with the line-up for our opening season, we revealed the location:

Things are starting to bubble, as the North prepares for twelve weeks of warehouse parties. With the venue now revealed as The Old Brewery, one of Manchester's most iconic landmarks, it's time to start spreading the word. Everybody from Manchester knows this legendary site, with its towering chimney peering out over the city. It was here that they made the legendary tonic for over 250 years ... Now, in 2006, and for three months only, we take a piece of the city's cherished history and catapult it into the twenty first century. We couldn't have asked for a more perfect backdrop for the first Warehouse Project.

People have been asking why the project will only last for these three months. The truth is, it will be something that is here, and then gone very quickly. While it lasts it will be truly amazing, and nobody will even get the chance to get bored of it. The idea for the project was revealed several months ago, with the tag line 'For twelve weeks, this city is ours ... Manchester is back.'

There were twenty-five events in that opening season, from the first night on 5 October till New Year's Eve. We booked Public Enemy to play the opening preview night, their first gig in Manchester for years, which was a big deal for us. The opening Saturday night was Mike Pickering presents 'Welcome to The Warehouse'. Seventeen years on since I had walked into The Haçienda and had my own moment on the road to Damascus, thanks to Mike Pickering (although I hadn't known at that moment who he was, or that he was the mythical figure in the DJ booth), now he was helping me to open the next step in Manchester's clubbing evolution. I don't remember dwelling on it too much that night though, I was too busy trying to get punters in from the chaos on Cheetham Hill Road. Pickering was joined on the bill with live DJ sets from Kasabian, Doves, Tom Findlay (of Groove Armada), The View, and Aim. I think that was Kasabian's first DJ set, Pickering had persuaded them to do it, as he had originally signed the band. It was a bit of a curveball for us but made for an interesting story. They didn't even want a fee, they just wanted paying in chips and gravy! Which, obviously, I was happy with. I would have even thrown in some mushy peas. Unfortunately, they had to pull out the night before, so they never did get their chips and gravy.

We had sold out the first few weeks before we even opened the doors, but we still didn't really know what to expect on that first night, especially as we hadn't established a proper queuing system yet. We did manage to correct that for the second week, but on the opening night it was a bit of a free for all, with 3,000 people in the streets, on Cheetham Hill Road. Right at the front of the queue was Pat Barrett, an ex-professional boxer who had a pretty big reputation around town, and owned a club in Collyhurst that was always kicking off and was now running his own security firm. When I saw him at the front of the queue, I began to wonder what we'd let ourselves in for.

Because of the lack of a proper queueing system, it was a real bun fight for the first couple of hours, and I was thinking, *Jesus Christ, maybe everyone who was telling me not to do this was right?* Two hours after the doors opened, when we just about managed to get everyone in, my phone started ringing. A withheld number. I ignored it at first, presuming it was someone trying to blag a last-minute spot on the guest list. But whoever it was kept ringing and ringing, and after about the sixth or seventh time, I thought I'd better answer it in case it was important.

It was the Governor from Strangeways Prison, which was just next door to The Warehouse Project. I've no idea how he got hold of my mobile number, but he was really annoyed.

'Is that Sacha? Right, can you tell me what time this bloody party is going on till tonight?'

'It's a live gig tonight,' I told him, 'So we'll be finished by 1 a.m.'

'OK.'

'But we're open till 4 a.m. tomorrow as it's a club night … '

'You're open again tomorrow???'

The Governor thought it was just a one-off event. 'Yes, till 4 a.m. tomorrow … and we're open for the next twelve weeks.'

'Oh God! You do realise the bass is coming out from your roof and reverberating around the whole of Strangways?'

Strangeways was an old Victorian prison, and to be honest none of the authorities had raised the prospect of sound leaking out into the prison prior to us opening. But it was clearly an issue. The Governor, to put it mildly, was not happy and remained so throughout the entire season.

The inmates, however, had a very different reaction! Within a week or two of The Warehouse Project being open, we started to get a few letters from Strangeways prisoners, on HM Prison-headed paper, saying stuff like, 'I could hear a bit of Annie Mac's set from my cell last night, and it sounded great, is there any chance you could send us a tape of her set?'

The Governor later went on record blaming us for a surge in drug taking within the prison, saying that drug abuse had rocketed during the period when The Warehouse Project was running.

Not long after I had that conversation with the Governor, a chafferer-driven Jaguar pulled up at the front door, and Mr Hakim got out of the back, puffing on a huge cigar. He looked around and took everything in, the type of clientele we had and how busy it was. He realised straight away that we'd pulled the wool over his eyes a little, but thankfully he didn't seem angry, he almost respected it. 'Sacha,' he said to me, slowly, in his very deep voice, 'you are a very *naughty* man.'

As a gesture, and a bit of a PR stunt, we invited all the workers who had been made redundant from Boddingtons to come down and check out what we had done with their old brewery one night and have a drink on us. Quite a few of them turned up, and we were shocked by just how much they could drink. *By 'eck!* To use Boddingtons old parlance. Quite a few of them had driven down, and we had to politely suggest that it might be better if they got a taxi home and came back for their cars in the morning, after they weren't six pints in.

Strangeways weren't the only people who had an issue with noise from The Warehouse Project that first year. Noise is a very difficult thing to control, it can leak out of the smallest, weirdest places, and it also travels in unpredictable directions. One of the biggest problems we had was with a block of high-rise flats in Salford, which was about a mile away. Somehow, the sound was leaking out of our roof, bouncing off the River Irwell and hitting this high rise a mile away. It sounded pretty unlikely when we first had complaints from there, but I went round there to check it out myself, and from the top of the high-rise you could hear the music almost as clearly as if you were on the dancefloor. We tried everything to mitigate it; we put in a second ceiling and insulated it with sound proofing, but the issue still remained.

After this, we then had the Environmental Health department after us because of the sound, and at one stage it really looked like they were going to close us down. I spoke to my lawyer, who told us that if they were going to serve us papers to shut us down, they could only serve them by hand to the Director. They had to physically hand *me* the papers, so I made sure I never gave them that opportunity. They used to park across the road from the venue every night and wait for me. Our Production Manager, Jon Drape, put a ladder over the back wall of the venue one night when we really thought they were going to try and serve me these papers, and I had my car waiting on the other side of the wall to make a quick getaway. We had this system set up where if they came into the venue to try and get to me, I'd run through the venue, up the ladder, over the wall, and drive off into the night. Somehow, we got away with it, and we managed to stay open for the whole twelve weeks.

On a couple of occasions, we had two nights running concurrently – one in The Racking Hall and one in The Box.

The most eventful of these was a Saturday night in October. In the more intimate Box, was The 3 Chairs Party, curated by Luke Una from Electric Chair, with Kenny Dixon Jr, Moody-mann, Theo Parrish, and Rick Wilhite, while Federation was in The Racking Hall – a pretty wild and no-holds-barred queer event. It's safe to say they attracted quite different crowds, with The 3 Chairs crowd being full of beardy crate-digging chin-stroking Northern Quarter types, and Federation, pulling the full-on, tops off gay crowd who were, they wouldn't be ashamed to admit, pretty promiscuous. There was only one set of toilets shared between The Racking Hall and The Box, and a few of the beardy 3 Chairs crowd saw some things in the shared toilets that night that opened their eyes a little and, to be honest, might have also made their eyes water a little!

We'd already finalised the line-up for New Year's Eve, when I got a call from Mike Pickering:

'Sach, can you do me a favour and put this new guy from Scotland I've got on your bill for New Year's Eve?'

'We're fully booked I'm afraid, Mike.'

'Can you just stick him on for an hour, early doors? As a favour to me? He's called Calvin Harris.'

Nobody had heard of Calvin Harris back then. Mike had just signed him to Sony, and his debut album *I Created Disco*, wasn't released till the following summer. As a favour to Mike, we juggled things around and put him on at 9 p.m. We didn't tell Calvin the doors didn't properly open till half an hour later, so he just thought it was quiet for the first half hour because it was early. We paid him £250 after his set, and then he presented his first-class train tickets to me to get reimbursed. I had to tell him I'd never agreed to pay first class, and just gave him the standard train fare instead. The following year, Calvin had Top Ten hits and was writing songs with Kylie

Minogue. Then he had a smash No.1 with Dizzee Rascal with 'Dance wiv Me'. Calvin gets an eye-watering amount for a gig now, and travels everywhere by private jet. They don't stick him on before the doors open anymore!

Lots of the artists that we had booked that first year, went on to be regulars at The Warehouse Project for many seasons. Annie Mac played that first season, and she was brilliant. She's played every single Warehouse Project season since, bar one and always pulls a great crowd.

Within the first week of The Warehouse Project, we really knew that we were on to something; we knew we had stumbled on something with huge potential. But within a few weeks it also became abundantly clear that the old Boddingtons Brewery could not possibly work as a long-term home for us. Despite myriad problems with the site, the prison next door, and especially the merry dance with the Environmental Health department, we somehow crawled to the finish line, although it was very touch and go.

In just twelve weeks, it felt like The Warehouse Project had established itself as a significant player not just in Manchester, but nationwide. We had pulled it off and made people sit up and take notice, which felt great. However, as soon as that first season had finished, we were homeless again.

It was time to begin the search for a new home.

Under the Paving Stones, the Beats

I'd already looked at most of the empty warehouses in the city centre on my first recce, so I started thinking more creatively – thinking outside the warehouse box. One of the things I googled for ideas was 'air-raid shelters' and I came across mention of one under Piccadilly station, on Store Street. We went down to have a look and it turns out it was the biggest air-raid shelter in Manchester city centre during the Second World War. If you go through the entrance on London Road there is still an old sign on the wall that says: 'Warden's office'.

Inside was an amazing cavernous space created by the huge Victorian brick arches. The only problem was it was currently in use as a car park, which was a slight issue. Undeterred, I set out to find the owner of the building, and by an unbelievable stroke of luck discovered it was Mr Hakim. Although Hakim had called me a 'naughty boy' at the start of the first Warehouse season at the brewery, by the end he was really happy with us, and didn't want to lose us as tenants. We began to get quite excited about this new space. It wasn't a warehouse, it was a car park, and the 'Car Park Project' doesn't have the same ring about it, but I took Sam and Jon Drape to see it, and we all thought we could do something very special there.

I didn't realise at first, but this place was also a link back to the first ever Manchester warehouse scene. Around the corner on Fairfield Street, there was another doorway, leading to a smaller space, which held a few hundred people, and that was where those seminal warehouse parties were held in the mid-1980s. The first three parties were held in 1985 by a guy called Steve Adge; this was before acid house had properly hit Manchester. The Adge is a legendary figure. There's plenty of real characters around Manchester, and then there's people like The Adge, who are next level. He'd been there, done that, and got the T-shirt, twenty years before everyone else.

Back in 1985, The Adge had somehow managed to get hold of this warehouse space, and Ian Brown from The Stone Roses remembers The Adge ringing him up and saying, 'I've got this place behind Piccadilly train station and I'm thinking of throwing a party. I'm gonna call it The Flower Show and I want a band to play. Are you up for it?'

The Stone Roses were still pretty unknown then, but they'd already put out some of the songs that would make up their 1989 debut album, and there's a clip on YouTube of them playing 'I Wanna Be Adored' from that first warehouse party in 1985. The Adge went on to tour-manage the Roses and he was there throughout their most pivotal moments. It was The Adge who took them to throw paint over their old record company offices, and it was he who handed Ian Brown the inflatable globe as he went on stage at Spike Island.

Chris and Antony Donnelly, the brothers behind Gio Goi, then held an early acid house rave at this space in 1989 called Sweat It Out. There were only about 300 people there, but it was a much smaller scene then, so a lot of the important faces were present, including the Mondays and the Roses, and early Haçienda regulars. Chris and Antony built a rudimentary stage from scaffolding, and Mike Pickering and Jon Da Silva from The Haç DJed. Tony Wilson turned up with a video camera and shot some footage of it, which is on YouTube these days, including a clip of Shaun Ryder, who is trying to persuade Wilson to 'lend' him money to buy drugs. Wilson lapped it up because he loved anything anarchic. The police were totally unaware of what was happening, and didn't turn up till 9 a.m. the next morning, when Chris and Antony were sweeping up, to find a lone pile of water bottles. The police were like, 'What's going on here?' Chris said, 'We've just had a private party, officer, but as you can see there was no alcohol, and Tony Wilson from *Granada Reports* came down as well.' The police were like, 'OK, fine'. They didn't have a clue.

It was early 2007 when we first saw the location, and we decided to test the water to see if we could make it work as a venue before we made the jump and installed The Warehouse Project there. Initially, we put on three parties over the Easter weekend. We didn't want to connect those three events to The Warehouse Project, so we called them Beneath the Streets.

Somehow, we had to find a way to work around the fact that the place was still an operational car park Monday to Friday – a huge logistical challenge, to say the least. I arranged with Mr Hakim to get the keys to the space at 6 p.m. on Friday, when it closed as a car park, and hand the keys back at 5 a.m. on the Monday morning. That meant we only had four hours on Friday evening to turn a car park into a groundbreaking nightclub, between 6 p.m. when we got the keys, to 10 p.m. when the doors opened. Afterwards, we would then have to convert it back to a car park and leave no trace that a nightclub had been there by 5 a.m. on the Monday. We must have been mental to even consider it, but we didn't have many other alternative sites to consider. In fact, we didn't have any. But if anyone could turn a car park into a nightclub in four hours, it was Jon Drape and his team. It was a military operation. The production team would be waiting outside with everything on standby, and as soon as we got the keys, they would start loading production in. It was pretty hairy the first night, but the space worked really well. It went off. It was such a good night that within a couple of hours we knew we had found the new home of The Warehouse Project.

Though turning a car park into a nightclub in the space of a few hours was a nightmare, it also echoed those early warehouse raves, when the organisers would find an empty warehouse or space and convert it into a place to have a party the same night. Darren Partington from 808 State once told Luke: 'I didn't like it when acid house was badged the second Summer of Love and associated with Woodstock and hippies and all that. I hated that. For me it had fuck all to do with hippies. Me, Andy, and Eric spending Saturday afternoon sweeping out an industrial warehouse in the city centre and then installing a generator so we can have a huge party and have it right off that night – what the fuck has that got to do with middle-class hippies? Fuck the hippies – they had nothing on acid house.'

The Beneath the Streets weekend was sadly the last time I ever saw Tony Wilson. Wilson was good friends with Jon Drape, and he came down with his dog to check out the venue. He had already been diagnosed with cancer and I was shocked by how frail he was at this point; his suit was just hanging off him.

Despite his deteriorating health, Wilson was still in pretty good spirits and said how fantastic he thought the venue was.

It meant a lot to have him there, as it always felt like your event had been blessed by the spirit of Manchester's musical heritage when he came down.

On 10 August 2007, a few months later, he passed away. It's nearly twenty years ago now, but it's still hard to believe he's gone, his legacy is everywhere in Manchester. It was Tony, Rob, and Factory that made Manchester believe in itself again. No Tony Wilson, no Factory Records, no Haçienda, no Home, no Sankeys, no Warehouse Project, no Parklife.

The only mistake we made on those first three Beneath the Streets nights was the food. In those days, a condition of the licence was that you had to serve food. You don't have to now, that's changed, thankfully, but back then you had to have food available, even though no one was coming there to eat. So, we found a burger van – the type of van that lined the streets on the way to Old Trafford on match days – called Bob's Burgers. Pete Tong was the headliner that night, and we arranged for Bob to drive the van into the venue and set up in the first archway. It was a schoolboy error on our part. As the doors opened, Bob started cooking up his burgers and onions and stunk the whole place out. He also had this bright neon sign saying 'Bob's Burgers'. Sven Vath was the headliner that night, and I remember standing at the back of the venue and all you could see was the stage in front of you and then this big lit-up sign to the right stating Bob's Burgers. So, Bob had to go. We wanted to move him outside, but we didn't have the right pavement licence, so we just moved him to a quieter spot inside, and told him he wasn't allowed to fry anything, not burgers and certainly no onions, just boil the burgers and keep them warm so there wasn't any smell. The burgers were pretty grim, but like I said, no one comes to The Warehouse Project for a burger.

After the success of those first few Beneath the Streets nights, we knew we'd found our new home and we quickly pushed on with booking the winter season of 2007 for The Warehouse Project. Because of our good track record with the first twelve weeks of Warehouse nights, it was easier for Rich and Sam to book acts now. We announced the line-up and ticket sales flew; everything was looking great. The opening night featured Radio 1 live with Pete Tong from The Warehouse Project, which completely sold out of tickets weeks in advance. Everything seemed to be slotting into place. Or, at least, it did till a week before we were due to open.

One morning I got a phone call out of the blue from someone in the licensing department of the city council to say we had a problem. Our capacity was 1,800 and we had already sold that many tickets in advance. But after the latest site inspection, the council's fire officer declared that our capacity needed to be reduced to 1,200. A huge fucking problem. 'There has to be some confusion,' I said, 'we've already run the Beneath the Streets events at 1,800 capacity without any issues.' Sam and I arranged to meet the fire officer at the venue on the Monday morning to hopefully sort out the issue. When we got there, we walked around the venue and the fire officer explained that all our existing fire exits were on Store Street, so if there was actually a fire on Store Street we wouldn't be able to get 1,800 people out in time, so that's why he was insisting the capacity be reduced to 1,200 – unless we could create a fire exit on the other side of the venue, on the London Road side. 'It just isn't possible,' I explained. Because it was an old air-raid shelter, and the walls were 6ft thick, we couldn't just knock through to create a new fire exit. We didn't even own the venue anyway, it belonged to Mr Hakim.

'I didn't do the fire inspection for the events at Easter,' said the fire officer. 'I had no idea they were happening. If I had done, then there is no way I would have given you a licence for 1,800.'

'We've already sold 1,800 tickets for each night.'

'That's not my problem, I'm afraid. I'm issuing you with a Prohibition Notice for the venue.'

The notice he served to Sam and me basically meant that if we let just one more person in over 1,200-person limit, then we would go to prison, as it had been declared a danger to human life if we were to go over capacity.

We couldn't believe it and drove back to the office in shock. Sam, with his head in his hands, said, 'That's it. That's the end of The Warehouse Project.'

The only way out of the situation was to somehow knock through one of the 6ft walls to create an extra fire exit. And get it done in the next four days. The first thing I did was go with Kirsty to see Mr Hakim and explain the situation to him.

'Impossible,' said Mr Hakim. 'I don't even own that wall, Sacha. It belongs to Network Rail. And, have you not seen that there is a memorial on the other side of the it?'

'But if we don't put a new fire exit in, then we won't get the licence and we'll have to cancel the whole season.'

'What you ask is impossible, Sacha ...' Mr Hakim insisted.

Fuck. *That's it*, I thought. *The end.*

Driving back to the office, over the Mancunian Way, I was thinking we would have to call Radio 1 that afternoon and tell them the live broadcast was off; then we'd need to put a press release out and start the process of refunding all the tickets. I had no idea how much it was going to cost us.

Half an hour after I'd got back into the office though, I got a call from Mr Hakim.

'Sacha, come and see me by yourself. Come now.'

What now? I drove back to Mr Hakim's office alone. When I walked in, before I had a chance to say anything, Mr Hakim said: 'Whatever happens to that wall I don't know anything about it ...'

'What do you mean?'

'I mean, whatever happens to that wall, I don't know anything about it ...'

The penny began to drop for me. 'Do you mean ...?'

'I *mean* I'm not going to go down there this week and I don't know *anything* about whatever happens to that wall.'

That was all the encouragement I needed. I got back to the office as fast as I could. We needed to make a fire exit in a 6ft-thick wall and hope that Network Rail wouldn't notice. *How the fuck could we do this?* In the end we managed to find some builders in Salford who had a huge diamond-tipped drill. You may well wonder what a firm in Salford is doing with a diamond-tipped drill that can go through 6ft-thick walls. I decided not to ask too many questions. Take the Hakim approach. Whatever else they used that diamond-tipped drill for was on a need-to-know basis as far as I was concerned. Right then, we just needed a new fire exit.

Sam and I briefed the lads from the Salford firm. 'Right, this is the deal. We need to go through a 6ft-thick wall, that we don't own, on London Road, one of the busiest roads in Manchester, just below Piccadilly Station. We have to go through without anybody seeing what we're doing. Oh, and there's a memorial on the other side and we need to avoid damaging that.'

It was beginning to feel more and more like a bank job as we came up with the plan. We had three nights to get it done, so our idea was to wait for the car park to shut at 7 p.m. each night, then put up camo netting on the outside and start drilling from the inside, right through the night, till the car park reopened at 6 a.m. the next morning. Either Sam or I stayed up each night to keep an eye on the progress. Unbelievably, no one came to investigate what we were doing, or what the noise was, and towards the end of the third night, we broke through to London Road. We spent the next day tidying up the hole and turning it into a usable fire exit. The day after, the fire officer came back down; he could not believe we'd managed to do it. He was shaking his head in disbelief as he signed off the licence. We'd even managed to do it without disturbing the memorial. The new doorway had, still has, the two bronze pillars of the memorial either side. We nicknamed this new fire exit The Temple of Doom.

We still weren't in the clear, though. We were convinced it was just a matter of time before Network Rail noticed the new double doorway that had miraculously appeared on one of its walls.

Remarkably, sixteen years later, still nobody has ever noticed the new doorway. Every time I pass it, it reminds me how close we got to losing The Warehouse Project.

We never had to use the fire exit for the public in the end, because thankfully we never had a fire, but we did use it when there was ever any need for an ambulance, as it was the quickest way for the paramedics to reach anyone who fell ill in the club, so it definitely came in useful.

After a few weeks, Jon Drape and our production team had mastered the job of turning a car park into a nightclub in just a few short hours. They had it down to a fine art. Though there was always the odd issue to deal with. One night I got a call from Kim, our general manager, to say the car park had closed but there was still a car sat in the middle of what would soon be our dancefloor. Someone had forgotten the car park closed in the evening and not come back for their car in time. 'Don't worry,' I said, 'I'm sure they'll turn up soon.' Half an hour before doors opened I got another call to say the car was still there, and they were doing soundchecks and were ready to open. In the end, we had about five bouncers at each end of the car, and they just bounced it off the dancefloor. But just as they were doing that, this little bloke walked in carrying a plastic carrier bag, and shouted, 'My car!' and ran over. He didn't even ask what they were doing, I think he was in a bit of shock and just got in before driving away. To be fair to him, you don't expect to park your car and return three hours later to find that the car park has turned into a nightclub.

The other issue we didn't expect to face in that first season at Store Street was a battle with cocaine rats. A film came out recently called *Cocaine Bear*, a comedy based on the true story of a grizzly bear who discovers a drug dealer's stash that leads to comical consequences. Well, forget *Cocaine Bear*, we had Cocaine Rats, and a fucking army of them! And it wasn't a comedy; it was a nightmare. What would happen was that outside the club, in the smoking area, some customers would have dropped empty wraps or bags on the floor that had remnants of cocaine on them, and once the club was closed, the rats would come out and obviously be sniffing around and devouring anything that was on the floor, including all the discarded wraps. By the time The Lieutenant opened up the next morning for the cleaners, there was an army of rats on coke, ready to take on the world. It's the only time I've seen The Lieutenant scared in all the years I've known and worked with him. He's had to deal with organised-crime groups, gangsters, football hooligans, stag-dos, and all sorts. No problem.

But an army of coked-up rats? A step too far for The Lieutenant. In *Cocaine Bear*, there's one particular scene where a kid shouts, 'There's a bear, *and it's fucked!*' and that's exactly what The Lieutenant was like. 'There's an army of rats, and they're off their fucking tits! I'm not going anywhere near those nasty little fuckers!'

Store Street Goes from Strength to Strength

After the first season of The Warehouse Project, Jon Drape and his production team had got the art of turning the car park into a nightclub within a few hours down to a fine art. Sam and Rich were doing an incredible job curating the line-ups, and it felt like The Warehouse Project was really making waves. It had quickly become the favourite venue in the country to play for many artists, because the atmosphere was so incredible, the space was so unique, and they knew they would be playing to a knowledgeable crowd.

Because it was an old air-raid shelter under Piccadilly Station, still operating as a car park during the week, and everything we had to install was temporary, there were always some logistical problems with the venue. In 2009 we had an issue with the smell from Portaloos being a bit overwhelming, and no matter what we did, we couldn't get rid of it completely. In the end we used to send Harry, who did our merch, over to Affleck's Palace every week to buy a huge pile of joss sticks. One particular Friday we had a big drum'n'bass night on, and we noticed that the whole venue stank of weed. It wasn't just the odd whiff, that you might get, if one or two punters have smuggled in a cheeky spliff, it was throughout the venue. We got security to go through the crowd and try and find the source of it, but they couldn't find anyone smoking weed anywhere. It was only after about an hour that Harry must have gone to light some more joss sticks to get rid of the smell and came back embarrassed to admit that he had accidentally bought 'cannabis flavour' joss sticks, and that's what the smell had been all along!

James Cassidy had been the first licensee at The Warehouse Project, but at the start of the second season, as we started at Store Street, he decided to leave, so Kim had to step up. She was still reasonably young then, but really did step up to the plate and has been an integral part of The Warehouse Project ever since. She has been Operations Manager since 2008 and now runs all the bars operations at Parklife and The Warehouse Project and that side of the business. Kim and her team must have trained thousands of bar staff over the years. There are so many people now running bars, restaurants, and venues in and around Manchester who got their first training under Kim O'Brien at The Warehouse Project.

One of the artists I remember being really blown away with in those early Store Street years was a female singer we had booked for just £500. She was called Florence, and I didn't know anything about her, I'd literally never heard of her, and she was only booked to go on quite early. I saw her warming up backstage, taking it incredibly seriously, going through all these strenuous vocal exercises. I remember thinking she had an amazing voice, but that she was going a bit over the top, *It's the Warehouse Project, it's not the Royal Albert Hall, love.* But then when she went on, she absolutely smashed it. Within a year of that, Florence and the Machine were pretty much the hottest act in the country and went on to headline Glastonbury.

In 2009, Annie Mac was doing a documentary on club culture and wanted to come and film some scenes at Store Street. She was filming outside the club, where there were about a thousand people queuing up waiting to get in. Annie had to do this scene where she walked down the queue and past the sniffer dogs, while talking to camera. Unfortunately, one of the sniffer dogs wasn't well at all, and as she walked past him, the dog did a projectile diarrhoea across the pavement. I've never seen anything like it. Fortunately, that was the only such incident we've ever had with sniffer dogs, they're usually pretty well behaved.

We generally got on well with other promoters, although Sam and I did get invited over for a 'discussion' with Cream once, when they were pretty unhappy with one of our bookings and thought we were stepping on their toes. Sam and I went over to their office in Liverpool, to meet James Barton and his brother Scott. We were there for an hour, and it was a bizarre meeting. Sam and I were fully expecting a robust discussion about bookings, but for the first fifty-six minutes it was just James telling us his views on the benefits of colonic irrigation, and then in the last few minutes he said that if we ever did a booking like that again he would open Cream in Manchester and it would be a full-on war with us. Everything was fine between us after that, and Scott and I still laugh about that meeting now.

We had some bitterly cold evenings at Store Street. There was a period in 2010 when it was quite regularly down to about -5 degrees some nights. The location of the entrance to the club under that railway bridge could also be a wind tunnel some nights, meaning the wind chill factor made it seem even colder. The Lieutenant swears it was actually -15 degrees down there one night. The other thing about being under the bridge, was there would often be water dripping down from some-where, and when it was bitterly cold that water would freeze so quickly it would form stalactites, hanging above where the queue for The Warehouse Project would normally line up. Some of those stalactites looked like daggers of ice, so we would worry that the heat from the queue underneath would detach them, and they could fall onto the punters and possibly hurt someone. In the end, the unorthodox solution we came up with was to bring a football or two in, then The Lieutenant and the security guards would volley the balls as hard as they could up towards the stalactites, to try and break them off, and keep doing that until they were all gone.

One night when it was particularly cold, I sent The Lieuten-ant back to my house to pick up my patio heater. I don't know why I hadn't thought of that earlier. We stuck it outside the entrance and fired it up, and The Lieutenant, me, and a few of the police on duty that night were all huddled round it, warming up. After a while, there was a funny burning smell. 'Can you smell that?' we asked each other. 'What a weird smell? Smells like burning rubber or something …' The Lieu-tenant then went 'Shit, it's your fucking helmet!' One of the policemen had huddled too close to the patio heater, still wearing his helmet, and the top had melted and just folded in on itself. I'm not sure how he explained that to his superiors.

He wasn't the only police officer to lose his helmet at Store Street either. We ended up quite friendly with the police who regularly worked the door, and now and again I might take one of them to the side of the stage while the headliner was playing, so they could experience it. One night when David Guetta was playing, I was taking one of the officers to the side of the stage, and one of the punters at the front of the crowd grabbed his hat while he wasn't looking and just disappeared.

By the time the officer turned round, the culprit and his hat were well gone.

David Guetta was one of the artists who would pull a slightly different crowd to The Warehouse Project; him and Swedish House Mafia in particular. They were a bit more mainstream than our usual bookings and would draw in more of an out-of-town crowd. We might have up to twenty coaches on some of those nights, from all over the country, especially northern cities like Liverpool, Leeds, and Newcastle. We had big digital screens in place at Store Street, and some of the artists would bring their own visuals, but lots of them were happy to use our in-house visuals. Guetta's team would use them to try and excite the crowd before he arrived. They would flash up messages before his set saying, 'David is ten minutes away' then 'David is five minutes away', then they had this countdown and with three minutes to go it would flash up 'David is in the building!'. It was pretty cheesy but it had the desired effect in getting the crowd worked up for his set.

Every night after the club closed, the staff would obviously do a sweep to make sure that everyone had left, but there was one Friday night when they missed someone. The cleaners came in on Saturday morning and started cleaning, when all of a sudden one of the Portaloo toilet doors opened and out fell this young girl, who they said didn't look older than about nineteen, wearing a tiny black dress. How she didn't freeze to death being in there all night, I don't know, but thankfully she was fine, and the cleaners helped get her a taxi home.

One morning, Kim came into the office looking like she'd seen a ghost. She had picked up the float for The Warehouse Project, which was about £10,000 in cash, then decided she needed to stop off in Didsbury and pop into a shop there. She parked her car and stupidly left her bag on the passenger seat that had the float in it. She was only in the shop ten minutes, but in that time, someone had smashed the window and grabbed the bag. I bet the thief couldn't believe their luck, when they found £10,000 in cash in there. That wasn't the only incident with Kim and a float either. We had to order the float a couple of days in advance and then Kim would pick it up from the HSBC on the corner of Oxford Street and Charles Street. She was in there one day picking it up, when she suddenly noticed her car rolling down the street, through the bank's full-height window. She'd forgotten to put the hand-brake on. She ran outside to find her car had rolled down Charles Street and smashed into a police van full of officers. She started apologising and explaining she had just been to pick up the £10,000 from the bank and that's why she had parked right outside. They then questioned what she was doing with £10,000 in cash, so she explained it was for The Warehouse Project and that broke the ice, as one of the officers said, 'Ah, I DJed there once! Do you work with Sacha?' It turns out they were a bit of a DJ in their spare time, and they'd played an early slot at the first season of The Warehouse Project.

The police who work on The Warehouse Project always have a soft spot for Kim anyway. It's a running joke that we don't think there's one police officer who has worked on The Warehouse Project who hasn't asked Kim out at some stage, and that includes the married ones!

2010s
THERE IS A LIGHT
THAT NEVER GOES OUT

Mad Ferret: The Birth of Parklife

In 2009, we were approached by the guys behind a student festival in Manchester called Mad Ferret, which took place at the end of the summer term in Platt Fields. There were originally five students behind the event – five ferrets – and despite not having much of a budget or experience they had managed to get to nearly 10,000 students, and book acts like Finlay Quaye, and The Streets. But they'd gone as far as they could with it. They had run up some debts and they didn't have the experience or knowledge or infrastructure to take the event any further. Like Kendal Calling, they had the bones of a good idea, the makings of what could be a decent festival, but things had escalated beyond their control and experience, and they desperately needed some investment to take it to the next level.

Mad Ferret was basically an end-of-year party, run for students by students. The concept wasn't bad, but the infrastructure and business side of the festival needed a lot of work. It felt like it was an event run by students, because that's what it was.

The first year of Mad Ferret hadn't really been on our radar. We were aware it was happening, but from what we had heard through the Mancunian grapevine it was logistically, meta-phorically, just about held together with Sellotape. Dave Vincent had just bought a double-decker bus at the time, which he used to encourage students to go to Sankeys and ferry them to and from the club. Let's just say it was a 'party bus'. The Mad Ferret production guys had only put basic fencing around their site, which was not very secure, and apparently Dave paid his driver to simply drive the Sankeys bus straight through the fencing, knocking it down, and then just parked, waiting to take students to Sankeys for an after party. An absolute piss-take.

By the second year of Mad Ferret, things had obviously gone seriously awry, because they rang me three days before the event, and they were desperate. They told me they needed £100,000 immediately or the event wouldn't go ahead. They were in a real mess and wanted me to lend them the money. I think it's fair to say I wasn't exactly 'mad for it'. 'Why would I lend you £100,000?' I said, as I didn't really know them at all. They tried to convince me by saying I could sit by the tills at the event and take back the first £100,000 they took. The whole thing seemed farcical, and they had obviously lost control of the business.

They also tried a few other people who ran event companies in Manchester, but since the Mad Ferret guys didn't really have any collateral, none of them were prepared to lend them the money, especially at such short notice. Eventually, they managed to convince Joel Wilkinson to bail them out. Joel started out with a small venue called Trof in Fallowfield, in the heart of Manchester's student land, then opened a second Trof in the Northern Quarter, along with The Deaf Institute (he later went on to open Albert Hall, Gorilla, and Diecast). Joel's house in Fallowfield literally overlooked Platt Fields, so maybe that influenced his decision to lend Mad Ferret the money, as he wanted the event to work.

So, the event went ahead, with Joel sat by the tills, pocketing the first £100,000, just as the Ferrets had suggested I did, and he got his money back, but loads of suppliers weren't paid. Out of the five original Ferrets, three of them disappeared, but two of them – Ben Paget and Jack Gutteridge – faced the music. Fair play to them, they could have walked away, too, but decided to face their portion of the bills.

By this time, I'd been running larger scale events for a decade and, impressed that Ben and Jack had wanted to pay the people they owed, I was pretty confident we could turn Mad Ferret into something much more professional with wider appeal. Sam and I met with Ben and Jack and worked out a deal to form a new company to turn the event into a proper festival. The new company comprised of me, Sam, Rich, Kirsty, Jon Drape, Steve Smith and David Norris from Ear to the Ground, Gareth Cooper, and the two Ferrets. We did have discussions with Joel about him being part of the new company as well but couldn't agree anything. Ben and Jack, the last Ferrets standing, are both really lovely guys, and are still shareholders in what became Parklife.[7]

We weren't keen on the Mad Ferret name at all, and we decided to rename it Parklife. Sam came up with the name, inspired by a festival in Australia, not the Blur song. The first actual Parklife was held in Platt Fields in the summer of 2010.

---

[7] I didn't find out this till quite a few years later, but it turns out Ben's full name is Benedict Dashiel Thomas Paget and he's the Earl of Uxbridge! His father is the Marquess of Anglesey, owns half of Anglesey, and at the coronation of King Charles in 2023, he carried the standard of Wales. A far cry from the 'broke student' vibe Ben gave out when we first met!

Ben and Jack, looked after the decor and all the fluffy stuff: the flags and all the creative dressing-up that turns a large expanse of grass like Platt Fields into a festival site. Jon Drape took over as Production Manager and made sure everything was running more professionally, while Sam and Rich took over the booking, and Kim took over the bars. One of the major costs of putting an event like Parklife on is the production, so it doesn't really make sense to build a site like that for just one day, so we decided to put a second day on, aimed at a slightly different crowd. If you look at most urban festival sites now, a lot of them do something similar. All Points East share their production in Victoria Park, East London with Field Day; The Mighty Hoopla share their production with Cross The Tracks and a few other events in Brockwell Park, South London. It just makes sense, you split the costs. We decided to book Ian Brown for the Friday night, for a more Mancunian crowd, and then Calvin Harris to headline the Saturday night for the more student-friendly Parklife crowd.

It was quite an eventful first year, to say the least. We had to deal with the local Rector, the biggest guest list in Manchester's history (including lots of wrong 'uns), and a gang stealing one of the bars (not the takings from the bar, but the actual bar itself), I ended up getting stalked by a weird policeman, and on top of all that, I had to sack my Mum.

One of the issues with Platt Fields was the Holy Trinity Platt Church, located within the park itself, which means there are restrictions on noise when there is a church service on. Jon Drape and I had to go and see the Rector, Steve James, to discuss the issue. Jon and I are quite lucky in that we work well together in those situations; the dual approach usually helps us get what we want. But the Rector was not for budging. We got our licence for the event, but on the condition that there was no audible music between 6 p.m. and 7 p.m., when there was a service on, which was obviously going to be an issue. It's just weird if the music suddenly goes dead for an hour in the middle of the festival, and who knew how the crowd would react.

We were lucky, that first year, though, and that was down to the good weather. When the weather is good, and you've got a beer in your hand, the sun on your face and your shades on, it's a lot more difficult to get annoyed about anything. Whereas if it's pissing down, you're cold and wet, your new trainers are getting trashed, there's nowhere to sit down because everywhere is wet, everywhere undercover is rammed, then you're going to be pissed off already. In the end, thanks to the weather, a lot of people didn't even realise that we had turned the sound off, they were too busy having a laugh and a beer and a buzz, and a fair few of those who were quite refreshed just kept on dancing, even though there was no music. It was like a huge silent disco. Nobody realised the sound had gone. As a festival organiser, the last thing you want is wet weather. Aside from all the production issues it creates, it also makes it hard to keep your crowd happy, and then you're in trouble. Young kids will put up with standing or dancing in the rain if they're watching some band or DJ they're really into, but if there's no band or DJ, then they're standing in the rain just to get wet on purpose. But though we were lucky that year, the following year would prove to be a different story.

The other institution that's located within Platt Fields is Manchester High School for Girls, an historic independent school that opened in 1874 and was the first girls' school in the north, and one of the first in the UK. We reached out to them to try and maintain a good relationship and offered to show some of their pupils around the site and explain how a festival runs. The school said that would be great, so the day before Parklife started, Jon and I took a group of fifteen-year-old girls around the site, happily explaining it all to them, till we got to the silent disco area, and I couldn't believe what I was seeing. Unbeknownst to me, the Mad Ferret decor team had decided to decorate the silent disco area with huge wooden phalluses. Jon and I were both speechless. We had no idea they'd done this. The girls just giggled, but the look on the teacher's face was priceless as they surveyed this field full of 6ft wooden cocks and balls.

The first summer of Parklife was also the centenary of Platt Fields Park, so we had arranged with Manchester City Council to commemorate the date by planting a tree and having a little ceremony on the first day, when Ian Brown was headlining. Ian had kindly agreed to be there for a photo opportunity with some of the Parklife team and members of the council. Unfortunately, Ian, as you might expect, has what you might call a flexible approach to timekeeping, so I wasn't that surprised when he didn't turn up on time for the photo call. We had the council and everyone else waiting so I kept ringing John Ward, AKA Little John/LJ as everyone calls him, to see where they were.[8] Every time I rang LJ he kept stalling, saying, 'We've been held up, we'll be another ten mins.' In the end they turned up an hour and a half late. 'What happened? Where you've been?' I said to LJ. Ian Brown overheard me and said, 'Oh, we stopped off for a Buzz Rocks on the way!' Buzz Rocks is a famous Caribbean takeaway not far from Platt Fields in Hulme, started

---

[8] Little John (LJ) used to work at The Haçienda, and he has tour-managed Ian Brown, been his right-hand man, for years, going round the world several times with The Stone Roses when they reformed.

by Basil 'Buzzrock' Anderson, who got his name because: 'They used to say that I would make my dumplings so tight. Tight like rocks!' So, Ian had kept the city council and the police waiting for an hour and a half, but at least he's got his jerk chicken, rice and peas, and fried dumpling!

We got the photo done in the end, with Ian Brown, me, Kirsty, Eamonn O'Rourke from the City Council, and a couple of Greater Manchester Police, one of whom was a copper called Michael Waters, who would later behave very oddly towards me. Eamonn O'Rourke and the council were happy, and they got their picture in the *Manchester Evening News*. Unfortunately, not long after the tree was planted, Dr Loos, who supplies the Portaloos for our festival, were a bit careless on site, and one of their Portaloos fell off the back of their truck and flattened the commemorative tree. I don't think anyone has noticed yet.

The other issue with Ian Brown is that he wanted a guest list of 1,000 people, the biggest guest list in Manchester's history. As if that wasn't enough, they didn't supply it in advance, as we always request, and it wasn't even one list – LJ handed me various scraps of paper on which 1,000 names were scribbled in pencil. They weren't in alphabetical order or anything and we had to try and make sense of it all. It was a nightmare. The first thing that was apparent was these names were a who's who of all the people you *don't* want at your gigs. Or at least people whose reputation precedes them. Luckily enough, Kim had Leroy Richardson running one of our bars, and Leroy knew all the characters, so he could look after them, and make sure they were happy and there was no trouble. Leroy was the original bar manager at The Haçienda, he started on day one there in 1982, and was there till it closed fifteen years later. Leroy is one of a select few people in Manchester, like The

Adge and The Lieutenant, who are invaluable, as they know most of Manchester, and of all the dynamics or politics between different groups that we need to be aware of. Because they have been around and seen everything, they also have respect from people, who know they're stand-up guys.

That 1,000 people on Ian Brown's guest list cost us quite a bit of money. I think people who are not involved in events think that sticking people on the guest list doesn't cost the organisers anything, but it absolutely does. Firstly, you've got the lost tickets sales – a ticket for Parklife is now £129.50 so if you've got 1,000 people on the guest list that's £129,500 of lost tickets sales, if those people would otherwise have paid for a ticket. But there's also the extra production you have to put in for the increased numbers. You still have to provide toilets, security and all the necessary infrastructure for those extra guests, even though they haven't paid, and Jon Drape reckons that costs us at least £50,000 at Parklife every year, on top of other costs.

As the crowd were leaving after Ian Brown's headline set, I was stood on the observation point, which is a raised platform that the GMP officers use to survey the crowd and spot any issues. We were watching the crowds leaving, when one of the police officers said to me, 'Is that the bar moving?'

He was pointing at a Red Bull caravan that had been turned into a bar.

'Nah, how can it be moving ... Hold on, you're right it is.'

I couldn't believe what I was seeing. As the crowd were moving slowly out, the bar was moving with them. I know Red Bull gives you wings, but bloody hell. It turns out that a gang from Salford had literally lifted it up and were walking out with it, complete with all the stock, fridges, and till. The police decided it was better to just let them walk off with it, than start an altercation while we had thousands of people trying to leave the site.

That first year of Parklife, we'd booked Grandmaster Flash, the legendary New York DJ, who must have forgiven us by now from the Tribal Gathering photo shoot with the tepee.

We put him up in the St John Hotel, which was the newest and best hotel in Manchester at the time, and shortly before his set I sent Jon Caine, our driver, to go and pick him up. When he was round the corner from the hotel, Jon rang Flash's room and said, 'Hi Flash, it's your driver here, I'll be at the hotel in two minutes, if you could come down when you're ready.'

'Have you got security for me?' asked Flash.

'Er, no ... '

'I'm not coming down till you get me some security, man. I just looked out the window and there's too many fans waiting outside, I'm gonna get mobbed!'

'What do you mean you're not coming out? You're due on in forty-five minutes.'

Jon had no idea what Flash was going on about, but when he turned the corner to the hotel, he saw that there were hundreds of young girls outside. Jon quickly realised that Take That, who were headlining the Etihad stadium were also staying in the same hotel as Flash. Poor Flash had no idea, he'd probably never even heard of Take That, and he presumed all the fans were for him. Jon rang up to Flash's room and assured him that he wasn't going to have a problem with being mobbed. When he came down to get into Jon's car, the Take That fans didn't give him a second glance.

Despite all the incidents we had to deal with, the first Park-life was a real success.

We've had police on the doors of our events since the first Warehouse Project in 2006, when we thought that if we were going to start a big rave in Cheetham Hill, it might be wise to have police on the door. I've always got on pretty well with them, and in all those years, we've only had one dodgy copper, and that was the first year of Parklife. He was a PC called Michael Waters; I got on reasonably well with him, and I can't remember why, but he had my mobile number, though that's not unusual since lots of people working on the event would have my number. The Tuesday after Parklife he said, 'I've got something for you' and said he'd come down to my office and drop it off. He walked in and dumped a huge back holdall with 'GMP' on the side on my desk.

'There you go, that's a gift for you ...'

'What is it?'

'I've nicked it from the station for you ...'

I opened the holdall and there was a full riot gear outfit, including a helmet. *What the fuck? Why would I want this?* He thought I would love it, but I just thought it was a really odd thing to do and felt really uncomfortable about having it. I did take it, but I didn't know what the fuck I was going to do with it. It's still in my office now. Not long after that, he texted me and said, 'Me and my mate have got United season tickets, and he's going through a heavy divorce and needs the money, do you want to take on his season ticket?' I was a big United fan, and I didn't have a season ticket at the time, so I thought, *Why not?* and took it on. The thing was, it was in the middle of The Warehouse Project season, so most weekends I wasn't getting to bed till 6 a.m. and sleeping most of the day, so I never went to a game for the first few months. After The

Warehouse Project season finished on New Year's Eve, United were at home to Liverpool in the FA Cup on 9 January, so I said to him, 'Can I use the tickets for the Liverpool game?' but he said, 'No, sorry I'm going to that one.' I thought, *You cheeky bastard, I've not been to a game all season.* So, I kind of fell out with him after that, and stopped answering his calls and texts, and that's when he went a bit weird. I started getting offside texts from him saying stuff like, 'You've just arrived at the Trafford Centre' and it was obvious that he was tracking my car via the police's ANPR (Automatic Number Plate Recognition) system, which is pretty dodgy behaviour, and surely illegal. I don't know where he is now, but I think he's still in the police force. Hopefully not abusing the ANPR system to follow other members of the public around.

On top of all the other issues we had at the first Parklife, I also had to sack my mum. She was working in the cash office for us, helping count the money as it came in from the box office and the bars and everywhere else. For some reason, she had a box of cash under her desk, waiting to be counted, and she kicked her shoes off, put her feet in it, and took a picture with her phone. How do I know this? Because she posted the bloody picture on social media, with the caption, 'Using Sacha's money to keep my feet warm!' I couldn't believe it! At any event back then, or now, you want to keep the cash side of the operation as quiet as possible, otherwise you're asking for trouble. So, I had to tell her, 'Mum, you can't do this', and in the end decided it would be better if she wasn't involved. Well, she decided and I agreed.

Sink Holes and the Missing £250,000 in Cash

Having been blessed with good weather for the first year of Parklife, we were cursed with wet weather for the second. The bill included Chase & Status, Mark Ronson, 2ManyDJs, Skrillex, DJ Shadow, Annie Mac, and a whole host of other artists. There was definitely a bit more of a Warehouse Project influence coming in, and it wasn't so completely focused on the student market. We had sold a lot more tickets than the first year and knew early on that the weather wasn't going to be great, so unlike the first year, an hour without music was going to be a big problem.

Before any major event like a festival, there is what is called a SAG meeting, which stands for Safety Advisory Group, which is attended by representatives from all the relevant authorities. For Parklife, this meant the festival organisers, police, City Council, Environmental Health, NHS, licensing for taxis, Transport for Greater Manchester, and Head of Parks. We hold the first SAG meeting three months before the event, and then have one a month up to the week before the event, when we have them daily, to raise and tackle any looming concerns. During the event itself we then had them twice a day, so that every department could give an update and flag any potential issues that might arise. There will also be a representative from all those authorities in what we call Event Control. The 'silent hour' we got away with in the first year was obviously a potential issue, especially when we could see from the weather forecast that it was going to be wet. Discussing it in the SAG meeting in the week before the festival I asked the police: 'What happens if it kicks off in one arena during the hour that sound has been turned off, what would you do?'

'Well, we'd have to assess the situation, but we may make the decision to turn the music back on in the arena where the incident was.'

'But you can't just turn the music back on in that one arena,' I explained, 'because then all 20,000 punters will be trying to get into one arena, which only holds 3,000 people.'

'Yeah, that's a good point. Well, we'd just have to assess the situation at the time ... '

I knew we needed to do something, so Sam and I came up with a plan. It was our idea, so I won't blame Jon Drape or anyone else. We just thought, if we've got 20,000 people in the rain and we turn the music off, there will be a riot. It will boot right off. So, what we did was round up a few mates, and mates of mates, put them all on the guest list, and instructed them to stage fights almost as soon as the music went off at 6 p.m.. It was co-ordinated, so that just after 6 p.m., these little groups started two staged kick-offs in different parts of the festival site. Security then radioed through about the incidents to Event Control, where I was and where the police were, keeping an eye on everything. I said to the police, 'We need to do something, there's a danger of this escalating ...' knowing full well that there was little chance of it escalating, as they were just manufactured scuffles. In the end, the police made the decision to turn the music back on after only eleven minutes. So, most of the punters there probably didn't realise it had stopped. It was a little underhand, I'll admit, but it also did possibly stop some trouble. Some of the people who were in the SAG meeting and Event Control that year are still part of the SAG meetings for Parklife now, and they never knew I did that, so apologies to them. The first they'll know about it is if they're reading this book. If you are one of them, I can assure you that year was a one-off, and I've never pulled a stunt like that since!

The weather also caused us other huge problems that year. First, we had a temporary bridge that collapsed. Jon Drape and his production team decided to build one over the stream in the middle of the park, to ease the flow of festival-goers around the site. Unfortunately, the weather was so bad that within a couple of hours of the site opening, the bridge was beginning to sink, and in the end, we had to cordon it off and stop using it.

As if that wasn't bad enough, a sink hole then suddenly appeared in the middle of the main field. A bloody sink hole! It was about 8ft wide, and it was so deep that you couldn't see the bottom of it. We had no option but to fence it off, and then have a ring of security staff stand around the sink hole for the rest of the weekend to make sure there was no incidents. 'Students lost down sinkhole' was not a headline we wanted in the *Manchester Evening News*.

I think that was the worst year we have ever had with weather at Parklife, and it's fair to say Jon Drape and his team had their work cut out, constantly firefighting and dealing with various issues.

If you go to a festival as a punter and it's wet, you're exhausted by the time you get home and everything you're wearing is soaked. As an organiser of a wet festival, you come home feeling like you've been at war.

A few days after that second year of Parklife, just when I felt I had finally recovered, I got a phone call which almost sent me straight back under. I was walking through the Arndale centre with Kim, on the way to buy some running trainers, when my phone rang. I can picture exactly where we were in the Arndale because the call stopped me in my tracks. I could not believe what I was hearing. It was my bank manager at HSBC.

'Hello Mr Lord, I don't want to worry you, but I'm afraid we think G4S have lost £250,000 of your money.'

'What?!'

'Like I said, I don't want you to worry you unduly, but it seems they have misplaced a quarter of a million in cash somewhere.'

'You don't want to worry me unduly? What the fuck? They've lost £250,000 of our money! How can they lose a quarter of a million in cash?!'

I felt sick.

'This does happen occasionally, and it usually turns up.'

'What do you mean, it usually turns up? It's not even our cash. That's money that we need to pay all our suppliers. We've got to pay all the production crew, the PA and lighting, the staging …'

When I put the phone down, I was in shock. *How the fuck do you lose a quarter of a million in cash?* Funnily enough, this was around the time when G4S were in the news quite a lot because they had lost a few prisoners. But this wasn't 'funnily enough' to me. We couldn't take this hit, we couldn't just lose a quarter of a million pounds, this could be enough to sink our business. I spent the next three days on the phone every hour, to my bank and to G4S, chasing them to see if there was any news yet. I couldn't sleep.

After three of the longest days of my life, G4S finally rang and said they had found the money, 'it had been dropped in one of our warehouses in Salford'. That was seriously their explanation. Where do you start with that? What sort of operation are you running that you can be so blasé about losing a quarter of a million pounds in cash of a customer's money, when that person is paying you specifically to guard their money? You literally had one job. Also, I thought, just how much money is floating around in the G4S system and warehouses, that they can lose track of this much cash, and it doesn't even seem like a big deal? It goes without saying, that I was just relieved that they finally found it. If they hadn't then that was another moment that could have been the end of Parklife and The Warehouse Project. The first thing we did was pay all the suppliers and crew from Parklife.

After that, I finally managed to get a decent night's sleep for the first time in days.

I vowed never to use G4S again, and we never have.

The *Annus Horribilis* Project

More than a decade on, I still find it hard to get my head around the extreme events that happened after we made the decision to move The Warehouse Project to Victoria Warehouse. By the end of the 2011 season, having done four years at Store Street, it felt like we had outgrown the venue. By now, The Warehouse Project was firmly established, both with the crowd and the industry, and we desperately needed more space. We had been thinking of moving for a while, but as ever with The Warehouse Project, the bigger we got the harder it was to find a suitable new venue. Especially as the redevelopment of Manchester continued apace. Thirty years ago, we could have had our pick of warehouses in the city centre, but with its reinvention we were competing with property developers.

One morning I got a call from a guy I know called John Rennie, who is a bit of a character around town, and has owned various businesses. He said he'd seen a space owned by a family called the Cohens that he thought would be great for The Warehouse Project, and did I want to go and have a look? Always interested in looking at potential new spaces, I went to check it out. I saw straight away that it had huge potential. It was a vast warehouse (The Warehouse Project would actually be back in a Warehouse!) on the Old Trafford side of Salford Quays. When it was built in 1932, during the heyday of industry in Trafford Park and Salford Quays, the vast building had been a storage facility for the Liverpool Warehousing Company. Later, in the 1980s, it suffered a huge fire and had been derelict till the Cohens took it over. I remember it as a disused warehouse when I used to go and watch United as a kid, because there was a huge Trafford Park-themed mural by Walter Kershaw on the side of it featuring Manchester United players and references to the area's industrial heritage. Walter Kershaw was a Rochdale-born artist who's known as the first British graffiti artist but is, in fact, a muralist. His colourful murals were dotted around Northern mill towns in the 1970s and 1980s, often on the gable ends of terraced houses. The one on the side of the Victoria Warehouse was his largest ever mural, it must have been 80ft high.

I met the Cohens, and at first I was reasonably impressed with them. They seemed like serious business people. And over the course of several meetings, we agreed a deal to move The Warehouse Project to Victoria Warehouse. It was a great idea in theory. We desperately needed to grow, and moving there allowed us to more than double in capacity, going from 2,000 capacity to 5,000 capacity. On paper it looked like a great move for us. But unfortunately, it turned into a nightmare.

I should make it clear that Victoria Warehouse is now run by a different operator, who have nothing to do with the ones we had to deal with. The new operators do a great job with Victoria Warehouse and it's now a really successful venue, but back when we first went there it was a different story. Chalk and cheese.

Looking back now, a decade or so later, I can safely say that those two years at Victoria Warehouse were the worst years of my professional and adult life. My business partner Sam would say the same, as would Kim, Jon Drape and all of those close to the business.

We had the horrible experiences of the death of poor Souvik Pal, who somehow ended up dead in the nearby Bridgewater canal, after visiting The Warehouse Project earlier in the evening of New Year's Eve 2012, and also the death of Nick Bonnie, a thirty-year-old charity worker, who died after a night out at The Warehouse Project on Saturday, 28 September 2013. They were both tragic events, and it was the first time we'd ever had to deal with the deaths of people who had been to The Warehouse Project. It's something their families will obviously never get over, and it also left an indelible mark on everyone in our business. Nobody should go for a night out and not come home again.

There were also a succession of horrible things going on behind the scenes, most of which the public and Warehouse regulars had no idea about, and still don't to this day. Most of these things I'm going to talk about here for the first time. There was a co-ordinated campaign to close the club down, an armed robbery in which our staff had machetes pulled on them – we also lost £130,000 – and we were separately targeted by a Romanian organised crime group. And there was much, much more. Most of these stories have never been told before.

Before those awful events, though, the building needed a lot of work to make it ready for The Warehouse Project – and even at that stage, alarm bells were starting to ring about the Cohens. For a start, they had no experience of running a venue like The Warehouse Project, and they just didn't listen to us when we suggested where the toilets should go. In our minds the Cohens were just the landlords, whereas we were the ones who should be running the venue because we had the expertise. It became very clear early on that these boundaries were somewhat blurred in the eyes of the Cohens.

The opening night was an indication of what was to come. We ended up with the fire brigade on site all night – never a great look – because there was an issue with the recently installed fire alarm. There were also some major issues with the flow of people into the building. One of the main acts came off at midnight, and hundreds of people who were watching them then tried to get out to the smoking area. But it had just started pissing down outside, so those hundreds of people desperately tried to come the other way. The Lieutenant says that's one of the few times he's been really scared about a crowd at The Warehouse Project, as it was obvious the layout was wrong and couldn't cope. Fortunately, no one was injured and after that night we made some adjustments to make sure it didn't happen again, but there was also a rumour spreading that someone in the crowd had a knife, and though thankfully that rumour proved to be false, it caused some panic. It was just a hugely stressful opening night, and a portent of things to come. Even though most people were blissfully unaware of the problems, and the shows were doing really well, selling out, behind the scenes there were all sorts of issues.

That very first night at Victoria Warehouse, The Lieutenant and I were stood outside, as we usually do, but with the owner's son stood next to us. Right next to us, just watching us, noting everything. The next week, he turned up again, and again stood next to us, but he was dressed exactly the same as me. I've always dressed very much in the same way – I have a kind of uniform, especially for The Warehouse – and at that time it was black converse with white toes, black jeans, black T-shirt and a three-quarter length black bubble jacket with a fur collar. The owner's son was dressed *exactly* like me: black converse with white toes, black jeans, black T-shirt and a three-quarter length black bubble jacket with a fur collar. The Lieutenant just whispered to me, 'He's come dressed as you … what the fucking fuck?'

During that first season, it became increasingly clear that the Cohens, who were getting excited about the numbers coming through the doors, were trying to find out more and more about the way our business worked. For example, I turned up one night and they had installed an electronic counter on the door, to track the number of people we had in each night. In pulling stunts like that, they basically destroyed any remaining trust in the business relationship we had with the Cohens, and because of that we realised that the Victoria Warehouse couldn't be the long-term home for The Warehouse Project. We would have to start looking, *again*, for a new home.

One of the other problems we had at Victoria Warehouse, is when we started getting high numbers of mobile phones stolen. You might get one or two stolen, but all of a sudden we were getting up to fifty phones a night stolen from customers. We couldn't work out what was happening. One night it happened again, so we decided to shut the front door and put a system in place to search everyone on the way out. The Lieutenant was stood by the door just observing and saw a guy come out and clock the searches and panic, this guy went behind a burger van and was about to try and climb over the wall to get out, when The Lieutenant, in his own words, 'smashed him from behind, and he went down like a sack of spuds'. The police searched the guy and found forty-three mobile phones down his trousers. Turns out he was part of a Romanian organised crime group who were not just targeting us, but lots of other venues across Manchester like the Arena and the Apollo. Apparently they could get hundreds for each phone back in Romania, so it was a really lucrative business.

That New Year's Eve, in 2012, we had reports of a customer missing. This had happened to us before, as it has with all large-scale events. I'm sure a lot of people reading this book will recall being out in a big group and having one of their mates disappear; but there's usually an explanation for it – they've peaked a bit too early, and have taken themselves home, or perhaps they got lucky and ended up back at some new friend's house, unaware that everyone is wondering where they are. That sadly wasn't the case with Souvik Pal. The nineteen-year-old Manchester Metropolitan University student came to The Warehouse Project event on New Year's Eve with his friends. At one stage he became separated from them and, after charging at a member of staff to try and get past the one-way system, he was asked to leave the club. His flatmate reported him missing the next morning, and the last confirmed sighting of Souvik was on our CCTV camera at 11 p.m. Shortly after that, two people were caught on another nearby CCTV camera, and one of them appeared to be trying to climb a fence next to the Bridgewater Canal. Police frogmen searched the canal in the days after he went missing, but didn't find anything, and it was only three weeks later when they went back into the canal that they sadly found Souvik's body. The inquest and the post-mortem showed no injuries, and the cause of his death was given as drowning, so the Trafford Coroner, Joanne Kearsley, recorded an open verdict. It was just tragic.

Our second Easter at Victoria Warehouse we did another three events over the bank holiday weekend. Good Friday, Easter Saturday and Easter Sunday. They all sold out, so we did really well. I was at home resting on Easter Monday morning, when I got a call to say there had been an armed robbery. At 10 a.m., we had staff in the cash office – an office lady, who was working for us, Jason Argyle, and Scott, who still works for us now. They were cashing up after the weekend, preparing for the security guards to collect the cash, who were due to turn up at 11.30 a.m., when suddenly a gang burst in, armed with crowbars and knives, and threatened them into opening the safe. Thankfully, none of the staff were injured, but they were obviously all traumatised.

It was pretty obvious, because the armed gang knew exactly where the cash office was and what time to come on Easter Monday when there were three days' worth of takings bagged up and waiting to be collected by the security van, that it was an inside job at some level. We didn't suspect any of the people who were working that day, but I knew someone connected to The Warehouse Project must have supplied information to the gang, which put us in a horrible situation because we started to look at everyone who worked there in a different light.

I got down to the warehouse as soon as I got the call, and obviously all the staff were in shock. The local police that day were pretty useless. I'll never forget being sat in Victoria Warehouse talking to the police, as two lads on mountain bikes and wearing balaclavas just rode nonchalantly past the entrance to the building, almost as if they were laughing at us. I said to the police, 'Aren't you going to go and speak to them?' They said, 'We can't stop and search people for wearing balaclavas.' I said, 'Don't you think it's a bit weird that we've just had an armed robbery and lost £130,000 in cash, and only an hour later, two lads wearing balaclavas are slowing down on bikes, to see what is going on here?'

GMP is a different beast nowadays, and we have a really good working relationship with them, particularly since the new Chief Constable Stephen Watson took over. But back then they never found out any information on who was behind the armed robbery, but we did manage to find out something ourselves quite a while later, on the underground Mancunian grapevine. An associate of The Lieutenant's was doing a short stint in Strangeways and overheard someone boasting that a connection of theirs had done over The Warehouse Project. We had never told anyone there had been an armed robbery, so only a handful of people inside our business, and the police who handled the case knew it had even happened. Along with whoever had done the robbery, of course.

The associate of The Lieutenant rang him up and said, 'You've not had an armed robbery at The Warehouse Project, have you?' And that's how we found out who was responsible. We drew a few connections, and by process of elimination we were pretty sure it was one of the bouncers who had supplied the inside information. Needless to say, he didn't work for us after we worked that out. Kirsty Smith found the whole experience at Victoria Warehouse so traumatic, that she decided to leave the business, and Sam and I bought her out.

While we were still reeling from Souvik Pal's death and the armed robbery, the Cohens were also making life very difficult for us. They had upped the rental for our second season, which made it harder for us to make the venue work for The Warehouse Project. We didn't immediately sign the contract, and then David Cohen just stopped taking our calls. We had already announced the new season of The Warehouse Project and put it on sale, but we couldn't get hold of the landlord to confirm the venue. It got to within two weeks of the opening night of that season, and we still didn't know for definite if we had the venue confirmed. I think the Cohens just wanted to make us sweat. In their eyes, it would make us realise how much we needed them, and they would regain some power over us. In the end, Sam and I went for a meeting with Bowlers, another venue just down the road, to make sure we had a back-up plan in place. The very next morning, David Cohen rang me back for the first time in weeks.

Sam and I went and met with the Cohens at their hotel, but at this stage I didn't trust them at all, so I took a recording device with me to record the conversation. I think they must have known we would try and record the conversation as they sat us under a speaker that was blaring out music, so when I listened back to the recording later all you could really hear was the music. We managed to agree a deal for the imminent season of The Warehouse Project, which involved us giving them a million-pound guarantee for the season, but I think it was clear to both sides that this relationship had run its course. It certainly was to me, anyway.

In the early hours of Saturday, 28 September 2013, we then had another tragic incident at The Warehouse Project. Nick Bonnie, a thirty-year-old charity worker, collapsed and was treated by our on-site medics. He was transferred to hospital but tragically later died.

On some nights, I would leave before the event ended, as I wasn't hands-on responsible for anything, so I had actually left the building when Nick was taken to hospital. The first I knew about it was when I turned on Sky News first thing the next morning and saw it there. One of the first calls I got that morning was from a police officer who we worked with called Simon

Collister, who said the Head of GMP Trafford, Mark Roberts, wanted to see me. Kim and I went together to meet him at the station, and he just wanted to reconfirm the facts, as we knew them, and speak to us face-to-face, as it was obviously a terrible incident. Roberts could tell we were shaken up but was really reassuring and said to us that from what he could tell, we had done everything we could, and nothing wrong. He warned us that the press would be all over us, and there were already some journalists outside the police station, so he let us leave through the back door to avoid them. It just so happened that it was the Tory party conference in Manchester that weekend, so as soon as the news broke, several politicians predictably jumped on it to try and score a few points, but it did also mean that there was more national press than normal in the city that weekend.

The Warehouse Project was due to open again the following night, and there was never any suggestion from the police or the authorities that it shouldn't, although Sam and I did discuss among ourselves whether it was the right thing to do. A death like that affects everyone involved in the business, from the bar staff to security, and we didn't have a dedicated HR department to support all staff members, so it was up to us as management to deal with it as best we could and Kim, in particular, was in the thick of it. It's very hard to know exactly what the right decision is to make at times like those, but once you are running large scale events – football matches, theatre productions, shopping centres even, not just live concerts and nightclubs – you're going to have to face incidents where people get injured. Anywhere that has a large footfall is going to have to deal with incidents at some stage. In the end, Sam and I decided to open the following night but with increased safety and security, though that caused a bit of backlash from customers because it took some people hours to get in due to the increased level of searches on the door and there was also a lot of press and TV outside, filming people as they went in. But rather that and know that we'd done everything we could to keep people safe.

We later found out that Nick had worked for The Prince's Trust and his mum, Pauline, worked for a Stroud dog support charity called The Nelson's Trust. I never met her or Nick's dad, Andy, personally, but they seemed to handle the whole situation brilliantly, or as well as any parent can handle the tragic death of their child, and they never ever put blame on The Warehouse Project. They put out a statement saying, 'Nick Bonnie lost his life tragically, senselessly and needlessly in a nightclub in Manchester on a 'lads' weekend. This has devastated the lives of [his family and friends]. Everyone who knew Nick was aware he loved life, lived it to the max and in making one stupid mistake he has cost himself his life. We hope that after reading this, we may have gone some way in helping anyone/everyone in the realisation that drinking, and the use of any illicit drugs, are a killer with consequences that will devastate lives for ever.'

Andy and Pauline may not have blamed us, but as that season went on there seemed to be intense public pushback against The Warehouse Project. We've never had anything like that sort of concerted campaign to muddy our name before or since, and at first, I had no idea who was behind it, or where it was coming from.

Then, one night at The Warehouse Project, I was stood with Jon Drape at 2 a.m. when my phone rang. It was a guy I knew called Graeme Bell who owned a few venues in the Gay Village and had been in business with The Lieutenant at one stage. Graeme was very distressed and upset and said to me, 'Sacha, I've been really bad. You've always looked after me, but I've done something really, really bad. I need to meet you.'

I had no idea what he was talking about, but I was really worried by the sound of his voice. I could tell it was something serious, he sounded in a right state.

'Graeme, what's going on? What's happened? You're panicking me a bit ...'

I arranged to meet him the next day at the Four Seasons hotel, but at the last minute I switched the location to the Bowdon Hotel, as I'd become so paranoid after everything we had been through in the preceding months. Sam, Jon Drape, The Lieutenant, and I met Graeme in the bar of the Bowden Hotel, and he looked half the man he used to be. His hands were shaking so much that The Lieutenant got him a glass of white wine. When he told us what had been going on I could not believe it. Graeme said, 'I've been paid £500 a week by your landlord to create this campaign against The Warehouse Project ...'

We sat there as he explained exactly what had been going on and handed over all his emails, which backed up everything he was saying. It was all there in black and white. It seemed the Cohens thought they could get rid of us and basically run The Warehouse Project themselves under a different name, that seemed to be what their idea was. It goes without saying that was never going to happen.

I tried to help poor Graeme as best I could, as did The Lieutenant and Jon. We got him away from Manchester and rented him a place in Glasgow, away from all the stress, in the hopes that he might be able to rebuild his life – Graeme had been a really successful entrepreneur at one stage. Tragically, though, his worries and demons must have got too much for him, and a few months later he took his own life. That hit all of us really hard, as Graeme really had been such a force of nature, before things started to escalate out of his control.

Without a doubt, those two years at Victoria Warehouse were the most traumatic of my lifetime. It was horrible and it all really affected me for a long time. Kim and I had become an item in 2011, but we had decided it would be best to keep it under wraps as it might not look too professional to some people. It came about because we were the only two on The Warehouse Project that weren't really into going to after-parties at the time. We didn't want to go partying after working all night at The Warehouse Project, but at the same time, you need to wind down for a couple of hours before you can sleep, so I started to invite Kim around to my house for a picnic after The Warehouse Project. I know that sounds a bit weird, a picnic at 5 a.m., but that's what we used to do. Scotch eggs, cocktail sausages, mini pizzas, and a few dips! We were together for a few years, and I thought we'd done quite well to keep it on a need-to-know basis, till I was working on this book, and I said to Luke, 'You probably don't know this, but Kim and I were together at one stage …' and he rolled his eyes and replied, 'Sacha, *everybody* knew.'[9]

We were obviously a lot more stressed and affected by it all than we thought, and one day Kim just decided she'd had enough. She was round at my house and told me she was looking for another job. She was so integral to the running of The Warehouse Project at that point that when she said she was leaving it triggered a panic attack in me. I'd never had a panic attack before, so I didn't know what was happening to me. I thought I was dying. Kim was really concerned and rang an ambulance. Two paramedics turned up and I think they

---

[9] I guess the fact that we used to always go on holiday at the same time was a bit of a giveaway. Although we're not together now, we're still best friends.

thought I was overreacting: 'You're not dying, it's OK, calm down, you're just having a panic attack.' If you've ever had a full-on panic attack, you'll know it's a really scary experience. Once the paramedics found out we ran The Warehouse Project, they seemed more concerned about getting on the guest list for the following weekend than my condition! They told me to just chill out for the rest of the day and have some comfort food, whatever my favourite food was. So, Kim ordered me a Chinese takeaway and we watched *Nanny McPhee* and tried to calm down.

As I mentioned, earlier, it's now run by completely different operators, one of the most respected in the country. It couldn't be more different. But back then, we just had to get out. After the last night at Victoria Warehouse, we made sure we got everything out of the building. All the production, the lot. It took a few days, and then it was time to make a couple of calls. On 6 January, I picked up Sam and together we called everyone who we knew had been involved in the campaign against The Warehouse Project. We had proof of what they had all done in the emails that Graeme had given us. When I spoke to David Cohen, I told him, 'Just so you know, Graeme Bell has been working with us since the beginning of December and has passed us every email with details of what has been going on.'

There was silence at the other end of the phone. But it was a silence that, to me, spoke volumes.

All we wanted at that stage was to move on and get The Warehouse Project back to what it is supposed to be. I don't think I will ever feel more relief than I did in the early hours of New Year's Day, after the last event of that Warehouse Project season. I drove home at 5 a.m., almost shell-shocked, walked into my house, fell to my knees and burst out crying. I was literally on my knees, sobbing.

I've never felt relief like it.

I didn't know where The Warehouse Project was going to go at that stage, but I knew we would be back.

Most importantly, I knew the nightmare of the past two years was over.

We're Gonna Need a Bigger Park

By the third year of Parklife, Platt Fields was bursting at the seams. It was no longer a student event, it had crossed over and become a mainstream event, attracting young people from all walks of life, not just from all over Manchester and the satellite towns, but from further afield. We had managed to get to 32,000 by doing everything we could to increase the capacity. To be fair to Manchester City Council and the rest of the authorities, they were as helpful as they could be. Everyone could see that Parklife was becoming a really important part of Manchester's calendar, and they wanted to support us as much as they could. It really was beginning to feel that Parklife was too big for Platt Fields though. Parklife had become too-big-for-this-park-life.

One person who certainly thought she was too big for Platt Fields was Kelis. She turned up with a slight cold and a huge attitude. She made a huge scene and refused to go on till we got a doctor to give her a B12 injection. She threw a big hissy fit, acting like she was the main act, even though she wasn't. The mighty De La Soul were.

I was reminded of Kelis's hissy fit a few years later in 2015, when Grace Jones was one of our headliners at Parklife, after we moved to Heaton Park. When Grace Jones arrived in Manchester, flying in from Australia, she really was ill, and she'd just got off a twenty-four-hour flight. But Grace was an absolute trooper and argued that the kids have bought the tickets to see her perform, so she was determined to do that. I was so impressed by her attitude. What's more, Grace was sixty-seven at the time, more than twice Kelis's age, which makes it all the more impressive.

In the end, Kelis ended up going on late after all her shenanigans, which was problematic. Every festival has a curfew, an agreed time with the authorities when the music has to stop, and if you go past that curfew then you get a huge fine. So, you have to stick to stage times at a festival. Letting one act over-run their stage time then has a knock-on effect on all the other acts, particularly the headline act, who'll potentially have to play a shorter set. And when you have more than one stage you also try and 'flip-flop' the stages, which means that the 'changeover' periods between acts are at different times on different stages, to make sure there are always acts on stage at any time in the festival. If one act goes over, then that knocks everything out of kilter. We had warned Kelis before she went on that we couldn't let her eat into De La Soul's stage time, but she ignored us and carried on playing. In that situation the first thing we would do is probably speak to the act's tour manager and try and get them to get their act to finish. If that doesn't work, the last resort is to pull the plug on the act. And it really is the last resort, because it's not a good look.

In the end, we had to pull the plug on Kelis, and she was absolutely furious with us. It was like her debut single 'Caught Out Here' when she screams 'I hate you so much right now'. She got in her driver's car and was still ranting as he drove off, calling us 'the most unprofessional promoters she's ever worked with', and that wasn't the worst thing she said. It's the only time we've had to pull the plug on any artist at Parklife, but it was the right thing to do, and most festivals have had to do it at least once.

A few years before our incident with Kelis, I was watching Glastonbury 2009 on television, and they pulled the plug on N*E*R*D* on the Pyramid Stage on the Friday afternoon. Pharrell Williams was as furious about it as Kelis was at Parklife (funnily enough, Pharrell and The Neptunes had produced Kelis's early hits) but if you don't get artists to stick to stage times at festivals then it becomes chaos. We've only ever run over our curfew once at Parklife and that was a few years later at Heaton Park, when we had an incident with Frank Ocean, and we managed to get round the hefty fine on that occasion due to an incident on the Metrolink, but more of that later.

It was obvious after the 2012 event that Platt Fields was now too small for Parklife. We literally couldn't get any more people in. We were in discussion with Manchester City Council, who came to us and said, 'Look, if you want to expand it, why don't you think about moving it to another park?'

The thing is, at that stage, we still thought Manchester's huge student population was the key to Parklife, and Platt Fields was right on their doorstep. We weren't convinced how many of those students would travel to the other side of the city to a different location. Wythenshawe Park was the only park (at a push) in walking distance of the student areas and could hold 50,000. The problem we uncovered was that there was an ancient covenant on Wythenshawe Park. It turns out that the estate had been owned by the Tatton family till 1926, when the Hall and 250 acres of land were bought by Sir Ernest

Simon and his wife Shena Simon. Ernest Simon was an industrialist and had been Lord Mayor of Manchester – he was later one of the sponsors of the construction of Jodrell Bank. His wife Shena was a politician, as well as a feminist and writer – the Shena Simon campus of Manchester College is name after her. The covenant dated back to when they donated Wythenshawe Park to the residents of Manchester, and basically said the residents had a say on what did and what didn't go on in the park, which meant that if just one resident objected to an event, it couldn't go ahead. It was annoying as I remember there being a party in the park back in 1994, an event called Pollen, run by a guy called Rollo, but nobody must have clocked the covenant at that point.

It was Vicky Rosen at Manchester City Council, who has since retired, who first suggested we look at Heaton Park. She said, 'Look, The Stone Roses and Oasis have both done huge gigs there, and they've had 80,000 people, without major issues. We'll give you loads of free transport, loads of free advertising, you can use all the council boards around town.'

Factory records had put on a smaller festival at Heaton Park in 1991, called Cities in the Park, but – apart from the Oasis and The Stone Roses gigs – the last time a huge crowd had gathered there was for Pope John Paul II in 1982, when an estimated 200,000, including a then ten-year-old Liam Gallagher with his mum, Peggy, turned up to see him speak. 'Last time I was here I came to see the Pope,' Liam told the crowd, when Oasis were playing there in the early 1990s, 'he was all right, but he didn't have many tunes.'

We had some major reservations about moving to Heaton Park, the biggest being that we didn't think Manchester's students would travel that far. There's a bit of a North-South divide in the city, and the majority of the 60,000 students live in South Manchester, in an area based around the Wilmslow Road corridor of Fallowfield, Withington, and Rusholme. I'd say 90 per cent of students who come to Manchester never venture north of Victoria station, and rarely leave the Wilmslow Road corridor. Parklife was going to have to change all that if we moved to Heaton Park and take the students out of their comfort zone.

Parklife Moves North

It was a huge decision to move Parklife to Heaton Park, but after Wythenshawe Park was ruled out, it was the only real option if we wanted to grow the festival and cope with the increased demand for tickets. Heaton Park is huge, it's the biggest park in Greater Manchester and it's also the biggest municipal park in all of Europe. It has a long and rich history including hosting the Heaton Races – the early horse races held there from 1827 to 1838, after which they moved to Aintree, where the Grand National is held today. The park was also an army base in the Second World War, and after the war, prefab housing estates were built there for Manchester residents who had been displaced by the war. Mark E. Smith of The Fall spent his early years growing up in the park, living in one of those prefab houses.

Heaton Park had undergone a huge renovation in the late 1990s, and was also served by the Metrolink, the tram-rail service that would help get people to and from Parklife. The council were key in the move. To be fair to Manchester City Council, their events strategy over recent years has been really forward thinking. Much more forward thinking than other UK cities.

While other cities like Liverpool would bid for one-off events like hosting the Eurovision Song Contest or Capital of Culture or such events, Manchester decided that it actually wanted to create and support its own unique landmark events that were part of the fabric of the city, such as Parklife or Manchester International Festival. Events that Manchester *owned*, and would return year after year, and support the economy and drive tourism.

The council agreed a 50,000 capacity for the first year of Parklife, with a plan in place for it to increase to an 80,000 capacity if everything went well in the first couple of years. Oasis and The Stone Roses had already held huge gigs there, so we knew the park could cope, but we were still very nervous about the move. It was a big step up from the 32,000 we'd had at Platt Fields. There was a big demand for more tickets, but we just didn't know if all the audience would make the jump with us to Heaton Park.

There were a few reservations from local residents, it has to be said, but there had also been reservations about the Oasis and The Stone Roses gigs that were held there. Whenever you put a gig or a festival on in a public space there is always a small number of local residents who object. I do understand. I do get that its disruptive, but on the other hand, it does bring in millions of pounds to the local economy (£12 million a year now) and it is for only one week a year.

With Greater Manchester Police, we had meetings with the residents before we moved there, and we continue to have annual residents' meetings, but some of them can get quite testy. One particular, feisty, attendee actually tried to punch Jon Drape at a meeting once, and GMP had to step in and calm things down. I do like to think we've got most of the local residents on board now, and like I say, we do appreciate that it's disruptive for them.

Obviously, in the first year, we had no idea how the move to Heaton Park would go, but since Parklife was established there we have done everything we can to consider and respect the local community, such as the huge Jewish population there, who we work closely with.

The Jewish community have their own technical boundary, called an Eruv, which if you had no idea what it was, just looks like a wire – a power cable, or a telephone wire – strung across an area. But it is hugely important and sacred to the Jewish community, basically expanding the area in which practising Jews are allowed to do activities on the Shabbat – the Saturday – such as carrying things, that they would not normally be allowed to do outside their home on that day. The Eruv for Crumpsall and Prestwich crosses that side of Heaton Park, and as we put additional entrances in that side of the park for the festival, it has to be delicately handled, working with the local Rabbi, to make sure the Eruv remains intact. We give the Rabbi one of our site buggies to help him get around each year, although I must say, he doesn't stick to the strict speed restrictions on site! All the site crew are safely adhering to the speed restrictions backstage, and then you'll see this speeding Rabbi go shooting past! He's very pleasant, though, and always gives our site manager a bottle of whiskey to say thanks. It makes sense all round to maintain good relationships with your neighbours.

There are plenty of local residents who completely embrace Parklife and lots of them have decided to use it as a money-making opportunity – from Airbnb-ing their spare bedrooms, to putting printers in their front gardens and charging people a fiver to print off tickets. Asian families might sell homemade samosas from their front gardens, and a few people with decent-sized back gardens have really gone for it and turned them into 'glamping sites', putting up bell tents or tepees and installing toilets and hot showers. Some of them manage to charge about £300 a night!

The first year, Sam and Rich managed to pull together a great bill, including Plan B, Example, and Professor Green – who were pretty much the biggest artists in their field in the UK at the time. Other artists included Rita Ora, Maccabees, Disclosure, Iggy Azalea, Rudimental, Erol Alkan, Horrors, Temper Trap, Shy FX, Joker, Benga, Todd Terje, Toddla T, Julio Bashmore, and Cyril Hahn. Example loved Parklife so much he decided to hang around and partied so long into the night that he missed his gig the following day. There were some incredible performances, but it was Disclosure who stole the show, they were amazing that year, and their performance was one of the greatest Parklife moments to date. It felt like it was a tipping point for Disclosure as they were just exploding at the time as their song 'Latch' with Sam Smith had been huge. It was a real 'glad I was there' moment, anyone who was at the first Parklife at Heaton Park will tell you that.

We put a lot of effort and money into turning the park into a proper festival site, too. As well as a big wheel and various other rides, we even bought in a log flume! I think we might be the only festival in the world to have one on site. The day before the event, we did the final walk around with Greater Manchester Police, who couldn't believe we had a log flume, and loved it. They insisted it needed to be tested, and all took their hats off and gave it a go, which was a brilliant comedy moment. Sadly, I don't think anyone took a picture. We had the flume for the first two years, but unfortunately it took up a lot of space, and as the festival grew we had to get rid of it.

My business partner Sam hates the rides, mainly because of the terrible music they generally blast out, and I can totally see his point. Sam and Rich and their team carefully curate a brilliant bill of cutting-edge musical talent, meticulous planning the changeovers between the acts, and balancing what is on the other stages at the same time, and then when you walk around the site you get snatches of this terrible Happy Hardcore or Bounce music blasting from dodgy speakers on some of the fairground rides.

We also had a big Nando's stall, which was hugely popular and rammed all day. They had a DJ set up there and Rudimental ended up playing a secret set on the stall, which went down a storm. The other thing that happened there was that, unbeknown to us, the actress Maisie Williams, Arya from *Game of Thrones*, had come to Parklife just as a normal punter. Maisie was at the Nando's stall when someone spotted her, and word quickly got round that she was at the festival. The kids lost it, and she was getting mobbed. Security had to rescue her and bring her backstage for her own safety and sanity.

Anyone who has ever run a festival will tell you that you never know what you're going to come up against each day. You try and predict the issues, but there will always be something that crops up. I certainly didn't predict the issue we would have with The Lieutenant on the first day of Parklife at Heaton Park. As I drove on site that morning, one of The Lieutenant's crew ran up to my car, holding out his phone, and said, 'It's The Lieutenant, he needs to speak to you now.'

I could tell by his expression that this was not good news. I took the phone and heard The Lieutenant's voice on the other end of the line, who told me he'd been arrested and was in a cell in central Manchester. Probably best not to go into finer details too much here but, suffice to say, The Lieutenant had

219

been stopped by the police and they found something in his car that shouldn't have been there, so he had been taken into custody. It was obvious straight away that it was pretty serious.

The Lieutenant used to sometimes call me 'Daddy'. In jest. Or at least I hope it's in jest. He had used his one phone call to reach Daddy. I reassured him I'd do whatever I could to help him, but it was the last thing I needed on the opening day of the biggest event I had ever run: one of my right-hand men being arrested and banged up. With hindsight, maybe someone else would have reacted differently, and blown their top at him for making such a mistake, but my knee-jerk reaction was *The Lieutenant's in trouble, he needs my help*. I got on to my solicitors right away and had them arrange to send one of their top barristers down. That done, we had to just get on with running the show, without The Lieutenant.

The case ended up going to court a few months later and The Lieutenant was so convinced that he was going to be sent down to spend some time at Her Majesty's Pleasure and wouldn't be coming home for a while, that he took a little bag containing his toothbrush and a few other personal items with him to court. Fortunately, the brief I'd arranged for him had done a brilliant job, not only in defending his case but also by pulling in some character references, including from high-profile Manchester musicians, and, perhaps more importantly, a couple of police officers. We had all spent so many long, cold nights with the police on the door of The Warehouse Project, that we'd got to know each other well – we'd even been to the football together. So, a couple of those officers were prepared to vouch for The Lieutenant. In the end, The Lieutenant got off with a suspended sentence and was, in his words, 'A very lucky boy'. But there was no group celebration on the steps of the courts, like in *Goodfellas*, where they all clap the young

Henry Hill on the back and say, 'Hey, you broke your cherry!' I'm pretty sure The Lieutenant's cherry had been broken a few years prior to that anyway, to be honest. He's been around that block and got the T-shirt. It did strengthen the working relationship between me and The Lieutenant though. He knows, without question, that I've got his back, and he has proved to me on several occasions that he's got mine.

In the end, our worries about moving Parklife north to Heaton Park were unfounded. We were helped by the weather, which was a lot sunnier than the previous years, but moving to this new location proved to be a brilliant decision. It had made Parklife more of a destination festival, and it meant we could now be much more ambitious for the following years.

You Don't Get a Town Like This for Nothing

The month after the first Parklife at Heaton Park, we put on New Order for the first time, at Jodrell Bank in Cheshire – Jodrell Bank Centre for Astrophysics, to give it its full name – a pretty cosmic place for Mancunians. The centre is part of the University of Manchester and was established by astronomer Bernard Lovell after the Second World War. It's dominated by the huge Lovell Telescope, the world's largest steerable telescope when it was built in 1957, and still the third largest in the world today. Many Mancunian musicians have been fascinated by the telescope, not least Doves, who used a picture of the telescope on the cover of their first record 'Space Face', back when they were called Sub Sub, and later used it to bounce a guitar riff off the moon. It doesn't get more prog rock than bouncing a guitar riff off the moon. In 2010, Luke Bainbridge got Doves to do an acoustic performance for the *Guardian* at the Jodrell centre, and shortly after that we began to put on gigs there.

For New Order nowadays, Jodrell Bank is actually more of a local gig than Manchester, as Bernard Sumner lives round the corner in Alderley Edge, and Steve Morris and Gillian

Gilbert live on a farm just outside Macclesfield. Steve has lived in the area all his life and once told Luke that his earliest memories of visiting Jodrell Bank were when he was a kid and used to go to the farmers' market there with his mum and dad in the late 1960s.

A few days before New Order's gig, we got told that the band wanted to arrive by helicopter. I couldn't understand why they needed a helicopter when they all lived a stone's throw away from Jodrell Bank. It's literally on the doorstep. But if the headline act wants to arrive by helicopter, you need to make it happen.

The only issue was that the nearest available helicopter was at Barton Aerodrome, which is half an hour's drive away in Eccles, Salford. So, we ended up driving the band to Salford, to fly them back in a helicopter, which seemed slightly self-defeating! The relationship between the band and Hooky – Peter Hook, New Order's original bassist – was a bit strained at the time, and he also lived near Jodrell Bank. I had a sneaking suspicion that it was more to do with Hooky being able to hear them arrive in a helicopter.

Another issue was that because the band had only requested the helicopter the week of the gig, we had no landing space organised for it at Jodrell Bank. A slight oversight! Jon Drape realised twenty minutes before they landed and had to send security out into the farmer's field next door to tread the long grass down in to a 'H' shape.

At the gig itself, Johnny Marr warmed up for them and I think I'm right in saying it was the last time the legendary Joe Moss, who'd managed both The Smiths and Johnny, saw him play. Joe sadly passed away a few years later. Bernard Sumner came on during Johnny's set, and they performed 'Getting Away with It' by Electronic – the band they'd formed together in 1988 – which was pretty special.

New Order were on fantastic form and played songs they rarely play live, like 'World', and five Joy Division songs, including 'Ceremony', which Bernard Sumner introduced, deadpan, as 'The song we wrote as Joy Division, before our singer inconveniently died.' We projected the band's visuals onto the 76-metre dish of the Lovell telescope, which felt like a futuristic celebration of electronic music legacy, and the band seemed to love it. 'Thank you to Jodrell Bank', yelled Bernard at one stage, 'it's a stately institution – just like us!'

A few years later, in the winter of 2015, we booked New Order to play Store Street, and that felt like another defining moment. Bearing in mind the band's legendary status, the pivotal role they have played in dance music and clubbing culture, both in Manchester and internationally, to have them play The Warehouse Project at Store Street was like booking electronic music royalty.

Because it was a live gig, we actually undersold it by 200 tickets, partly because we knew New Order would have a reasonably sized guest list, as it was a hometown gig, which they did – though not an Ian Brown-sized guest list, but we were still within capacity. Within half an hour of the doors opening, however, Sam and I knew we had a problem. New Order's crowd is different to the normal Warehouse Project crowd, not just in age and demographic, but in its actual physical size. The Warehouse Project usually attracts skinny, eighteen- to twenty-five-year-old students who don't wear bulky clothing as they are there to dance all night; and even if it's cold outside in the Mancunian winter, it won't be cold inside. But a sizeable number of the New Order crowd at those Store Street gigs was considerably bulkier than your normal Warehouse Project punter, all wearing big jackets, too, which meant they were taking up nearly twice the space of our usual crowd. Even though we were officially just under capacity, it felt over full. Not dangerous, but definitely uncomfortable.

We got through the two shows, but a lot of people were unhappy or angry with us because they thought it was too packed and busy. I remember the poet, Mike Garry, leaving quite upset, as did a few other people. Even though the gigs themselves were fantastic, as you don't often get the chance to see New Order in a space like Store Street, it was a lesson learnt for us – and apologies to anyone who was at that gig who wasn't able to enjoy it properly. We've never made that mistake again.

Because a few people had put in official complaints about the gig being overly busy, the licensing department was all over us and I was dragged in to speak to the fire officer that week. Kim and I were completely upfront about it and explained the whole situation and said that we had actually been *under* our official capacity, but we had underestimated the effect that the different demographic would have. I had an inkling they would want to come down and double-check on us, and sure enough, the following weekend a Greater Manchester Fire and Rescue vehicle turned up. One of the big bosses wanted to have a walk around and check out Store Street for himself. Fortunately for us, the show that he came down to, Jungle, was the only night of that whole season that hadn't sold brilliantly well, so he could see there was actually plenty of free space, not too lively or shoulder to shoulder, and it didn't feel packed or remotely uncomfortable. I think he was quite surprised at how civilised it all was and couldn't under- stand what all the fuss and complaints had been about. To our relief, he left saying everything was perfectly fine.

New Order at Store Street was really special, but perhaps even more special was when we put the band on at Heaton Park in

2021. New Order created a video montage of their career and Manchester over the last forty years, which showed on the big screens just before they went on stage. It feels special to have promoted New Order's biggest ever headline show, but really it's testament to the staying power of the band and their incredible career. Not many artists can say they played their biggest gig by far in their fourth decade as a band.

Snoop, Your Mum, and Aitch

In 2014, we booked Snoop Dogg as one of our headliners for Parklife – which felt like a real step up. Snoop was our first real global superstar and it felt like a statement booking, like Parklife was putting its flag in the ground as one of the major festivals in the country.

Our social-media team are always looking for innovative and interesting ways to engage with the audience and reach new people, and at the time they were experimenting with some new software which allowed us to send a text to everyone on the Parklife database, but change the name of who the text was received from. When it popped up on your phone it would look like you had received a text from 'David Beckham' or 'Ronaldo' even though they obviously weren't in your address book. We tried this first with a message from Snoop Dogg, that just popped up in people's phones with the message – 'It's Parklife, biatch!' – and a link to buy tickets, which actually ended up going viral.

A couple of months later, I was driving from home into work one morning, when my phone suddenly starting pinging like mental with notifications. I didn't know what was going on, so pulled over to have a look. At the time we were giving a big promotional push to some of the Parklife after-parties and unbeknown to me, our social media team had decided to use the same text technology that we had used with Snoop to send out a message to the Parklife punters that came up as if it was a text from 'Mum'. It simply said 'Some of the Parklife after-parties have already sold out. If you're going, make sure you're home for breakfast!'

It was meant purely as a light-hearted way of engaging with our Parklife audience, but it backfired horribly. Some people just saw it for what it was, but others, who'd recently lost their mum, were estranged from their mum, or perhaps never even knew their mum, were terribly upset. Some of them were quite vocal about it, including Sir Ian McKellen's nephew, who lived in Chorlton and had been to Parklife a couple of times previously. Sometimes you have to admit you've misjudged something and got it wrong, even if there was no intent to upset anyone.

Quite a few people complained to the press or made official complaints. In the end we were fined £70,000 by the ICO (Information Commissioner's Office, the independent authority set up to 'uphold information rights in the public interest'). The ICO's reason for fining us was because 'the identity of the person behind the text' we sent to customers was 'disguised or concealed'. Steve Eckersley, Head of ICO enforcement, said: 'This was a poorly thought-out piece of marketing that didn't appear to even try to follow the rules or consider the impact that their actions would have on the privacy of individuals. It made some people very upset in an attempt to sell tickets to a club night. The fine sends a clear message that using this type of marketing is unacceptable.'

We put out a message saying: 'The communication was intended as a fun way of engaging festival-goers. However, the festival acknowledges that this was not an appropriate theme for everyone. The Parklife Weekender wants to apologise for any offence caused by the SMS marketing message sent to their customers earlier this year.'

We've all sent texts that we regret afterwards, though most of us don't get fined £70,000 for doing so!

We just wanted to draw a line under it, so we paid the fine straight away. I even managed to get a 20 per cent reduction for paying it immediately, and we haven't used the technology since.

That same year, 2014, we also began to have real problems with people jumping the fence. Parklife had become such a huge event that it's inevitable that we were going to attract some fence jumpers. There are so many trees in Heaton Park that one of the ways to try and get in free to the festival was to climb one of the trees whose branches overhung the festival perimeter fence. We would obviously try and put the fence away from any trees, but that's not always possible in Heaton Park, where there are so many trees. There is one specific tree on the edge of the festival site that had a TPO (Tree Protection Order) – an order made by a local planning authority to protect certain trees that are deemed to be of specific merit. In our case it meant that this tree was protected, and we couldn't do anything to it. We couldn't damage the tree, cut any of its branches or anything. Frustratingly, the tree had quite large branches, which extended over the perimeter fence, and in that first year of Parklife it was used by quite a few fence jumpers to get into the festival without paying, which really pissed me off. So, for the second year of Parklife, we decided to adjust the site map of the festival so that the police compound was below the tree, inside the festival fence. Any fence jumpers who used that tree and thought they had made it into the festival – congratulating themselves on jibbing into Parklife – got a bit of a shock when they jumped down.[10] The looks on their faces were priceless as they realised they had simply jumped into the police compound, and were quickly apprehended by GMP.

Nowadays, only about ten manage to fence-jump into the festival, but in the first year or two we might have had about forty to fifty people doing it, including one of our recent headliners, Aitch, who boasted that he'd done it when he was younger. Aitch is from nearby Moston, and we booked him to headline in 2023, which was announced just before that year's Brit awards. Aitch proudly told the press on the red carpet that it was beyond his wildest dreams to headline a festival that he used to have to jump the fence to get into.

Back to 2014, and the moment Snoop Dog came on for his headline slot was unforgettable. I can remember exactly where I was: standing with Sam at the side of the stage. As Snoop came on stage to a crowd of 50,000, we looked at each other and were like 'Woah, we've created a festival.' That moment felt like a huge leap – Parklife was now a major event, not just a little student festival. Moments like that don't come very often, believe it or not. Usually, everyone working on an event – and that includes me, Sam, Jon, Kim, and The Lieutenant – is usually too busy making sure everything is going to plan to

---

[10] 'Jib' is Mancunian for getting in for free. A group of Manchester United fans who pride themselves on getting the train to away games without paying, call themselves 'The Inter City Jibbers'

register big triumphs. We very rarely get to stand back and enjoy our success as it happens.

Sadly, that special moment coincided with a tragic event in the audience that neither Sam nor I knew anything about at the time. Just before Snoop Dogg came on stage, there was an altercation in the crowd as someone was hitting a girl on the head with a blow-up doll. The girl's boyfriend, Robert Hart, then intervened and asked them to stop, but the person obviously didn't appreciate that and punched him. Robert was nearly knocked out and collapsed. The medics arrived on scene and Robert seemed to be fine at first, apart from a small bruise above his eye. The medics later said he was alert and talking and didn't meet the criteria of a major trauma. But any head injury or chest pain incident at a festival is treated with standard procedure and that person is taken to hospital to be checked out. Because the medics found Robert Hart was alert and talking, he was sent to North Manchester hospital rather than Salford Royal, which specialises in brain and head injuries. What happened after that we only found out at the inquest. A CT scan was carried out on Robert at the hospital and sent digitally to Salford Royal, but a wrong interpretation of his brain scan led to a delay in his transfer to Salford Royal. That delay was fatal, and tragically Robert died four days later.

Everyone connected with the festival was devastated. I spoke to his girlfriend to pass on our condolences, and she kindly said she didn't blame Parklife. We were keen to find the person responsible, though, and after speaking to his girlfriend and the police we announced a £20,000 reward for any information leading to an arrest. GMP ran a massive public campaign to try and find the individual who attacked Robert, and when the person responsible still hadn't been found by the time of the following year's Parklife, GMP handed out leaflets to everyone to try and trigger memories, but again no one came forward. All we know is the person had a Scouse accent. The police were pretty adamant that whoever attacked Robert must have had protection around them, to keep everyone quiet.

Return to Store Street

After two pretty traumatic years behind the scenes at Victoria Warehouse, it was a huge relief to all of us when The Warehouse Project returned to our spiritual home at Store Street in 2014. It's impossible to describe how heavy a weight it felt had been lifted off our shoulders. Not just for Sam and me, but for everyone who worked with us and for us, from the production staff to security. Thankfully, most of the punters had no idea what had gone on behind the scenes at Victoria Warehouse, as obviously we had done everything we could to make sure it didn't affect the experience of those coming to The Warehouse Project for an incredible night out. But those two years really had taken a toll on everyone who worked behind the scenes.

Moving back to our spiritual home at Store Street, we felt like we were waking from a nightmare. As Joni Mitchell lamented in that song, 'Big Yellow Taxi', 'they paved paradise, and put up a parking lot'. Sorry Joni, but we could not have been happier to be going back to a parking lot, that *was* paradise for us after Victoria Warehouse. Or as The Lieutenant said, 'It felt like coming home after the worst shitty holiday you've ever had.'

The Warehouse Project was now too big for Store Street, we were more than halving our capacity by going back there, so the initial idea was only to return for one year, while we found a new permanent home in time for our 10th anniversary. As Sam said at the time, when we announced the line-up, '2014 is about The Warehouse Project going back to its roots. Smaller capacity, more intimate — an opportunity to revisit our spiritual home for one year only before we take the next step … before we get to that, one year only back beneath the streets.'

In the end, we ended up staying there for four seasons, and they were arguably the most joyous seasons we've ever had at The Warehouse Project. The atmosphere was incredible every week. We were back in a space which we knew so well. The crowd was also a little different as almost every show would sell out really quickly, which meant that you really had a hardcore crowd of dedicated music lovers. The bigger your events get, it stands to reason that the crowd is diluted a little and you need to have broader appeal, which has its pros and cons. But when we were back at Store Street with a smaller capacity, almost every night felt like a crowd of real dedicated music lovers, because you had to be pretty dedicated to get a ticket for most shows as they would sell out so quickly.

It was still a difficult space to work with, the logistical problems were still there as there's a lot of restrictions on the Store Street space – not just the capacity, which means there were some artists we couldn't book because the numbers wouldn't stand up, but also on a production level. The relatively low ceilings create a great atmosphere and help it feel intimate and underground – if it wasn't for the police on the front door it would feel like an illegal rave – but they are also restrictive in terms of the show you can put on: the size of screens and all sorts of other production issues for artists. After every season at

Store Street, we would sit down and say, 'Right, what can we do to make the experience better next season?' I didn't just mean the line-up: we were always trying to improve the sound, the lights, even the toilets, or the customer experience of getting in.

We had so many highlights in those seasons back at Store Street. In the first season alone, some of the nights that stand out were three-hour sets from the Chemical Brothers, the late great Andrew Weatherall and Bicep on the same night, a special Bugged Out twentieth anniversary night, and a night curated by Jon Hopkins and Jamie XX.

It wasn't just the punters that loved Store Street, for many of the DJs and artists it was also the favourite place to play, because of the atmosphere and the fact they knew we had such a knowledgeable and up-for-it crowd. Many DJs said that playing The Warehouse Project was one of the highlights of their year, and for some of them the partying when they got to Manchester was one of their highlights of the year as well. There was a time when we used to put some of our headline acts up in a hotel with suites in the Northern Quarter called The Light. One particular night, our headline DJ was booked into the penthouse suite, which had a hot tub on the balcony. It was known as the Simon Cowell suite, as he used to stay there when he was filming *Britain's Got Talent* in Manchester. Our headline DJ finished his set and decided he wanted to carry on the party back at his suite and invited some of the female bar staff back. It all got quite debauched and out of hand, and the DJ ended up in the hot tub with some of our bar staff. Simon Cowell might not have been staying there that night, but unfortunately, according to hotel management, someone from the show was, and they heard the commotion outside. When they looked out of the window they must have been pretty shocked at what they saw, as allegedly they reported it to the management, and The Warehouse Project was then banned from The Light.

Store Street was also the first time we had Elrow at The Warehouse Project, which was an incredible night for everyone. Well, everyone but our cleaners. On the nights when we used confetti canons at The Warehouse Project, we would probably use 5 kilos of confetti. Elrow absolutely went to town and came fully armed with 75 kilos of the stuff, *fifteen times* what we would normally use. Their show was amazing and memorable for everyone there, but it was memorable for the cleaners for another reason. Customers literally had to wade out of knee-high confetti on the floor on their way out. The cleaners took one look at the state of the venue and resigned *en masse*. We were still finding remnants of confetti from that night for a year later.

The Warehouse Project is not really a celeb hangout, and we've never wanted it to be. We don't have a proper VIP area or cater for celebs, which probably puts off any of them who are not really coming for the music, which is fine by us. Although we don't have a VIP area, there's been a couple of times when we've had to make sure someone didn't get mobbed or hassled. Gary Lineker has been down a few times, as we have a mutual friend called Jonathan Downey, and he's always been really friendly and down to earth. He came to see Groove Armada, and I took him up to the lighting desk as it's the best view in the house, and he loved it, but when the lights went up, the crowd spotted him and started chanting 'There's only one Gary Lineker', so we had to escort him out as we didn't want him to be hassled and it was also stopping the crowd from leaving.

The Warehouse Project has always been about looking forward, but we do usually have one Haçienda night a year. It's our nod to the clubbing heritage of Manchester and recognition that we're standing on the shoulders of giants. The

Haçienda nights have quite a different demographic to the usual Warehouse Project nights though. It's twenty-six years since The Haçienda closed now, so obviously anyone who was old enough to go there when it was still open is now probably in their fifties. If you were eighteen the day The Haçienda closed, you're now forty-four for fuck's sake, that makes me feel old. On our Haçienda nights we quite often get families coming together, dad and son, mum and daughter, all partying together. I can't imagine partying and dancing all night with my mum. We sometimes even get three generations partying together at the Hac nights – gran, mum and daughter, all off their tits together. Or grandad, dad and son coming in together, which is slightly embarrassing on the door when you see either the granddad or dad gets stopped when security finds a wrap of coke on them. The two other things that stand out on Haç nights are it's pretty much the only night where quite a few people want to pay cash on the bar. Every other night the punters use contactless to pay, but quite a few of the Hac punters carry cash, so we have to organise a float especially. We also need to order extra ear plugs, because we get more punters going to welfare asking if they've got any earplugs.

Store Street was a forgotten bit of Manchester before The Warehouse Project first moved there. An unloved side street under Piccadilly. Not many people know that Manchester Piccadilly station was originally called Store Street. The actual station name was Store Street when it opened in 1842, it was renamed Manchester London Road in 1847, and only became Manchester Piccadilly in 1960. I didn't know that before starting work on this book! But in the last few decades before we moved there, Store Street had almost fallen off the map. Taxi drivers didn't even know where it was when The Warehouse

Project first opened there. I think the club put Store Street back on the map. It's still a car park during the day, and the car park attendant told me that he often gets people taking selfies outside or walking in and taking a video clip of it. Although we may have put Store Street back on the map, we may have made it harder for some people to find it, as we took the two Victorian street signs down for posterity when we left. They were 25ft up on the wall, but I got The Lieutenant to go up a ladder and remove them. I had one in my house and Sam had the other in his. A bit naughty to nick the street signs, but Store Street had been such a huge part of our lives that we wanted something to remember it by.

Laurent Garnier played the final ever set at The Warehouse Project at Store Street and as he dropped his seminal track 'The Man With The Red Face', it was one of those really emotional special moments, looking around at all the faces in the crowd, where everyone in the building was connected, on the same wavelength and in the same moment, and it felt like the perfect soundtrack to end that chapter of The Warehouse Project.

Grace Jones and the Stolen Police Buggy

Mancunians don't generally look too reverently at many other cities, but the nightlife and clubbing culture of New York has had a huge influence on Manchester. It was New Order's wild nights out on their early trips to New York, being shown around clubs like Danceteria, The Fun House, and smaller places like Better Days, by people like the legendary New York producer Arthur Baker, that inspired the group, Rob Gretton, and Tony Wilson to think 'Why hasn't Manchester got any clubs like this?' and then come home and build The Haçienda. Personally, I've always been obsessed with Studio 54 and its reputation for excess and debauchery, the impossibly glamourous clientele, and photographs that remain of it. I don't think I've ever seen any image of Studio 54 that didn't look incredible. Grace Jones – the first black supermodel – always looked amazing, iconic, pictured there – so you can imagine how excited I was when we booked her as one of the headliners of Parklife in 2015.

Grace was flying in from Australia for Parklife and her team sent a message to say that she was really under the weather. She was staying at The Lowry – the five-star hotel in central

Manchester favoured by most popstars and by Manchester United at that time.

I'd never watched Grace Jones live in concert before, and when you see her for the first time it really is something else. She ended up performing topless, apart from tribal make-up, and did an incredible seven-minute version of 'Slave to the Rhythm', while hula-hooping. It was an amazing set by anyone's standards, but for a nearly seventy-year-old with a fever it was staggering. When Grace finally walked off the main stage at the end, she literally collapsed in her dressing room. I don't think any other artist has ever given their all at Parklife like she did that night. She left it all out there on the stage.

I rarely ask artists for selfies, or to meet them, but Grace was such a living legend and I was so blown away by her performance I just wanted to say hello and thank you. Her manager said, she's exhausted so won't want to do any photos, but she'd like to invite you into her dressing room. When I walked into the dressing room she was only wearing men's boxer shorts and a white see-through T-shirt. On her rider, she had demanded vintage champagne, brandy, and very specific rare oysters and a particular kind of oyster knife. She suggested I sit down and have a glass of brandy, and I didn't have the nerve to tell her I never ever drank when I was working. I felt like a little boy, and just couldn't say no to Grace Jones, and I also thought it might calm my nerves a little. It's still the only time I've ever drunk at any of my events.

I've dealt with gangsters, having guns pulled on me – and death threats – but I don't think I've ever felt more intimidated than I did by Grace Jones in her dressing room that time. I've heard so many legendary and possibly apocryphal tales about her, and her fierce reputation preceded her. She stared at me really intensely, while cracking open her rock oysters and then slurping them, which in itself was pretty unnerving, while I just stumbled over my words and tried to think of something intelligent and interesting to say to her, the Grace Jones. We ended up having a nice chat and laughing about her infamous appearance on the Russell Harty show, when she attacked him because she thought he was turning his back on her.

The footballer Micah Richards was still playing for Manchester City at the time, and he came to Parklife that year, and was one of the first big Premier League players to come down to the festival. He is a really, really lovely guy, he's just everything that you want and expect Micah Richards to be. Larger than life, physically and personality wise, with that huge laugh. He did have some mates with him who were not as entertaining. In fact, one of them was a bit of a dick, who, when another mate of theirs went to use a Portaloo backstage, pushed over the Portaloo with his mate stuck inside. I've never understood why people think that is such a hilarious thing to do.

That year at Parklife, we also very nearly had a serious medical incident with poppers, or amyl nitrite, which are legal in the UK, and give people a short euphoric high when they sniff them. We sell them at Parklife, through individual vendors around the site. I was in Event Control when we got word that we had five very poorly customers within the space of half an hour. They had all individually necked a bottle of poppers, which is a really weird thing to do, but also very dangerous, and were being treated by medics. I thought everyone knew that you're supposed to just have a quick sniff of poppers, and certainly never drink them, but it turns out there was a young member of staff selling them that day who didn't know what they were. He obviously hadn't been listening properly when he was briefed, and thought they were energy shots. You can buy energy shots in garages and other places that look a little similar to poppers bottles. Anyway, obviously most of the people buying them off this young lad knew what they were, but a handful must have asked, 'What is it?' and when he told them they were energy shots, they'd bought some, and just downed them. That could have been very serious, but fortunately the medics were able to deal with it really quickly, and everyone affected was fine in the end.

That was also the year that Greater Manchester Police managed to have their buggy stolen, embarrassingly for them. We have dozens of buggies on site at Parklife, and they are all assigned to different departments or individuals who need them. GMP had their own buggy with 'GMP' on the front. At one stage, two police officers had gone to North Gate, the busiest entrance to the whole festival, to collect all the drug confiscations. When customers are searched on their way into the festival, any small amount of drugs found, which are obviously just for personal use, are confiscated. As we have 80,000 people on site, all those small confiscations can mount up, and over the weekend we probably confiscate drugs with a total street value of anywhere between £40,000 and £50,000.

That day, for some reason, having picked up the big bag of drug confiscations from the main entry gate, the police then parked their buggy outside the police command area, with the confiscated drugs just sitting on the back of the buggy, and nipped inside to grab some paperwork. When they came out, the buggy was gone, and so were the drugs. I was in Event Control with Gold Command, who are the head of police on the event, when these two shame-faced officers came in and had to confess that they had lost the police buggy and around £30,000 of confiscated drugs. Gold Command were not best pleased, to put it mildly. We had to put a call out on the site radio to all the production staff, asking if anyone had seen GMP's buggy.

What a lot of people don't realise is that the buggies we use at Parklife don't have unique keys, one key will work any buggy. It turns out that someone had taken one of the cleaner's buggies, so the cleaner had simply taken GMP's buggy, not realising that it belonged to the police. They'd gone off round the site blissfully unaware that they had £30,000 worth of drugs just sat on the back seat, which anyone could have grabbed. Fortunately, the cleaner was quickly tracked down, and the drugs were returned to the police, but I don't think those two police officers will be leaving their buggy unattended ever again.

Live Nation and the Parklife Fountain

In January 2016, I was in Rome for a short holiday with Kim after that year's Warehouse Project season. I usually try and take a break to recharge my batteries at that time of year because The Warehouse Project is so draining, but the Rome trip that year didn't turn out to be very relaxing.

First, I woke up to the news on 10 January that David Bowie had died. I've always been a huge fan of his, and I thought the way he released his final album *Blackstar*, on his 69th birthday, two days before he died, was incredible; with all the hidden messages and meaning in the music, artwork, and videos. I particularly loved the cover artwork of Blackstar, which had a deconstructed star spelling out 'B.O.W.I.E.'[11]

The other thing that happened when I was in Rome was I got a call to say that Live Nation were interested in buying 50 per cent of Parklife and The Warehouse Project. We did a call with Live Nation on 22 January, and it all sounded really promising, so then myself, Sam, Rich, and Simon Moran went

---

[11] I even got a tattoo of it on the inside of my foot, which is still the only tattoo I've ever had.

down to London and met with Denis Desmond from Live Nation for lunch at the Pollen St Social Club. We got on really well, he clearly knew our business well, and knew what Live Nation could bring to the table. Denis suggested that we come up with a figure of what we wanted for 50 per cent of the business. Sam, Rich, and I bought some cans of gin and tonic from Marks & Spencer, got back on the train to Manchester and sat round a table on the train: we came up with a figure. It was a lifechanging amount of money and we had no idea what Live Nation would say in response; half of me thought they might have laughed at the figure. But they didn't. They came back within forty-eight hours and agreed on the figure, on condition the deal was completed within twenty-eight days. That was twenty-eight of the most stressful days of my life. There was no reason for the deal to not go ahead, but till it was finalised, I was nervous that for some reason it would all fall through. It was like the stress of buying a house, times a thousand. You know when you're stuck in limbo – you've had your offer accepted on a house that you really want, but then you're left in limbo for weeks or months waiting for the paperwork and the solicitors to pull their finger out. John Rennie, who owns quite a few bars in Manchester, had given me a jeroboam of vodka for Christmas, which is a huge three-litre bottle. That vodka helped me through those weeks.

With any deal there's always some last-minute things that need to be sorted. One of the issues was the 'S building' on Station Approach, above Store Street, that used to be owned by the NHS, had been turned into a hotel, and they were kicking off about the sound from The Warehouse Project. In the end we had to do a deal with them to book out the whole first four floors of the hotel for every night The Warehouse Project was on, which was eighty-four bloody rooms. They charged us £130 a room, which is nearly £11,000 each night, which is a big hit to take. Obviously, we needed some rooms for DJs and crew, but we didn't need anything like eighty-four rooms, and we ended up re-selling them to Warehouse Project punters where we could.

The other issue was Network Rail needed to put a huge new generator into the Store Street site, which was more or less in front of the main entrance. It didn't look great aesthetically, but the real issue is that it would reduce our capacity by 600, from 1,800 down to 1,200. This would basically mean The Warehouse Project wasn't financially viable, which would jeopardise its future and mean the whole deal with Live Nation was off. It was an incredibly stressful time, but thankfully our Health and Safety Officer Mike Atkinson, with the help of Kim, came to the rescue, not for the first or last time. Mike is a lovely bloke and has been our Health and Safety Officer since we launched The Warehouse Project back in 2006, another long-term member of The Warehouse Project family. Mike found a new fire company who managed to find some more space by restructuring the layout of The Warehouse Project. I'm not sure how he and they did it, but he undoubtedly saved The Warehouse Project, and the Live Nation deal.

On the day that the deal was to go through, all the shareholders came together at Pannone, our solicitors on Deansgate. Their offices are in the church at the end of Deansgate, opposite Atlas bar, which actually used to be recording studios owned by Pete Waterman. Everyone from Kylie Minogue to the Manchester United team have recorded in there. One of the Pannone's staff wheeled a trolley into the room with champagne on it, but I said, 'Nobody is touching a drop till the deal is completed.' It was supposed to go through in the afternoon, but it didn't actually go through till two hours before midnight.

By that stage, the feeling was almost extraordinary relief, rather than celebration.

We did receive some criticism for doing that deal, as I knew we would, with people accusing us of selling out or cashing in. I won't deny that I, and the other shareholders, did well out of the deal, but it wasn't just about us cashing in. It was also imperative we did that deal to give The Warehouse Project and Parklife financial security, and allowed us to build, and grow both businesses. As I've talked about, there were several times before we did that deal that we had come perilously close to losing The Warehouse Project.

The Live Nation deal gave us greater security. We had no idea that Covid was going to hit us when we did that deal, for instance, but if we hadn't gone into partnership with Live Nation, I honestly don't think The Warehouse Project and Parklife would have survived the pandemic.

Predictably, the first Parklife after we did a deal, there was an incident that meant the festival nearly didn't happen that year, which would not have been a great thing for us to have to tell Live Nation. Neither Manchester City Council nor North West Water had told us that there were two water main pipes running under Heaton Park that served over 200,000 homes, about half of North Manchester. Jon Drape and his production crew had a map with all the various drainage pipes and utilities marked on it, but these two water mains weren't on there. The week leading up to the festival, one of the Big Top contractors arrived to start erecting one of the huge Big Tops, drove a steel tent pin down into the ground, and fractured one of the Victorian cast iron pipes. There was a huge fountain of water. I have never seen anything like it. It was like the Bellagio Fountains, or the sort of comedy water fountain you see in a cartoon. Which is the last thing you want in the middle of your festival site, three days before opening. Jon Drape and the production crew were straight on it, and called out United Utilities, who were a bit useless at first. They kept sending more and more senior people, but all they seemed to do is look at this huge fountain of water and stroke their chin. One guy suggested they would have to get a collar custom-made to fit over the gap, and that could take ten days. *What are you talking about?* I thought, *Ten days? We've got a huge festival here in THREE days!*

Thankfully another guy arrived, who was more of a problem solver, and he just said to Jon, 'Have you got a digger? Let's have a look at what we're dealing with here.'

One of the production crew used a digger to expose the pipe and found out that the hole was actually only about 5 inches wide, but this huge fountain was coming out of it. This latest United Utilities guy, who was pretty no-nonsense, just said, 'Let's just try and plug it with a fence post.'

Which seemed a ridiculous idea, and no one thought it would work. But, against the odds, it did. They hammered a fence post into the hole and remarkably it stopped the fountain of water. The site crew quickly filled the earth back in over the top, and unbelievably it held. So, to this day, half of the people of North Manchester have got a fence post to thank for their supply of water. And we have a fence post to thank for not having to pull Parklife that year, which would have been a nightmare.

That Parklife was also the second year running that Greater Manchester Police had their buggy taken. Not by the cleaners this time, but by two punters from the festival. It went viral on social media, because the two guys stupidly posted pictures of them speeding round Heaton Park, outside the festival site, on it. Thankfully, GMP had not left the drugs amnesty bag on the buggy that time. The police eventually found the buggy abandoned in Prestwich. They've never had their buggy stolen since, but a few officers got a bit of a bollocking that year, and I imagine they make pretty sure they don't just leave it lying around unmanned nowadays.

The Arena Bomb and the Mancunian Response

On Monday, 22 May 2017, I was at home having a chilled evening, when I started hearing reports on social media of an explosion at Manchester Arena – at that evening's Ariana Grande concert. My very first reaction was that maybe a speaker had blown or something, I didn't immediately presume it was something serious. The last thing I suspected was that it would be terrorist attack. Nobody did. As I've mentioned previously, when you're planning a huge gig or event you always have SAG (Safety Advisory Group) meetings with all the relevant authorities beforehand, to run through planning for various possible scenarios. The authorities want to make sure arrangements are in place for worse-case scenarios. But up till that horrific night at Manchester Arena, we had never been asked to have a specific plan for a terrorist attack. Sadly, such plans are now vital.

As the news rolled out that night, it quite quickly became apparent that what had happened at the arena was really serious. We later learned that as the concert ended and people started leaving, Islamic extremist Salman Abedi, had detonated a nail bomb in his backpack in the arena foyer, killing twenty-two people and himself, injuring 1,017 others. It was the most serious act of terrorism and first suicide bombing in the country since the 7/7 bombings in London in July 2005. And though Manchester had already been victim to an IRA bombing in 1996 – the biggest bomb the IRA had ever exploded on the British mainland – that caused huge damage to the city centre, thankfully nobody had been killed in that attack.

There were so many shocking things about the incident. Obviously, the loss of so many innocent lives, and the severe injuries to many others, but also that Abedi seemed to have deliberately targeted young people and children having fun at a concert. That felt like a first in this country, and it made it all the more shocking. The fact that Abedi had grown up in Manchester and had gone to school here, quite possibly with some of those injured or connected to people who'd died in the attack.

What was absolutely incredible, and still astonishes me to this day, was the response to the arena attack from Manchester as a city. Completely united. Parklife was the first large scale event in Manchester's calendar after the arena attack – just under three weeks later. First thing on the morning of 23 May, when the arena attack was all over the international news, and Mancunians and the rest of the country were still reeling, I got a call from Greater Manchester Police. It was Ronnie Neilson, the Head of Licencing for GMP, and he told me he had been asked to ring Parklife on behalf of the council. 'This is a message from the top,' Ronnie told me. 'It's business as usual. We're not cancelling any events. We're not bowing down to terrorism.' It was an amazing response really, and just showed the determination of Manchester to stand proud and defiant in response.

In the following days, there were incredible scenes across the city, from the thousands of people at the vigils in Albert Square outside Manchester Town Hall, to the one in St Ann's Square, a week after the event, where after the minute's silence one woman started singing 'Don't Look Back in Anger' and the crowd joined in. Nobody living in Manchester will forget how the city came together after the tragic incident, and I know I've never witnessed anything like that in my fifty years of living in this city.

The music industry also put on a united front. Just two weeks after the bombing, Ariana Grande, Simon Moran (SJM Concerts), Melvin Benn (Live Nation), and the American music executive Scooter Braun put on a benefit concert called One Love Manchester at Old Trafford Cricket Ground. Ariana Grande, along with Simon, Melvin, and Scooter basically opened up their black books and called on everybody, from Justin Bieber to Pharrell Williams, Katy Perry and Miley Cyrus to Chris Martin and Liam Gallagher to Take That. I was at the One Love gig, and it was amazing. The atmosphere was incredible, and, I'll be honest, it's probably the most starstruck I've ever been. I was backstage in the dressing rooms, and *everyone* was there; Pharrell Williams even opened the door for me. But even though there were all these global icons present, there was one moment that stopped everyone in their tracks. The door opened and in walked Liam Gallagher, in this bright orange cagoule. Liam's got such a presence that all these other iconic music artists just stopped and stared.

The whole One Love Manchester concert was broadcast on BBC One and BBC radio, it was televised in thirty-eight countries around the world, and raised nearly £20 million for the British Red Cross.

As incredible as One Love was, it was very much a global response to the attack, and I decided we should have a more personal, *Mancunian* response, a week later, at Parklife.

Andy Burnham had only been appointed Mayor of Greater Manchester a few weeks previously, and I'd never met him, but I contacted his office and asked him to make a speech from the main stage at Parklife, and we also invited representatives from Manchester City Council. But most of all, I really wanted to invite representatives of the first responders, paramedics, police, and fire on stage, as they were the real heroes of the event. It was a hugely emotional moment.

The mood was understandably very nervy backstage on the morning of Parklife and in the days leading up to it. We turned up at that show half expecting something to happen. We'd had countless SAG meetings and other high-level meetings with the police and authorities to prepare. The police had put a large number of security measures in place that we knew of – including roadblocks and a ban on any drones – and we were told if anything was spotted flying about Heaton Park it would be shot down by the police. But there were a few extra security measures even we weren't told about. Such as none of us knew till the day that police marksmen were stationed in the trees around Heaton Park. Thankfully, the day went off without any incident, but it was without doubt the most nervous any of us have ever been before an event.

As if we hadn't had enough stress to deal with that weekend, there was then an incident with Frank Ocean's headline set. He's an incredible artist, and we were made up to have him headlining, but he's also pretty particular and specific about his stage show. He'd already cancelled his appearance at that year's Primavera festival in Barcelona, citing 'production delays beyond his control', and had done the same at another couple of shows, so we were nervous before he turned up, in case there was a repeat of that. Frank had asked for a specific stage, which we had to build for him, and also had a huge light show, using LED screens at the back of the stage. As most people know, huge LED screens are actually made up of lots of tiny screens and there was one tiny screen in the bottom left that wasn't working and Frank Ocean refused to go on till it was fixed. He was due to go on just before it was dark, but I think he wanted to find an excuse to not go on till it was dark because, remarkably, coincidentally, as soon as it got dark, the screen magically started working again. Funny that. He went on twenty-two minutes late, but since he was the headliner closing the whole festival, his management insisted he did his full set as Frank wasn't prepared to cut it short. This meant he would be finishing at 11.22, which meant we would be in breach of our licence and would get a huge fine. We had no option but to agree, though, and figure out how we would deal with it afterwards.

Ten minutes after Frank had gone on stage, and still wondering how we were going to resolve going over time, I was back in Event Control when we got word that the Metrolink was down. There had been an incident at Victoria Station: two homeless people had a fight and one of them had pushed the other one on to the tramline, which was horrible. Metrolink had been shut down while the incident was dealt with, and it was going to be at least twenty minutes before it was up and running again. I was stood with Jon Drape, the police and all the other authorities, all of whom were unaware of the other issue we had with Frank Ocean. 'Look,' I said, 'If the Metrolink isn't going to be running by the time the festival finishes, then we need to stay open for a little while longer, for safety reasons, otherwise we're going to have tens of thousands of kids starting to walk back to Manchester city centre, which is a health and safety nightmare.'

Egress is one of the most delicate parts of organising a festival, making sure that everyone gets off site safely, so there was truth in what I was saying, but there was also the ulterior motive of avoiding a penalty for breaching our licence. Fortunately, the authorities agreed, and allowed us to extend the licence by thirty minutes. Even so, it was a stressful end to what was probably the most draining and emotional Parklife we've ever had.

Liam and Parkalife

After being reminded of his incredible presence and how he stood out even among all the other stars at the One Love Manchester concert the previous summer, we booked Liam Gallagher to headline Parklife in 2018. It was his biggest ever solo hometown gig. Liam was having one of his regular rows with his brother Noel at the time and kept referring to him in interviews and on social media as a 'potato' and 'Mr Potato Head'. Noel had also just released a record which included a French female musician playing 'scissors', which Liam couldn't get his head around at all. When Noel then performed on *Later with Jools Holland*, with the French woman playing scissors, Liam found it hilarious. He put a tweet out asking fans to 'peel some spuds' at his next gig.

I decided to have a bit of fun with it and put out a press release saying that we'd had to ban potato peelers from Parklife after announcing Liam as the headliner. *Manchester Evening News* picked up on a story and ran with it, including a quote from me saying we'd been 'blown away at how many people have asked to bring in potato peelers for Liam's main stage performance'. 'Let's not forget', said the *Manchester*

Evening News article, in all seriousness, 'they're sharp implements which is not ideal in a crowded situation.' The MEN then quoted me on whether people could bring potato peelers to Parklife: 'In case you're wondering – the answer is most definitely no.'

Of course, not one person had asked to bring in a potato peeler, it was just a joke, but the *Evening News* were happy to run with it.

Liam joked with his fans online about the name of Parklife, as obviously Blur had a huge hit with a song of the same name back in the 1990s (although our festival is definitely *not* named after the Blur song!). Liam tweeted 'Rite up for this festival in Manchester … not sure about the name though', then followed that up by tweeting 'Stick an A in the middle of the K and the L and we're there PARKALIFE sounds better already', so we temporarily changed the name of the festival on our social media accounts to Parkalife. We normally have about three to five 'headliners' at Parklife, so people rarely buy a ticket to see one act, they're buying into the festival, but with Liam Gallagher, there was definitely a large contingent who had come to see him, and they weren't disappointed, he put on an incredible performance.

The other jokey news story at that year's Parklife was The Piccadilly Rats on the main stage. The Piccadilly Rats were a band of street buskers, who used to play in and around Piccadilly Gardens in Manchester and had become infamous for their appearance, and rough and ready cover versions. The drummer and bass player would wear rat masks when they were playing, which is how they got their name. In early February of 2018, the lead singer had tweeted me saying, 'Hi Sacha can you get us a five-minute slot on the main PARKLIFE 2018 stage we don't want paying! Just need a few butties and a bottle of dandelion and burdock for Tommy 😎👍🎸🐶🎸❤️🍺'. I then jokingly tweeted from the official Parklife account, saying: 'Thinking of getting these local legends involved this year what do we reckon?' with a video of them busking. I went downstairs to the toilet and by the time I came back it had already gone viral. After seeing that reaction, I thought, why not? I got in touch with The Rats and agreed to put them on first on the main stage. There was only about fifty people there to watch them when they performed at 1 p.m., and The Rats got absolutely hammered backstage. We found one of them comatose in one of the dressing rooms. The hilarious thing was, they were making a film about The Piccadilly Rats at the time, so they filmed their performance, but when I saw the finished film, they had cut their performance with shots of Liam Gallagher's audience for his headline slot, so it looked like 70,000 people were going crazy to The Piccadilly Rats!

Sadly, the following April, one of The Rats, seventy-seven-year-old Ray Boddington, died after he was hit by a tram near the Arndale centre. One of the other Rats got in touch with me after he died, to say that they couldn't afford a gravestone for him, and asking for my help, so I gave them £500 to pay for the headstone. The only thing was, they got back in touch the following week to say they needed an extra few hundred quid to pay for the engraving!

Like having Liam Gallagher to headline, when Sam and Rich booked Cardi B as the main act at Parklife the following year, we knew lots of the audience would have booked tickets specifically to see her, as she doesn't play that often in the UK. So, when she pulled out of a few of her other gigs the month before Parklife, we started to get nervous. The reason she gave for cancelling the gigs was because her breasts hadn't healed after having plastic surgery, which was a new one on me. She posted on Instagram, saying, 'You know I hate cancelling shows because I love money. I'm a money addict and I get paid a lot of money. A lot of money for these shows, like I'm cancelling millions of dollars in shows. But like health is wealth, so I have to do what I have to do ... My breasts gotta fucking heal and it is what it is.'

We were still being told she would make Parklife, but then in the end she pulled out just days before the event, which was a massive pain in the tits for us, as well as for her. It's really not a great look to lose your headliner on the week of the event, and we were really nervous about how the audience would react, but when the news went out there was a bit of a backlash, but it was more against her than towards Parklife. We rejigged the schedule and Rich persuaded Mark Ronson to DJ in the Cardi B slot. It was really good of Mark to agree to do that last minute, but it didn't really work well on the day, as only a small audience turned out for him, and Mark was really pissed off with us. He's really good friends with Rich, so Mark took most of his frustration out on him. They're still good friends to this day, but I'm not sure Mark has ever totally forgiven him for the Cardi B episode.

At that year's Parklife, we also had one of the most bizarre medical issues we've ever had. A young lad, who can't have been more than twenty, presented himself at the medics' tent within the first hour of the doors opening. He was really worried and came completely clean about what the issue was. He had put fifty ecstasy pills in a balloon and stuck them up his bum, in order to get past security on the gate. The problem was the balloon had gone too far up inside him, and he couldn't get it out. The medics were obviously really worried, because if the balloon had popped inside him then he would have died. The poor lad spent two hours bent over, with medics prodding gently further up his bum. They managed to get the balloon out in the end, but as soon as they did, the poor bugger (no pun intended) was arrested by the police for possession of drugs. We honestly think he wasn't an actual dealer; he was just the mule for his group of friends and carrying the drugs for them. It was a bum deal, in more ways than one, and he won't be doing that again in a hurry.

King of the North

After he appeared at Parklife in 2017, I kept in touch with Andy Burnham and his office, and Kevin Lee, who is the Director of the Mayor's Office, and Gareth Williams, in particular. I met with them a couple of times, and I think in retrospect they were trying to suss me out at first.

When it had been first announced that Greater Manchester would be getting a Mayor, I had followed all the candidates' campaigns, went to all the hustings and listened to their ideas. I also asked all of them if they would support the idea of something like a night-time economy taskforce. In my mind, I was imagining some sort of committee of people who represented that sector of society and industry. All of the candidates said they would support that idea, apart from Shneur Odze, the UKIP candidate. He was the only one that said he wasn't interested. But then he was a man who had quite particular and peculiar interests. He was quite an odd character, to put it mildly. He was friends with Nigel Farage and was a strictly Orthodox Jew who was married with four kids, and refused to shake hands with female political opponents on religious grounds. It was then later reported through social media and the press that he allegedly was pretty kinky on the side.

The reason I had come up with the idea of a night-time economy taskforce, was that over the previous decade or so, as Parklife and The Warehouse Project had grown and become bigger players in the night-time economy, I'd become increasingly pissed off that there was no unifying voice for us. By night-time economy I don't just mean nightclubs and bars, I mean restaurants, theatres, festivals, cinemas, and all of the wider entertainment industry. Then you also have the shift workers, and NHS and emergency services who work through the night. There didn't seem to be a voice for this huge sector. In Greater Manchester alone, that sector employs 494,000 people, nearly half a million people, which is nearly a fifth of the population, and they didn't seem to have a voice. Westminster just seemed so far out of touch with that whole sector of society, how they live their lives and what their concerns and worries are. Especially the incumbent Tory government (at the time of writing) who are so far out of touch with most working people's lives it's a joke. I've spent my whole adult life working in the night-time economy, so I know from bitter experience that decisions are continually made by those in power that are completely ill-informed about how the industry works and how people actually live their lives.

I was already part of the Night-Time Industries Association, and we had assembled our own Night-Time Commission, with members including BBC Radio 6 Music DJ, Mary Anne Hobbs, and Clint Boon, Inspiral Carpets keyboardist and DJ, to discuss and formulate policies that would make Manchester stronger and safer after dark; campaigning for a late-running Metrolink and other public transport services. London, Berlin, and Amsterdam already had a 'night czar' or similar role, and I thought Manchester really needed a similar champion to help it become a proper twenty-four-hour city.

After Andy Burnham became Mayor of Greater Manchester, and after he appeared on stage at Parklife, we continued these discussions for about six months. In the end, Andy asked me to take the chalice and become Manchester's first Night-Time Economy Advisor. Andy held a press conference and announced my appointment at the Clarence pub in Bury on 6 June 2018.

Burnham said: 'By appointing a Night-Time Economy Advisor and panel, I want us to build on our strong reputation to make it even better – for residents, visitors, and those who work in the sector. Sacha brings with him a wealth of experience. He's a real Greater Manchester success story and I'm thrilled that he's joining us as our first-ever Night-Time Economy Advisor.'

I got on like a house on fire with Andy immediately, and I have loved working closely with him over the past five years. In a time when we're saddled with the most out-of-touch government in living memory, Andy is a complete breath of fresh air. He's unbelievably passionate and hard-working, and his ideas and policies are based on solid foundations and are not grandstanding or the populism nonsense we see from Westminster at the moment. They are serious well thought through ideas that tackle the real issues that people face.

Not long after we had started working together, we went to do a talk with female students at Manchester University. As we came out, Andy and I walked back to the office together. On our walk, he stopped at one point and pointed across the road and said, 'Do you know the significance of that church?'

I didn't. 'I thought you were a Smiths fan?!' said Andy, 'That's the Holy Name church from 'Vicar in a Tutu'!'[12]

Andy has been brilliant for Greater Manchester. The three biggest things that he's done for Greater Manchester are – firstly, tackle rough sleeping. Secondly, take back public control of public transport, which has really resonated. Thirdly, apprenticeships – to stress that it's not just about going to university, and university doesn't suit everyone, so we need to have other routes in place.

Personally, he's also had a big effect on me. He's made me look at life slightly differently. Some of the things he's said to me have really stuck. I remember when he was talking to me about dealing with a particular tricky individual in government, and he said, 'Sacha, it's easier to work with people sometimes, if you want to get results.' That really stuck with me, as it's not always the approach I've taken in life, but he's absolutely right. Due to the difficult relationship with my dad, and then spending most of my career battling other promoters, a lot of my life has been spent in battle against other people, without probably realising it, and that's likely influenced my outlook and psyche. Working with Andy has helped me see that sometimes it's better to work with people than just battle against them the whole time. I'm at the stage of my life now where I thankfully don't have to worry about paying the leccy bill next week, whereas a lot of other people do, sadly. I hope

---

[12] The opening line of 'Vicar in a Tutu' is 'I was minding my business, lifting some lead off the roof of The Holy Name Church'. I had no idea it was that church, and Andy's knowledge impressed me.

that I've become a bit more relaxed and open in my views about things.

Andy has definitely been a huge influence in helping me to see life through a different lens, and I'd go as far as to say he's been as formative an influence as my old art teacher Mr McGinnis was, back in the day.

Spiked, Covid, and United We Stream

In early March 2020, we had a few Warehouse Project shows in the Depot, including Michael Bibi. My wife, Demi, and I had been for dinner one night, and afterwards we thought we would swing by The Warehouse Project and see what was happening. I never usually hang out around the DJ booth when I'm working, but that particular night I got us a couple of drinks and we were stood by the DJ booth watching Bibi perform. I was drinking Grey Goose and lemonade, and we only stayed for a couple of drinks, but by the time I left I was staggering all over the place. The Lieutenant was there, working, and he had to put his arm around me and help Demi pour me into a taxi. I don't really remember anything about the taxi journey home, or anything really from when I left the venue till the following morning. When I woke up the next day, Demi looked really worried, and said to me, 'Do you remember what happened last night?' I had no idea. Demi went back through the night before with me. She said when I got home, I went upstairs and was projectile vomiting everywhere and then collapsed in the bathroom, landed on our glass bathroom scales and smashed them, and hit my head on the wall with such force that it went through the plasterboard. Demi had managed to get me to bed and clean everything up, but she was obviously really worried. We tried to piece together what had happened, because I hadn't had much to drink, and remembered I had put my drink down by the side of the booth, while we stood there, so we could only conclude it had been spiked. Over the next few days, I tried to carry on as normal, but whenever I lay down the room started to spin, so I went to Wythenshawe hospital and got checked out. They couldn't find anything wrong with me, and I have no idea if I was purposely spiked, or I'd just picked up a drink meant for someone else. If it wasn't meant for me, then maybe it was meant for one of the Warehouse punters, and although it was a horrific experience for me, I'd rather it was me than some poor unsuspecting female customer.

We haven't had a specific problem with people being spiked, but there was a bit of a flurry of national media stories about drink spiking a couple of years ago, not at The Warehouse Project, but just generally, and after that people were more vigilant about it. We were the first club in the UK to introduce the on-site spiking test, which looks a bit like a pregnancy test, and the medics can tell immediately whether you've been spiked or not, so we did test a lot of people, but never had anyone test positive for being spiked.

It was while I was at the hospital after being spiked, that I saw a Portacabin outside with a sign on it that said 'COVID TESTING'. I remember thinking, *That seems a bit over the top*. Little did I know what was about to hit us. But then it's pretty clear from what has come out since, that the Prime Minister didn't really have a clue about the magnitude of what was about to unfold, either. Two weeks later, he was forced to announce to the country that we had to go into lockdown.

Like every other business owner, I was completely in the dark about how this might pan out. We had no idea if lockdown was going to be for a couple of weeks, or a couple of months. No one had any idea at that point that lockdowns would continue on and off, for eighteen months and that the long tail effect of Covid, on people's health, the economy, and hundreds of thousands of businesses, would last for years. There was no direct guidance or contact from the government at all, either to me as a business owner, or as Night-Time Economy Advisor. Throughout that time, I got constant calls and emails from people and business owners who were desperate for more information, but I was just as much in the dark as everyone else. The first we heard of any coming lockdown or change to the tier system was when we read it in the press or on BBC News like everyone else. I was fielding constant calls from people who were desperate, whose businesses were going under, and there was nothing useful I could tell them.

The constant chopping and changing of guidance was an absolute joke. Matt Lucas, the comedian, summed it up with a bumbling impression of Johnson that went viral, saying, 'Go to work, don't got to work, don't use public transport, if you can use public transport, go to work …' In the end people didn't know if they were coming or going, or allowed to come and go, or what to believe. The pandemic was a first, none of us had experienced anything like that before in our lives, so I think much of the country initially had sympathy and patience for the government, because we knew it was a first for them, too, but their dreadful mishandling of it, soon erased all that goodwill.

In 2020, during the first summer of lockdown, there were two huge illegal raves in Manchester, one for 2,000 people and one for 6,000 people. The Mayor's office was concerned that more needed to be done to entertain people, to try and keep them in their houses and stick to the guidance, particularly young people. Andy Burnham rang me up and said, 'Sacha, I've been thinking about this. You're the promoter, can you find a way to entertain everybody? To try and keep them occupied and in their houses? Just put your thinking cap on.'

I started to investigate and found that in Berlin they were already streaming techno sets from a closed nightclub and calling it United We Stream. You could watch it for free, but you could also donate a few Euros if you wanted. It was the bones of a good idea, so I thought we could do something similar, but we'd do it on steroids. I rang Andy Burnham back and said, 'Andy, this is what we're going to do, an online stream called United We Stream, and we'll take charity donations. I need your backing on this, and your help to find a venue, and to allow artists to be allowed to travel there so they can be part of it.' I'm pretty convinced Andy didn't understand what I was talking about, and in fact he later openly admitted he didn't know what I meant, but he agreed to help. He arranged for us to use The Met theatre in Bury, they gave us the keys, and everything was filmed and streamed from there. Andy's office gave me a letter for all the artists involved in the filming for the stream, so that they could prove to the police that they were allowed to travel, in case they got pulled over by them. I knew we'd put something really good together, but I had no idea how it was going to go, because I'd never done anything like that before. My whole career has been about getting people out of the house and into a nightclub, not encouraging them to stay at home. But the response was mental.

In the end we did ten weeks of streamed shows, and had twenty million viewers in total, raising £612,000, which was distributed to freelancers and local charities across Greater Manchester. The biggest show we did was the all-day Haçienda party in the second week, which was really special. The stream went down when it started, at 2 p.m., because so many people were trying to watch it, which was a bit hairy, and I had Andy Burnham on the phone asking what was happening, but we got it back up quickly, and it was a huge hit. I was getting sent videos of neighbours dancing next to each other in their gardens and messages from everyone from Angela Rayner, 'This is amazing!' to Gary Lineker, 'This is unbelievable!' As the day went on, and I had a few drinks, my ego got the better of me, and I put my 'I love Manchester' T-shirt on and put some clips out on social media asking people to donate money, as if I was some acid-house Bob Geldof or something! Demi had to rein me in a bit.

I'm still immensely proud of not only what we pulled off, but how much the money raised helped freelancers and artists who really needed it. Neither London nor any other city in the country did anything like that to support their artists. The Mayor's office took all the requests for support, and they distributed all the money. I didn't have any part of that, and everything was confidential, but I do know there were some well-known names who received support. It all hit home just how bad the pandemic had hit our sector.

As the months went on, it was clear there was something very wrong going on with the handling of the pandemic. I felt the hospitality industry and the night-time economy were really hung out to dry by the government. They didn't receive the support that other sectors did and were particularly messed about by the chopping and changing of the rules when it came to tiers, and absolutely ridiculous things like the 'Scotch egg rule', which said you could only have a drink if it was accompanied by a substantial meal. After me and my team asked the government to disclose their Equality Impact Assessment Report to us, they asked me to sign a non-disclosure agreement. After this I accused them on social media of 'employing a bullying tactic to try to delay our case'. I thought the Scotch egg rule was particularly discriminatory as the majority of 'wet-led' pubs (ones that don't offer food) were in lower income areas, which meant people in Altrincham and Didsbury could go for a pint in their local upmarket gastro pub, but people in more deprived areas couldn't go to their local as it wasn't allowed to open because it didn't serve food. I felt so strongly about it that I ended up taking Matt Hancock in his capacity as Health Secretary to court, over the 10 p.m. closing rule and the Scotch egg rule. I personally brought the court case forward, and paid for it myself, but Andy Burnham's office were right behind me. In the end the government dropped the 'substantial meal' policy, but I didn't see it as me winning, I absolutely saw it, as I said at the time, as a 'landmark victory for the hospitality industry', which had endured some of the toughest restrictions of any sector since the beginning of the pandemic. I've got the court papers from 'Sacha Lord vs Matt Hancock' framed in my downstairs loo, and it gives me a little smile every time I go to take a piss.

Three years on, during the Covid enquiry in December 2023, Andy Burnham was called to give evidence and he made it abundantly clear that the government minutes showed that Tier 3 was imposed on Manchester as a 'punishment beating' for his defiance. He referred to a minute from the government's Covid-O committee, which was responsible for Covid operational matters, that said, 'Lancashire should have a lighter set of measures imposed than Greater Manchester since they had shown a greater willingness to co-operate. Tougher measures should be imposed on Greater Manchester that day'.

As Andy told the committee: 'Because we stood up for people in our city region who would otherwise have really struggled had they gone into that lockdown without the funds to help them, because we took that stand they decided to make an example of us. It's unbelievable for me now to look at evidence saying they knew it didn't work, they knew Tier 3 didn't work. They knew that, but they were still going to impose it on us without enough financial support.'

It was absolutely shocking, and I said so at the time. As Night-Time Economy Advisor, I thought I should stand up for the sector. I've done a huge amount of press, organised by my brilliant publicist Nina Sawetz. Andy and I were out one night in Manchester and bumped into Nihal Arthanayake, the great presenter from BBC Radio 5 Live, who is a regular at The Warehouse Project, and Nihal was joking that Andy and I were 'like The Kray Twins' the way we stood up to the government during that time. I'm fully aware that you're going to get online abuse once you stick your head above the parapet on an issue like that, but I didn't expect to get physically attacked for being outspoken. Demi and I were out one night in a place called One Central in Altrincham. It's a place that opened during the pandemic, it was outdoors with lots of good street-food traders, and DJs. Morrissey's nephews Alex and Jay, who I know, used to DJ there, so Demi and I used to pop down with Pickle, our dog, quite often. This one evening, Demi and I were sat down at a picnic bench, and I went off to the toilet. When I came back there were two blokes sat on the bench with her, but I didn't think much of it, as it's the sort of place where people share benches. I sat down and was just chatting with Demi, when a couple of minutes later, one of those lads suddenly stood up behind me and he just started raining punches down on the top of my head. I couldn't move away easily, as my legs were trapped in a bit by the bench legs, so all I could do was just put my hands up to protect my head.

It's the first time I've been randomly attacked like that, and it does shake you up. I didn't leave the house much for a couple of weeks. In the end, Andy Burnham was having some drinks at Freight Island to thank everyone who helped him in his leadership campaign, and he rang me up and said, 'Look, Sacha, I think you should come down, it will do you good to get out.' But even then, at an event like that, in a place owned by my friends, I still felt wary when I went to the toilet, I was thinking, *I could get jumped again here.*

I'm fine now, but it took me a while to get over it. If you're campaigning for something nowadays, you've got to accept you're going to get some abuse online, that comes with the territory, but there's no excuse for physically attacking someone.

When I later saw the CCTV of me being attacked, I couldn't believe Demi's reaction. She was sat opposite me, holding our dog Pickle under her arm, but as soon as this guy started raining down punches on my head, Demi launched herself over the table, and punched this guy full-on in the face, while still holding Pickle under her other arm. She absolutely flew at this guy. I've never seen her look more Scottish!

I first met Demi in 2017, in the gym in Hale Country Club. We starting seeing each other and she started staying over at my house on the weekends, and then you know how it happens. The toothbrush appears in the bathroom, and then it's 'Is it alright if I put some of my stuff in this cabinet?' We've now been together for seven years, and got married in April 2022 in a beautiful place in Capri, Italy. If you've never been to Capri, I can't recommend it highly enough. Get to Naples and then it's a forty-minute ferry from there. As soon as you set foot off the ferry it's like they've pressed pause on Italy in a glorious 1970s summer.

The wedding itself was held on a cliff edge (no symbolism intended!) and our wedding car was a tiny 1960s Fiat, which looked stunning, but it was a bit of a squeeze in the back for Demi and me!

Manchester Evening News ran a story on our wedding and predictably some guy commented underneath, slagging me off: 'You're supposed to be supporting Manchester's hospitality trade! You should be getting married here, not supporting Capri's hospitality trade!' I'm never going to reply to any online comments like that, but I was pleased to see someone else respond to him, saying, 'It's his wedding day FFS, give the guy a break!'

Demi is an incredible woman. She has been my rock over the last seven years – she gets me. We recently launched the Sacha Lord Foundation, which aims to support kids like me, who are a little bit lost after leaving school, and not sure what they want to do, to get into the entertainment and hospitality industry. Demi is going to head up the foundation. I know I can rely on her, and she also absolutely keeps me completely grounded. There's no danger of me getting above myself on Demi's watch. When I was invited on *Question Time* in January 2020 it was a big moment for me, so I recorded it so I could watch it back. A few weeks later, I went to rewatch it and Demi had recorded over it with *At Home with the Kardashians*! I was like, 'What the fuck, Demi?' She couldn't understand why I was so bothered: 'You've already watched it about seven times for fuck's sake!' That was me told.

One other example of how she keeps my feet on the ground: after Parklife in 2023, I was driving home in the early hours of the morning and I was absolutely done in. Not only is it a really long day, it's also difficult to describe the pressure of being ultimately responsible for the welfare of over 120,000 young people across two days, which doesn't really let up until you know that they are all off site and have got home safely.

I was driving home, absolutely exhausted, when Demi texted me: 'Are you on your way home yet?'

'Yes,' I replied, 'I'm shattered.'

'It's bin day tomorrow,' she replied, 'Can you make sure you put the bins out when you get home.'

NOW

The Depot, Homobloc, and Future Destinations

The Warehouse Project is now eighteen years old, so if you were born on the day we first opened its doors, then this coming season you will be legally old enough to come in. That blows my mind. Time moves fast on the dancefloor.

In 2018, we left Store Street for the final time, and moved to Depot Mayfield, a huge 10,000-capacity venue in a historic former railway station, only two minutes' walk from Store Street. We had tried to move to Mayfield previously, when we were having our *annus horriblis* at Victoria Warehouse, but it didn't work out.

The first sign we got that we may be be able to reignite the idea was when Manchester International Festival (MIF) used Mayfield for a couple of shows. They asked us to help run a couple of shows with them, including a ground-breaking collaboration between Massive Attack, the documentary maker Adam Curtis, United Visual Artists, Punchdrunk, and Es Devlin in 2013, and then some shows that Mary Anne Hobbs curated in 2017. As we were working with MIF, I asked them if they thought there was an opportunity to do more shows in the space, and they thought there was.

The site was run by a combination of Manchester City Council, Transport for Greater Manchester, and a developer called Richard Upton. Shortly after that conversation, Broadwick Venues, who also run The Printworks, and Drumsheds in London, took over Mayfield. We already had a working relationship with Broadwick, not least as Jon Drape is one of its directors – as is Gareth Cooper, one of the shareholders of Parklife – so we managed to do a deal with them to move The Warehouse Project to the Depot.

There was a lot of nervousness about moving away from Store Street again, because it really is The Warehouse Project's spiritual home, and the last time we had left Store Street precipitated the worst two years of my life. But after we had been back there three years, it had got to the stage where we really had refined the experience as much as possible, and there was nothing left we could do. We were bursting at the seams, and had outgrown the place, so the time had come to reluctantly close the door on that chapter of The Warehouse Project.

We were still nervous about the move, though. Either it was going to work, or it wasn't. If not, that would be the end of The Warehouse Project. We knew there would be a backlash from a minority that we had gone too big, but there is always a backlash from a minority when you make a change, and to be honest, if what you really want is a sweaty basement for 200 people then you are probably not going to come to The Warehouse Project anyway. The Warehouse Project is a coming together of tribes, and it's all about the communal, collective experience, it's not a niche basement rave.

Moving to Mayfield has also allowed us to collaborate more, so The Warehouse Project don't curate every single night, we also collaborate with other people on nights like Homobloc and XXL.

The opening night of the Depot, Sam and Rich booked Aphex Twin – the pioneer of experimental techno – to head-line, which was a bit of a statement: we might be moving to a much bigger space, but The Warehouse Project would still be booking the most credible and challenging artists in electronic music. Aphex Twin brought his own VJ with him to do his show, and there was one point halfway through the show where the screens started showing a succession of famous Mancunian faces, from Johnny Marr to Eric Cantona to Frank Sidebottom, and then, slap bang in this procession of heads, the face of Fred Talbot – the weatherman, who a couple of years previously had been disgraced – flashed up. I never found out if that was some weird bad-taste joke on Aphex Twin's behalf, or a mistake, but thankfully not many other people seemed to notice it.

Everything had to be scaled up when we moved to the Depot. Not just the production and the staff. When you start dealing with 10,000 people each night then you need to start thinking about counterterrorism measures, putting in place concrete blocks to stop any vehicle attacks and things like that. Everything moves to the next level. The security at The Ware-house Project is now as robust as any venue in Europe, but we also try and streamline it as much as possible for the customer. Along with the usual security staff, we have eight knife arches (metal detectors) and sniffer dogs, but also paramedics on the front door, keeping an eye out for anyone who might not be feeling too well. Once you're inside we have twelve 'roaming angels', who walk around the venue all night checking on people and making sure they're OK. If they do find someone who looks a bit the worse for wear, they will take them to welfare and maybe just give them a cup of tea, biscuits, and a chat, if that's all they need. But of course, the medics are always there if they need them. I don't think any other venue in the UK goes as far as we do when it comes to looking after customers.

We have that many staff now that there's also a security operation for them. There are sniffer dogs and searches on the staff entrance – even I get searched when I come in each night – there's no exceptions. Because it's now a bigger operation, we've been targeted by organised criminal gangs. One of the most brazen was the time recently when Kim caught a guy working behind our bar with his own PDQ (card payment) machine. Most of our customers pay by card now, and this guy had got a job working on the bar and bought his own card machine in, so when he served a customer drinks, he just presented his own card machine to them instead of ours. By the time we clocked it and stopped him, he had already done £11,000 on the one card machine in a week!

The Warehouse Project has a much wider catchment area now. Of the 10,000 people partying each evening, it's probably 50 per cent Mancunians, 20 per cent from across the North, and then the last 30 per cent national and international ravers. On some nights like Homobloc, people come from all over Europe.

Homobloc, run by Luke Una, is now one of the key shows of The Warehouse Project season. I first met Luke Unabomber over twenty years ago, when he was running the club night The Electric Chair with his partner, Justin Unabomber, and was one of the Cord crew, that cool Northern Quarter crowd that I wasn't part of, but I always got on well with him. He's a brilliant force of nature; one of the most gregarious characters in the nocturnal underbelly of Manchester.

When we used to book him to DJ at Sankeys, twenty years ago, he would turn up with a shopping trolley with his boxes of records, and the bouncers would have to help him in with them. He would wheel the shopping trolley all the way to Sankeys from his flat in the Northern Quarter!

Luke had curated a night with us at the first Warehouse Project at Boddingtons, and we'd always been talking about doing something bigger. We had various meetings about doing an Electric Chair festival over the years, but it never happened.

During Covid, Luke became an Instagram celebrity with his off-the-wall posts. He DJed for us for United We Stream during the pandemic, and I remember him turning up at an empty Bury Met theatre and he had this little puppet with him, and he put his puppet in the front seat of the auditorium to watch him DJ. It was off camera, so it wasn't for anyone else's benefit, just for his own benefit, so he could DJ to this puppet. When we moved to the Depot, Luke came to us with the idea for Homobloc. He'd been running Homoelectric for twenty years, but it was normally for just a few hundred people not 10,000, so it was a huge step up. But we really thought there was a market there for a huge LGBTQ+ warehouse party. Nobody had done anything remotely like it before, but we really thought there was an opportunity to do something special. Luke says that the night before tickets went on sale, he thought, *What have I done? 10,000 people? As if!* Even people on the LGBTQ+ scene were saying to Luke, 'You're off your head, you're never gonna get 10,000 people!'

But Luke had been banging on about this idea he had for a promo for Homobloc with this drag queen called Cheddar Gorgeous, and the first time I saw the finished promo clip I knew the event was going to smash it. The first Homobloc sold out within twenty-four hours, but we still didn't know what sort of crowd to expect. Luke remembers that, 'Seconds before we opened, I felt like Eddie the Eagle going down the ski slope – you're going into the unknown but it's too late to go back. I had no idea if the crowd would work, or if we'd get some knobheads ruining it for everyone. But the first three people through the door were this amazing older dude who looked like Gandalf, his daughter and her friend who was trans. As soon as they walked in, I knew it was going to be great.'

Homobloc doesn't really feel like any other Warehouse Project night, and we leave Luke and his team to get on with the creative side of it to keep it that way. It's Luke's night really, his vision, and we just provide the support to make it happen. The attention to detail that goes into trying to encompass everybody from that scene is phenomenal. We even bring specialists in to train security and bar staff, just for that one night, on how to address people, to make sure no one's offended. I thought it would be a good idea if all the bouncers on the front door wore glitter face paint, and they were surprisingly up for it! It reminded me of when Bowie persuaded his band The Spiders from Mars to wear glam make-up, although our lot were more like The Bouncers from Wigan, all saying, 'Ey up, pass us t'glitter, you daft bugger.' Kim also got all her bar staff to wear glitter face paint.

There are about 200 performers each year at Homobloc, not just the artists and DJs, but a whole host of other performance artists who make Homobloc unique. There's a huge backstage area for them all, and at the first Homobloc I wandered through it and people were walking around naked with their various bits hanging out. I've seen a few things in my time, especially at Paradise Factory back in the day, but it was still a bit of an eye opener. Homobloc is wilder than other

Warehouse nights. If you've never been to anything like it before, it is pretty debauched, so we do give all the staff a heads up, as there might be an eighteen-year-old student working on the bar who comes from a tiny village in Wales and has lived a bit of a sheltered life. It does get pretty wild. I didn't witness this happen, but I did see a tweet the morning after Homobloc last year, where one of the artists talked about achieving 'lifetime goals' when they rimmed their best mate *on stage*.

You don't get that at a Coldplay gig.

The Return and Future of Parklife

The pandemic meant that we were forced to cancel Parklife in 2020. We returned in 2021 but had to push the date back to later that year, due to Covid restrictions. When we confirmed the date, Saturday, 11 September, we were a little unsure about the move to late summer, but what no one could have predicted was that it would clash with Ronaldo's second debut for Manchester United! Rod Stewart was also performing at the Etihad stadium the same day, so town was absolutely heaving.

The whole of Manchester was even more rammed than usual. Luke remembers walking out of Piccadilly station, and it was the busiest he'd ever seen it. Thousands of people pouring out of the station, United fans singing 'Viva Ronaldo' and kids dressed for Parklife.

Because it was the second year of Covid, we had to make a lot of changes on site, including taking the roof off the Hanger, so it was open air. We also bought 25,000 Covid tests for punters to use, although we ended up using hardly any of them, so we donated all the leftover ones to the NHS.

Ronaldo scored twice for United that day. He didn't come down to Parklife afterwards to celebrate, but then he's never been much of a party animal, he's more of a machine, and he rarely drinks. A few of his teammates came down, though. Marcus Rashford came with Jesse Lingard (who had also scored that day); Darren Fletcher was also there with his family, who were lovely, and Paul Pogba arrived separately. Pogba is good mates with the Nigerian rapper Burna Boy who'd watched him at Old Trafford that afternoon, so Burna Boy returned the favour and invited Pogba to Parklife. Wearing a United shirt, with Pogba's name on the back, Burna Boy got Pogba up on stage with him, and the crowd went absolutely mental. Pogba obviously loved being on stage, as being up there once with Burna Boy wasn't enough: he also later jumped up on stage with D-Block Europe, too. Burna Boy's management hadn't told us he was going to the United game, otherwise we would have been a bit nervous about him making it across town to Parklife in time for his stage appearance. I still don't quite know how they managed it.

Pogba had arrived in a black Mercedes-Benz Viano, with an official Man United driver, and he left before the roads closed for egress. Nowadays, the police shut all the roads around Heaton Park at 9.30 p.m. and they don't open again till 12.30 a.m. It's to make egress as safe and painless as possible, so we can get everyone off site safely. Pogba might have got the memo, but Rashford and Lingard unfortunately didn't, or they forgot. I'm normally the first out when the police reopen the roads, and as I was sat in my car waiting, Rashford and Lingard were sat in Rashford's car next to me. I thought to myself, *There's no way if Alex Ferguson was still in charge at United, he would want his footballers out past midnight at a festival, a couple of days before a Champions League game.*

That thought came back to haunt me when I was watching United away at Young Boys in the Champions League two days later. In the last minute of added time, Lingard misplaced a back pass and Siebatcheau reacted quickest to slot home a winner and cause euphoria in the Swiss capital. My first thought was, *Fucking hell, if the manager knew he was at Parklife till the early hours of Monday morning, he'd do his nut.* I felt like it was my fault!

Mind you, when United players want to come down to Parklife they normally get Mary-Jane Dalton, who was Richard Arnold's executive assistant, to ring up and arrange it for them, so the manager would probably go even more mental if he knew it was someone in the club getting them on the guest list.

That same year of Parklife, there was talk of Drake turning up as a special guest. Drake had been at Wireless festival in London the night before, and rumoured to be coming to Parklife, which would have been incredible. We'd heard the rumour, like everyone else, but hadn't had any contact from Drake's people, although that didn't necessarily mean it wasn't going to happen last minute, so we were half expecting the call.

Early evening, I was walking backstage and saw a fleet of black Rolls Royces arrive through the artist gate, and my first thought was, *Ah, so Drake has turned up*, which was going to be a huge moment for Parklife. But it wasn't Drake, it was the Kamani family, the family behind BooHoo. I've no idea how they managed to get their Rolls Royces back stage, but I can only assume they rocked up at the artist entrance and the security on the gate thought, *Well it must be someone special, even if they don't have the right vehicle access passes, because they're in a fleet of five black Rolls Royces.*

We later heard that after he had appeared at Wireless, Drake had a party back at the Rosewood Hotel, a lovely luxury hotel where I sometimes stay. Some gangs turned up and tried to infiltrate the party, and when they weren't allowed in, they shot at the hotel windows. I don't think that ever came out or was reported in the media, but apparently Drake just thought, 'Fuck this' and went back to America, so he never made it to Parklife.

Parklife can't get any bigger at Heaton Park. It's now 80,000 capacity and we get over 200,000 people registering for tickets, but there really is no more space for us to use. It now takes over 1,000 people to build the festival site, with the first person starting work three weeks before the show, and the last person leaving two weeks after the show.[13]

Even by Parklife standards, 2023 was a bit of a crazy year. Sometimes it happens like that, it will have been all smooth in the lead up to the festival and then it goes crazy. We had Aitch headlining, which we knew was going to be massive, alongside The 1975, another local act. Just after we announced Aitch, he appeared at The Brit awards and (along with his story about fence jumping the festival when he was younger)

---

[13] We have also have 1,200 security staff and stewards, 1,000 bar staff and 200 police. There is 5 miles of perimeter fence, 1,000 toilets and over two acres of marquees. Over the weekend the food concessions serve 10,800 pizzas, 3,100 burritos, 3,600 gyros and 31,000 portions of chips. We also donate 337 kilos of leftover food to the food charity Open Kitchen MCR after the show.

he said some really nice things about being asked to headline Parklife, describing it as a 'real, genuine bucket list kind of thing'.

Other headliners on the stages included Fred again, Fisher, the Prodigy, Mercury Prize-winner Little Simz, Self Esteem, Raye, The Wu Tang Clan, and Nas.

In the week leading up to Parklife 2023, Angela Rayner, Deputy Leader of the Opposition, who I get on with really well, messaged me to say she wanted to come down with her son, so I said yes, of course. Angela said, 'Fisher is playing. I *love* Fisher, is there any chance we can meet him?' I said 'Yes of course, I can arrange that.' I arranged to meet Angela at half past eight on Sunday evening in the backstage hospitality area, and I then drove her over to the Artist Village on the other side of the site to meet Fisher. When we got there, Fisher was FaceTiming Jack Grealish, who was in the middle of his lost forty-eight hours partying after Man City won the European Cup. Grealish and Fisher were mates and Grealish was asking Fisher if he could come down to Parklife when their plane landed back in Liverpool. Obviously, I said yes, but then when the City plane landed in Liverpool, the players – including Grealish, Kyle Walker, Foden, and a couple of others – clocked a private jet sat on the tarmac, and they were like, 'Shall we just hire that and go to Ibiza?' Apparently, City had hired out a Chinese restaurant in Manchester City centre and only three players turned up because all the rest had flew off to Ibiza.

Jack Grealish didn't make it down to Parklife, unsurprisingly. I've met some real party animals in my life and anyone reading this book will know people who can go out and party really hard. But Jack Grealish has to be up there. It's quite refreshing in this day and age to have a footballer who has a bit of personality and likes to party, as most of them are really square. Jack might not have made it to Parklife, but he has become a bit of a regular at The Warehouse Project. He always turns up in a bucket hat to try and avoid getting mobbed, but then hangs at the stage where the crowd can see him anyway. He's also danced on stage with Fisher.

Angela Rayner asked me to take a picture of her with Fisher, and then she sent it to ex-New Zealand Prime Minister Jacinda Ardern, who was clearly a Fisher fan, too. Angela and Fisher obviously got on, because as he closed the Hangar stage, she was dancing on stage and he shouted on the mic to the audience, 'This is the future Prime Minister!' It was a pretty bonkers Parklife moment and at that stage I thought I'd better leave them to it.

A couple of weeks later, Angela Rayner was on holiday out in Ibiza, and I had got her on the guest list for CamelPhat and Fisher, and the *Daily Mail* did a piece on her partying in Ibiza, although they only got the information from her Instagram account.

Parklife is at capacity, but we can still add on an extra date on the Friday, like when we did New Order or The Courteeners. But a decade after we first looked at moving Parklife to Wythenshawe Park, we are finally starting to do shows there, after managing to work around the covenant. We're now hoping to do three large shows there every August bank holiday. The first one we did, in 2023, was with Noel Gallagher, which was great. In 2024, the two headliners will be New Order and Blossoms. The New Order show will be their second biggest Manchester gig ever, after the Heaton Park gig we did in 2021, which means we have promoted the band's two biggest ever Manchester gigs.

Andy Burnham came down to the Noel Gallagher gig. I introduced him to Noel backstage and they had a big old chat, and it turns out they've got a family connection: a cousin of Andy's does Noel's PR. Noel then dedicated a song to Burnham during his set, but he mustn't have been reading his setlist properly, and fucked it up. 'Dedicating this to Andy Burnham' he declared, and then played 'The Importance of Being Idle'. Everyone was like 'WTF?' 'Got the songs in the wrong order,' Noel apologised after the song 'didn't mean to say he was a lazy cunt. It was supposed to be this one,' and then he played 'Masterplan'.

The Warehouse Project is now settled at Depot, but we still want to keep moving forward. In 2023, we did our first over-seas Warehouse Project seasons, in Rotterdam and Antwerp. For years, we've had countless offers to take it to other venues, including different festivals, but it's never felt true to The Warehouse Project. It wouldn't feel right for us to just curate a tent at a festival and slap 'The Warehouse Project' name on it, when it needs to be in a bricks and mortar space, ideally a warehouse.

The first text I got when we announced The Warehouse Project Rotterdam was from Mike Pickering, the first DJ I'd ever seen at The Haçienda, three decades previously. 'Genius' he said, 'Brilliant to not go with the obvious choice of Amster-dam. Rotterdam is amazing.' I'd forgotten that Mike had lived in Rotterdam at the start of the 1980s, before he came back home to launch The Haçienda. The spaces in Rotterdam and Antwerp are similar to the Depot, huge industrial spaces but with a smaller capacity of 4,000, and we work in collabora-tion with local promoters out there. It's always tricky to gauge how many people actually get The Warehouse Project outside of the UK, but Rotterdam and Antwerp have shown that they really do, and that there is a huge appetite for it.

Otherwise, we've spent quite a lot of time and effort over the last two to three years looking at venues in New York, but we've never found exactly the right space. London is always on the radar too; we're always looking for the ideal space and opportunity there. The fact that we haven't done London or New York yet, proves how difficult it is to find the perfect venue, and that Manchester is The Warehouse Project's natural home.

So, the future is bright for The Warehouse Project, as it keeps pushing boundaries and pushing forward. In ten years' time, it could be in twenty cities across Europe. And we're not just restricted to Europe. As well as the US, we've looked at Australia and further afield.

But one thing's for sure, it was Manchester that made The Warehouse Project. At times I've questioned myself and the decisions we've made over the years, but one thing has never been in question. Manchester is in our DNA, and The Warehouse Project's home will always be in Manchester.

This couldn't have happened anywhere else.

A Map of Manchester Locations

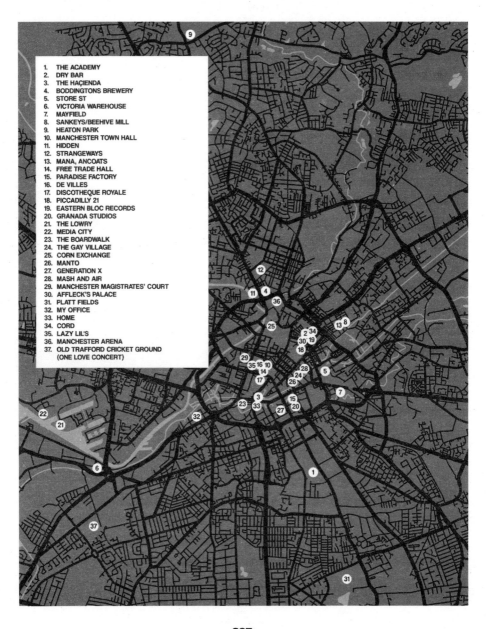

1. THE ACADEMY
2. DRY BAR
3. THE HAÇIENDA
4. BODDINGTONS BREWERY
5. STORE ST
6. VICTORIA WAREHOUSE
7. MAYFIELD
8. SANKEYS/BEEHIVE MILL
9. HEATON PARK
10. MANCHESTER TOWN HALL
11. HIDDEN
12. STRANGEWAYS
13. MANA, ANCOATS
14. FREE TRADE HALL
15. PARADISE FACTORY
16. DE VILLES
17. DISCOTHEQUE ROYALE
18. PICCADILLY 21
19. EASTERN BLOC RECORDS
20. GRANADA STUDIOS
21. THE LOWRY
22. MEDIA CITY
23. THE BOARDWALK
24. THE GAY VILLAGE
25. CORN EXCHANGE
26. MANTO
27. GENERATION X
28. MASH AND AIR
29. MANCHESTER MAGISTRATES' COURT
30. AFFLECK'S PALACE
31. PLATT FIELDS
32. MY OFFICE
33. HOME
34. CORD
35. LAZY LIL'S
36. MANCHESTER ARENA
37. OLD TRAFFORD CRICKET GROUND
    (ONE LOVE CONCERT)

Tracks That Made the Decade

1990s

1. 'Groove Is In The Heart' – Deee-Lite
2. 'Missing (Todd Terry Club Mix)' – Everything But The Girl
3. 'Can You Feel It? (In-House Dub)' – Todd Terry presents CLS
4. 'Bingo Bango (Latin Bango Mix)' – Basement Jaxx
5. 'Higher State of Consciousness' – Wink
6. 'Plastic Dreams (Def Mix)' – Jay Dee
7. 'U Don't Know Me' – Armand Van Helden feat. Duane Harden
8. 'Move Your Body (Club Mix)' – Xpansions
9. 'Playing With Knives' – Bizarre Inc.
10. 'Deep Inside' – Hardrive
11. 'Born Slippy' – Underworld

Tracks That Made the Decade

2000s

1. 'Shades of Jae' – Moodymann
2. 'The Revival' – Braxton Holmes ft. Mark Grant
3. 'The Way' – Global Communications
4. 'Fix My Sink' –DJ Sneak
5. 'I'm So Crazy' – Par-T-One
6. 'I'm A Disco Dancer' – Christopher Just
7. 'Hazin & Phazin' – Harry Romero
8. 'Where Ya At' – Derrick Carter
9. 'You Can't Hide From' – DJ Sneak
10. 'Boogie' – Stacy Kidd
11. 'It's Yours' – Jon Cutler
12. 'Play the Game' – Kenny Hawkes
13. 'Tub' – Grant Phabao
14. 'Indo Silver' – Bucky (Redlight Edit)
15. 'Lazy' – X-Press 2 feat. David Byrne

Tracks That Made
the Decade

2010s

1. 'Tribesmen' – Solardo
2. 'Glue' – Bicep
3. '(It Goes Like) Nanana' – Peggy Gou
4. 'Kids' – MGMT
5. 'Get Up' – Eats Everything
6. 'Eat Sleep Rave Repeat' – Fatboy Slim feat. Beardyman (Calvin Harris Remix)
7. 'White Noise' – Disclosure feat. AlunaGeorge
8. 'Move your Body' – Marshall Jefferson x Solardo
9. 'Forget' – Patrick Topping
10. 'Hungry for the Power' – Azari & III (Jamie Jones Ridge Street Remix)
11. 'Pjanno' – Eric Prydz
12. 'Losing It' – Fisher
13. 'Cola' – CamelPhat, Elderbrook
14. 'Around' – Solomun, Noir, Haze
15. 'Jack' – Breach

Acknowledgements

I've been lucky enough to work with some amazing people over the years, not least my business partners in The Warehouse Project and Parklife, Sam Kandel and Rich McGinnis, but also many others who, though less visible, are absolutely key to the success of The Warehouse Project and Parklife.

I've worked with Sam Kandel since 2000, when we first reopened Sankeys. Sam has been a massive part of The Warehouse Project, and he and Rich McGinnis have booked the majority of the acts for both The Warehouse Project and Parklife, since we first started out. Rich started off booking acts for Chibuku Shake Shake in Liverpool, and we first brought him in to work with us on the Tribal Warehouse in 2004, and he and Sam now share responsibility for booking talent for The Warehouse Project and Parklife, supported by the staff in our office.

Jon Drape has been essential in helping to building The Warehouse Project and Parklife. He is the man who can get *anything* done in Manchester, from getting streets cordoned off to turning a park into a festival site overnight, and we could not have done it without him and his huge arm of brilliant production staff and specialists.

I first met Kim O'Brien at Sankeys, when she was one of the regulars who partied well into the early hours of the morning. Since she joined The Warehouse Project she has been an integral member of the team ever since. As I will be stopping attending the late nights later this year, Kim will be stepping up.

My beautiful wife, Demi, who has to put up with so much… and sadly for her, will have to put up with it for many more years to come. Thank you for all your support and words of encouragement.

To my mum, Sandra, thank you for everything.

Elisa was a driving force behind the student nights we promoted together, and continues to work for The Warehoue Project and Parklife to this day.

Krysko started DJing for us just after we took over Sankeys and quickly became part of the family. He has Djed for us ever since, playing every Warehouse season and every Parklife.

The Lieutenant is not a man to court publicity, but he is my eyes and ears on the ground at The Warehouse Project and Parklife. My equivalent of the Wolf in *Pulp Fiction*. An acid house firefighter.

Dave Vincent is another person who I should mention here, even though we disagreed at times, he was (and still is) such a brilliant promoter and a huge part of my early success in this industry.

The list of people who I've worked with and who have helped me over the years, but aren't mentioned in the book, is extensive. I've tried to remember everyone but, undoubtedly, I will have missed many off who should be here.

Nina Sawetz, my publicist, who I know I drive mad. I would highly recommend her, but not if that means all her time won't be focused on me!

Great Influence: Amy, Ash, Claudia and Megan.

Manchester Grammar School: Mr Bohl, Mr Brown, Mr Davidson, Mr McGinnis, Mr Simpson, Mr Thorpe.

Student nights: Jason Argyle, Brian Cheetham, Si Frater, Jon Harlow, Ann McGrath, Shaun Wilson.

Live Nation: Scott Barton, Melvin Benn, Rory Brett, Jim Campling, Ian Coburn, Andy Copping, Matt Corbin, Raye Cosbert, Daniel Cuffe, Denis Desmond, Jo Dipple, Stuart Douglas, Geoff Ellis, Selina Emeny, Gary Ezard, Diane Fallow, Ele Hill, Paul Latham, Lynn Lavelle, Katie Moore, Andrea Myers, Nethelli Ordish, David Pepper, Peter Taylor, Jana Watkins.

SJM concerts: Rob Ballentine, Simon Moran, Conrad Murray, Randy, Chris York.

Accountant: David Shapiro

PR: Gemma Gore, Lisa Morton, Angie Towse, Tania Von Pear.

NTIA: Mike and Silvana Kill

Andy Burnham's Office: Karen Chambers, Amy Davies, Gill Doyle, Marie France, Joe Heyes, Kevin Lee, Michelle Waugh, Tom Whitney, Gareth Williams, John Wrathmell,

Greater Manchester Leaders and Councillors: Carl Austin, Bev Craig, Paul Dennett, Sean Fielding, Kate Green, Joe Heyes, Pat Karney, Alison Mackenzie Folan, Eamon O'Brien, Mike Parrott, Lucy Powell, Luther Rahman, Rebecca Never Becky, Tom Ross, Arooj Shah, Jeff Smith, Fraser Swift.

Ticketmaster: Andrew Parsons, Sarah Slater.

Kendal Calling: Ben Robinson, Andy Smith.

Hideout: Steve Allison, Wilf Prophecy

Mustard Media: Ed, Oli, Rob and Sian Bennett.

United We Stream: Marie Claire Daly, Colin and everyone at Badger and Coomes, James Monaghan, Vic from the Bury Met, Gareth Williams; every single artist and DJ who donated their time to both raise funds and raise everyone's spirits.

Sankeys: Darren Bisby, Bucky, Jason Furmidge, Greg Lord, Colin Oldham, Crazy Paul, Tidy, Greg Vickers.

Aitch, Bicep, Ian Brown, Blessed Madonna, Shaun Ryder for support on the book.

Industry allies: Steve Alton, Emma Maclarkin, Kate Nichols.

Wythenshawe FC: Carl Barratt, John Cotton, Chris Howard, Martin Howe, James Melville, Pete, Shane, Steve, all the teams and all the fans.

People who try to make me look good: Emma, Olivia Hammond, Dr Rosh, Abby Whittle.

My wife Demi's crew: mother-in-law Donna Mackenzie, Rhoddy Mackenzie, sisters-in-law Mia and Millie, Gary and Laura Stenhouse, Munroe and Wren, Carol, Paul, Tracey, Wendy, Arlene and everyone at The Bruce.

Primary Security: Thanks to all our labour partners and providers.

Harry Bayford, Lola Cameron, Charlie Lothman, Shamsun Khatun, Anil Patel, Dan Perry, Danny Tracey, Mark Turnbull, Lizzie Williams, Daniel Wolfendale.

Gemma and everyone at W.E.L.S.A.F.E

The Loop and MANDRAKE.

Printer: Kevin, Mike Lynch and Vinny Posters.

GMP: Martin Aylett, Andy Brookes, Paul Cocker, Shakey Dave, Dave Henshall, Andy Owen, Sarah Pickstone, Dave Smith, Phil Spurgeon.

All of our photographers, but especially Jody, Pippa and Sebastian.

Designer: Paul Hemmingfield for all of his work with Sankeys and early Warehouse materials.

WHP designer (and huge help with designs for the book): Katie Hamill.

Artist Driver: Jon Caine

All current office team, including Mark Abbott, Abi, Ashleigh, Kirsty Batchelor, Sophie Bee, Caolon, James Crossan (Croissant) Chelsea, Damo and all the artist liaison team, Daphne, Edite, George, Martin Goodwin, Katie Hamill (thanks for the map on p.292), Jess, Charlie Lothman, JP Mackey, James McGraw, Joe Redmore, Rod, Shamsun, Emma Zillman.

Bars/Office: Aaron the baker, Rachel Barber, Tom Booth, Will Bosworth, Simon Bryne, Joe Burke, cleaners Hannah and Anthony, Laura Connerty, Harry Feigen, Jonny Heyes, Tasha Hulme, Matt Lang, Chris Legh, Bruce Lerman, Scott O'Connor, Dan Pirie, Andre Proverbs, Frankie Rushden, Abbie Stein, Warwick Tams, Vicky Valdez. Every single member of bar staff who has worked at any of our events.

Christine Cort, David the tout, Farris, Rick Gordon, Matt the builder, Moussa, Will Orchard, Ollie Ryder, Lee Stone, Luke Walsh, Alex Poots, James Pyrah.

Fabric: Cameron Leslie/Keith Reilly

Cream: James and Scott Barton

Flyer crew: Sophie Eustace, Lewis Harrison, Raushan Kumar, Lucia Midda, George Mossman, Dave and Shauna, Colin and Yvonne, Yasmine, all the Toms, especially Tom Stalker.

Mike Parrott, the man who lets events happen in Manchester!

All the production staff involved in The Warehouse Project and Parklife, including Meg Ah-Tow, Jason Argyle, Cordi Ashwell, Mike Atkinson, James Brown, Max Cairnes Steve Collinge Jim Gee, Jon Green, Ben Johnstone, Alex Knight, Charlie Lister, Dr Loo, Will McHugh, The mighty Bruce Mitchell, Sheena Platt, Louise Renn, Sarah Rowland, Tom Sheals Barrett, Tom Sabin, Sausage Fingers, Stev.

DBN Audile, including Rob Ashworth, Rob Leach, Stephen Page and Peter Robinson.

Nat Lea at Depot, Broadwick. Clodagh Buckely and Steven Gilholme at TFGM, Mark Logan at Showsec.

A huge, huge thank you to Bucky, Graeme Park and Solardo, who have created sets to accompany each decade of the book.

I've never been one for self-analysis or therapy, so it's only through the process of writing this book with my co-author Luke Bainbridge that I started to reflect on some of the events that shaped my life. After some of the early sessions I had the best night's sleep I'd had in years, so I guess a weight must have been lifted! Luke helped paint the background to my story and Manchester, drawing the links from L.S. Lowry to Sankeys, God's Cop to Heaton Park, including plenty of things I hadn't even realised myself, like the fact that The Warehouse Project wouldn't exist if film director Michael Winterbottom hadn't got snowed in while doing a recce in a remote logging town in rural Canada. I first met Luke back in 1995, when he was a young writer for *City Life* (Manchester's answer to *Time Out*) and he came to one of my early nights at The Haçienda. He was there on the dancefloor to document Manchester's change in the late 1990s and 2000s, before moving to the *Observer* to launch *Observer Music Monthly*, the biggest music magazine this country has ever had. Over the years, he's been to most of the events mentioned in this book, so he was the perfect person to work on it with me.

Thanks to everyone at HarperNorth for believing in the book and the story.

Finally, I'm also using this opportunity to announce I will be taking a slight step back from actually putting on the shows for The Warehouse Project. I'll still be involved in the day-to-day running of the business. You won't see me on the door every night now. I'm fifty-two, I can't be doing 5 a.m. finishes every weekend these days! It's time to pass the reins over.

Picture Credits

Harper
North

Book Credits

HarperNorth would like to thank the following staff and contributors for their involvement in making this book a reality:

Fionnuala Barrett
Samuel Birkett
Peter Borcsok
Ciara Briggs
Katie Buckley
Sarah Burke
Matthew Burne
Alan Cracknell
Jonathan de Peyer
Anna Derkacz
Tom Dunstan
Kate Elton
Sarah Emsley
Simon Gerratt
Monica Green
Natassa Hadjinicolaou
Jo Ireson

Megan Jones
Jean-Marie Kelly
Taslima Khatun
Rachel McCarron
Ben McConnell
Alice Murphy-Pyle
Adam Murray
Genevieve Pegg
Agnes Rigou
Nina Sawetz
Florence Shepherd
Eleanor Slater
Hilary Stein
Emma Sullivan
Emily Thomas
Katrina Troy
Daisy Watt

For more unmissable reads,
sign up to the HarperNorth newsletter at
www.harpernorth.co.uk

or find us on Twitter at
@HarperNorthUK

Harper
North